Praise for *Mother Teresa: Come Be My Light*

'Mother Teresa's *Come Be My Light* will come to rank with St Augustine's *Confessions* and Thomas Merton's *The Seven Storey Mountain* as an autobiography proving that great religious figures must first climb through grave doubts.'

Daily Mail

'*Come Be My Light* is that rare thing, a posthumous autobiography that could cause a wholesale reconsideration of a major public figure – one way or another. It raises questions about God and faith, the engine behind great achievement, and the persistence of love, divine and human.'

TIME

'Nothing makes Mother Teresa's potential sainthood a more intriguing prospect than the collection of her private papers published on the recent anniversary of her death…These writings reveal a soul that lived through most of adulthood not only in the shadows, but in profound, spiritual darkness and pain.'

The Post-Tribune

D0488821

Mother TERESA

COME BE MY LIGHT

THE REVEALING PRIVATE WRITINGS OF THE NOBEL PEACE PRIZE WINNER

Edited and with Commentary by

Brian Kolodiejchuk, M.C.

RIDER

LONDON · SYDNEY · AUCKLAND · JOHANNESBURG

For those, especially the poorest of the poor, who
find themselves in any form of darkness, that they
may find in Mother Teresa's experience and faith,
consolation, and encouragement.

5 7 9 10 8 6 4

Published in 2008 by Rider, an imprint of Ebury Publishing
First published in the USA by Doubleday, an imprint of The Doubleday Broadway
Publishing Group, a division of Random House, Inc., New York, in 2007

Ebury Publishing is a Random House Group company

The Random House Group Limited Reg. No. 954009

Addresses for companies within the Random House Group can be found at
www.rbooks.co.uk

A CIP catalogue record for this book is available from the British Library

The Random House Group Limited supports The Forest Stewardship
Council (FSC), the leading international forest certification organisation. All our
titles that are printed on Greenpeace approved FSC certified paper carry the FSC
logo. Our paper procurement policy can be found at
www.rbooks.co.uk/environment

Mixed Sources
Product group from well-managed
forests and other controlled sources
www.fsc.org Cert no. TT-COC-2139
© 1996 Forest Stewardship Council

Printed in the UK by CPI Cox & Wyman, Reading, RG1 8EX

ISBN 9781846041303

Copies are available at special rates for bulk orders. Contact the sales development
team on 020 7840 8487 for more information.

To buy books by your favourite authors and register for offers, visit
www.rbooks.co.uk

St Mary's Convent
12ᵗʰ Jan. 47.

Your Grace,

From last Sept. strange thoughts and desires have been filling my heart. They got stronger and clearer during the 8 days retreat I made in Darjeeling. On coming here I told Fr. Van Exem everything - I showed him the few notes I had written during the retreat - He told me. He thought - it was God's inspiration - but to pray and remain silent over it. I kept on telling him whatever passed in my soul - in thoughts and desires. Then yesterday he wrote this * "I cannot prevent you from talking or writing to His Grace. You will write to His Grace as a daughter to her father, in perfect trust and sincerity, without any fear or anxiety, telling him how it all went, adding that you talked to me and that now I think I cannot in conscience prevent you from exposing everything to him".

Before I begin I want to tell you that at one word that Your Grace would say I am ready never to consider again any of those strange thoughts which have been coming continually.

During the year very often I have been longing to be all for Jesus and to make other souls - especially Indian, come and love Him fervently: to identify myself with Indian girls completely and so love Him as He has never been loved before. I thought it was one of my many mad desires. I read the life of St. M. Cabrini - She did so much for the Americans because she became one of them. Why can't I do for India what she did for Amer. She did not wait for souls to come to her. She went to them with her zealous

---

First page of Mother Teresa's letter to Archbishop Périer, found on page 47.

mind my feelings - Don't mind even - My pain If my separation from You - brings others to You and in their love and company - You find joy and pleasure. Why Jesus, I am willing with all my heart to suffer all that I suffer - not only now - but for all eternity - if this was possible. Your happiness is all that - I want - for the rest - please do not take the trouble - even if You see me faint with pain. - All this is my Will - I want to satiate Your thirst with every single drop of blood, that You can find in me. - Don't allow me to do You wrong in any way. Take from me the power of hurting You. - Heart and soul I will work for the Sisters - because they are Yours. Each and every one - are Yours. I beg of You only one thing - please do not take the trouble to return soon. - I am ready to wait for You for all eternity. Your little one.

Last page of Mother Teresa's letter to Jesus,
found on page 194.

If I ever become a Saint—I will surely be one of "darkness." I will continually be absent from Heaven—to light the light of those in darkness on earth—

—*Mother Teresa of Calcutta*

CONTENTS

PREFACE

For decades, Mother Teresa and her work received extensive public interest. In view of all the attention she garnered during her lifetime, and particularly at the time of her death at the age of eighty-seven, the question arises: What was the source of this attractive force drawing so many people to her? She would have certainly preferred to remain unnoticed. She considered herself just "a pencil in God's hand"[1] and was convinced that God was using her "nothingness" to show His greatness. She never took credit for her accomplishments and always tried to divert the attention she received to God and "His work" among the poorest of the poor. Yet it was not in God's providential plan for her to remain unknown. People of all creeds and walks of life recognized her selfless love and compassion for the poor; they admired her simplicity and genuineness and were attracted by the joy and peace that radiated from her. At the same time, all those who met her, even just once, were left with the sense that there was something more behind her penetrating gaze.

Mother Teresa could not hide her work among the poor, but what she did manage to keep hidden—and with astonishing success—were the most profound aspects of her relationship with God. She was determined to keep these secrets of love far from mortal eyes. The late archbishop Ferdinand Périer of Calcutta and a few priests were the only ones who had some insight into the spiritual wealth of her interior life, and even with them she constantly begged that they destroy all her letters regarding it. The reason for such insistence can be found in her deep reverence for God and His work in her and through her. Her silence now stands as a testimony to her humility and the delicacy of her love.

Providentially, Mother Teresa's spiritual directors preserved some of her correspondence. Thus, when testimonies and documents were gathered during the process for her beatification and canonization, the remarkable story of her intimate relationship with Jesus, hidden from even her closest collaborators, was discovered. In contrast to her "ordinariness," Mother Teresa's confidences reveal previously unknown depths of holiness and may very well lead her to be ranked among the great mystics of the Church.

Her life and message continue to fascinate. This book, then, is a response to the plea of many who knew, loved, and admired her and who desire to know the motive of her action, the source of her strength, the reason for her joy, and the intensity of her love. These pages unveil her interior life, with all its depth and drama, and add unsuspected riches to the spiritual heritage Mother Teresa offers to the world.

Father Brian Kolodiejchuk, M.C.

Postulator, Cause of Canonization of Blessed Teresa of Calcutta

Director, Mother Teresa Center

Introduction

"If I ever become a Saint—I will surely be one of 'darkness.' I will continually be absent from Heaven—to light the light of those in darkness on earth."[1] Taken as a kind of "mission statement," these words of Mother Teresa provide a key to the understanding of her spiritual life, and indeed of her whole life. "Come be My light," Jesus had requested, and Mother Teresa strove to be that light of God's love in the lives of those who were experiencing darkness. For her, however, the paradoxical and totally unsuspected cost of her mission was that she herself would live in "terrible darkness." In a letter to one of her spiritual directors she wrote:

Now Father—since 49 or 50 this terrible sense of loss—this untold darkness—this loneliness—this continual longing for God—which gives me that pain deep down in my heart.—Darkness is such that I really do not

see—neither with my mind nor with my reason.—The place
of God in my soul is blank.—There is no God in me.—When
the pain of longing is so great—I just long & long for God—
and then it is that I feel—He does not want me—He is not
there.— . . . God does not want me.—Sometimes—I just hear
my own heart cry out—"My God" and nothing else comes.—
The torture and pain I can't explain.—[2]

Aim of the Book

This book plumbs the depth of Mother Teresa's interior life seen
from the perspective of this "mission statement." Rather than a theological study, this work is a presentation of the previously unknown
aspects of her interior life, through which we gain greater insight
into her resolute faith and intense love for God and neighbor.

Three aspects of Mother Teresa's interior life revealed during
her cause of canonization are the private vow made while she was
still a Loreto nun, the mystical experiences that surrounded the inspiration to found the Missionaries of Charity, and her intimate
sharing in the Cross of Christ through the long years of interior
darkness. Each of these elements is connected: the private vow lay-
ing the groundwork for the call to serve the poorest of the poor, the
new call inviting her to embrace the spiritual reality of those she
served, and the vow again supporting her heroic living of the
painful darkness.

The book is divided into three parts. Chapters 1 and 2 cover her
interior life prior to her "call within a call." Love for God and
neighbor had been planted in her heart since her early childhood.
Her generous response already as a youth in Skopje, and particularly as a dedicated and self-sacrificing Loreto nun, reached its peak
in a private vow she made in 1942. This vow proved to be not only

the driving force behind her actions, but also a providential preparation for what lay ahead.

Chapters 3 through 7 deal with the inspiration she received on September 10, 1946, to found the Missionaries of Charity, the drama of waiting to start her new mission, and, finally, her leaving the Loreto order and beginning the work in the slums. Both in answering the "call within a call" and in the slow process of discernment that followed, she faced bravely the many sufferings that came her way and held firmly to her new mission.

When all seemed to be in place, the worst of her ordeals was only just beginning. From the time she received the call, she was convinced that her mission was to bring the light of faith to those living in darkness. Little did Mother Teresa realize that "darkness" would become the greatest trial of her own life, and a fundamental part of her mission. The depth of this mystical experience and the cost of living out this new call and mission are the themes of Chapters 8 through 13.

Her Legacy

Initially, the experience of darkness took her off guard. Since she had experienced a high degree of union with God, the change was not only surprising but also agonizing: unable to feel His presence as she had earlier, she was bewildered and afraid. Was she going the "wrong way"? Seeking possible reasons for God's apparent absence, when His presence to her had seemed so real, she at first attributed this absence to her sinfulness and weakness, concluding that the darkness was purification of her imperfections.

With the help of her spiritual directors, she progressively came to grasp that her painful inner experience was an essential part of living out her mission. It was a sharing in the Passion of Christ on the Cross—with a particular emphasis on the *thirst* of Jesus as the mystery of His longing for the love and salvation of every human person. Eventually she recognized her mysterious suffering as an imprint of Christ's Passion on her soul. She was living the mystery of Calvary—the Calvary of Jesus and the Calvary of the poor.

Her living of this inner experience was an integral aspect of her vocation, the most challenging demand of her mission, and the supreme expression of her love for God and for His poor. Beyond providing care for the downtrodden and outcasts of human society, she was willing to embrace their material and spiritual suffering, their state of being "unwanted, unloved, uncared for," of having no one.

Although this intense and ongoing spiritual agony could have made her despondent, she instead radiated remarkable joy and love. She was truly a witness to hope, an apostle of love and joy, because she had built the edifice of her life on pure faith. She glowed with a kind of "luminosity," as Malcolm Muggeridge described it,[3] which flowed from her relationship with God. In this book I hope to explore and illuminate the hidden dynamics of this relationship.

The Documents

Mother Teresa herself was well aware of the uncommon circumstances of her calling and the extraordinary way in which she was challenged to live it out. She always insisted that all documents revealing the inspiration behind the founding of the Missionaries of Charity be destroyed, for fear that she would be given a prominence that she believed was due to God alone.

> Father [Van Exem] has also many letters I wrote to him re—the work while still a Loreto Nun.—Now that the plan of Jesus entrusted to us is in the Constitutions—those letters are not

necessary. Please may I have them—as these were the very
expression of my soul in those days. I would like to burn all
papers that disclose anything of me in them.—Please Your Grace
I ask, I beg you to grant me this desire—I want God's secret
to me to remain ours—the world does not know and I want it to
remain so.—Anything re—the Society* you have plenty—I
have never told—not even in Confession—of how the Society
started.—You and Father [Van Exem] know it—this is enough.
I was His little instrument—now His will is known through the
Constitutions—all those letters are useless.[4]

When after a year, in 1957, Archbishop Périer had not yet com-
plied with her request, she found another opportunity to repeat her
appeal. This second request was similarly not agreed to. As time
went on and interest in her work increased, the possibility arose that
she and the work would be the topic for articles and books. This
proved to be yet another trial for her. Again she feared that Archbishop Périer and Father Van Exem, her spiritual director since
1944, might make the documents available:

I went this morning but you were not there. I have a very big
request to make to you.—I have never asked you for anything
personally.—From Monsignor E. Barber I heard that Cardinal
Spellman wants to write about me & the work. Bishop Morrow
is going to come and ask you for all the documents.—With you
and Fr. Van Exem I have entrusted my deepest thoughts—my
love for Jesus—and His tender love for me—please do not give
anything of 1946. I want the work to remain only His. When the
beginning will be known people will think more of me—less of
Jesus. Please for Our Lady's sake do not tell or give anything.

*The Society refers to the Congregation of the Missionaries of Charity.

I know they want to help the Society financial[ly]—I do not want money—my trust in God is blind—I know He will never let me down. In these few years lakhs* of rupees have passed through my hands.—I do not know how they came. I am perfectly happy and grateful to God for what He gives—I [would] rather be and remain poor with Jesus and His poor.—I prefer to beg & struggle with little—Let him write about "the work" and our poor suffering people—help me to pay for the schooling of our poor children & give the clever ones a chance in life.

Rev. Fr. Martindale S.J. wants also to write & he sent word through [Captain] Cheshire—I have said no.—I am only His instrument—why so much about me—when the work is all His. I hold no claim to it. It was given to me. . . .[5]

Three years later she had yet another occasion to request that the documents be destroyed. To obtain pontifical recognition of the Missionaries of Charity, the archbishop of Calcutta had to present a formal application to the pope, outlining the history and work of the congregation under his care. This new scrutiny concerned her.

Your Grace,
Now that you are looking through the file of our Society—I beg you to destroy any letter which I have written to His Grace—not connected with the Society.—"The Call" was a delicate gift of God to me—unworthy—I do not know why He picked me up—I suppose like the people we pick up—because they are the most unwanted. From the first [day] to this day—this my new vocation has been one prolonged "Yes" to God—without even a look at the cost.—My conviction that "the work is His"—is

*One lakh is equal to 100,000 rupees. Here Mother Teresa is acknowledging that a large sum of money has passed through her hands.

more than the reality.—I have never doubted. It hurts me only when the people call me foundress because I know for certain He asked—"Will you do this for Me?" Everything was His—I had only to surrender myself to His plan—to His will—Today His work has grown because it is He, not I, that do[es] it through me.

Of this I am so convinced—that I would give my life gladly to prove it—[6]

Even so it was the conviction of Archbishop Périer and his successors in office that the documents should survive, although Mother Teresa did manage to destroy a good number. Father Van Exem likewise struggled for years against Mother Teresa's insistence to destroy the documents. He tried to persuade her to keep them for the benefit of the future generations of her followers. In 1981 he wrote to her, "A last point for me has been a shock: I do not know what happened to the documents kept by Fr. Henry. When I went to St. Teresa's last year, I could find nothing anymore. Where are the documents now? I surely do not want this to happen in my case." Finally he gave in. Shortly before his death in 1993, Father Van Exem described the details to Archbishop Henry D'Souza, the archbishop of Calcutta at that time:

Your Grace,
I am returning with thanks the documents you sent to me before leaving for Hong Kong.

Re the copy-book of Mother Teresa I add the following:
Mother wrote this herself. It is apparently a diary but it is not. It was surely written in part some time after the events. Did Mother have any notes I do not know. It is possible since she puts so many dates. In some places I added the month and the year. At the beginning of the Congregation Mother after answering the letters she received used to give them to me to keep them for her.

After some time—it may have been in Creek Lane—she wanted to burn all the letters I had received from her. I had by then two trunks of letters from her, one trunk of letters from benefactors and one of other correspondence. I refused to give permission to destroy the letters and told her she should apply to Archbishop Périer superior general of the M.C.'s [Missionaries of Charity]. Mother went to Archbishop Périer who told her: "Mother, write the history of the Congregation and Fr. Van Exem will give you all the letters." Mother started writing the present book with data from 21st December 1948 till the 11th June 1949. In the evening she was so tired that she could not continue the history for long.

When Archbishop Dyer took over from Archbishop Périer Mother went to him for the same permission. He asked her what Archbishop Périer had decided and told her to do that. Then came Archbishop Albert Vincent who was emphatic in his refusal. In 1969 Archbishop Picachy came to Calcutta and Mother told me not to mention anything about her letters to him. She knew what he would say.

In the seventies and the eighties she continued to insist on destroying the letters. Mother was the elected General Superior of a Pontifical Congregation since 1965 and there was no ruling from any Archbishop. So I sent the trunks of letters to Mother but in a long letter I explained to her that some of the letters did not belong to her but to her Congregation.

The copy-book of Mother remained with me till I sent it to Your Grace.

Today I send back the documents I received from you.[7]

Although knowledge of her inspiration remained the privilege of Father Van Exem and Archbishop Périer, a number of priests over the years came to know of Mother Teresa's spiritual darkness. She revealed her interior state only because she felt God urging her to do so. Her own personal preferences did not matter; Him she could not refuse. These priests proved to be valuable helpers—real "Simons of Cyrene" on this "way of the Cross."

The recipients of these letters were the first ones to realize that the darkness was an essential element of her vocation, and they foresaw that making it known would offer precious testimony of Mother Teresa's holiness and help continue her mission beyond her lifetime. Father Neuner explained:

> Against her explicit request to burn these pages after I had read them I felt I had to preserve them as they revealed an aspect of her life, the real depth of her vocation, of which no one seemed to be aware. All saw her courageous struggle in establishing her work, her outgoing love for the poor and suffering, the care for her Sisters; but the spiritual darkness remained her secret. She seemed cheerful in her daily life, tireless in her work. The inner agony would not weaken her activities. With her inspiring leadership she guided her Sisters, started new centres, became famous, but inside she was in utter emptiness. These pages reveal the supporting power on which her mission rested. It would be important for her Sisters, and many others, to know that her work had its root in the mystery of Jesus' mission, in union with him who dying on the cross felt abandoned by his Father.

On some of the letters and notes about her interior darkness, Mother Teresa had written "matter of conscience." For Mother Teresa every word she wrote about her interior darkness (whether indicated or not) would fall into this category. One of the priests who knew about her darkness sheds light on the reasons for preserving and revealing these documents:

> Would Mother, now that she is no longer with us on earth, still object to these letters having been preserved by Cardinal Picachy

and now, after her and his death, brought into the open? By now she no doubt has understood that she belongs to the church. It is traditional teaching that the mystical charism of God's close friends is meant not primarily for themselves but for the good of the whole church. Many people who go through similar trials may gain courage and hope from these letters. There are probably many more such persons than we think—though in various degrees of intensity.[8]

As to Mother Teresa's expression "Part of my Confession," it should be understood that what she meant was not part of the Sacrament of Reconciliation. One cannot make a sacramental confession by writing one's sins on a piece of paper and sending it to a priest. The priests, recipients of her letters, understood her well—she had written what she was not able to say when she went to meet them for spiritual direction. It was her way of indicating that the matter was confidential; for her it meant the same as "matter of conscience."

In addition to the letters, excerpts from Mother Teresa's other writings are also quoted here, among them the journal she kept at the beginning of her work in the slums, her instructions to the sisters, and her public speeches. Other sources have also been used: excerpts of letters written during the time of discerning whether her "call within a call" was of divine origin, mainly those of Archbishop Périer, Father Van Exem, and her superiors; testimonies gathered during Mother Teresa's process of canonization, for the most part from her surviving spiritual guides and members of the Missionaries of Charity; and testimonies about her from published sources.

Organization

The documents have been organized chronologically. As a result the same or similar expressions reappear, but these repetitions, especially in her writings regarding her interior state, are precisely what reveal the progression, intensity, and duration of her darkness. They are, therefore, invaluable. For her part, Mother Teresa could only speak of the reality within her and her repeated mention of her pain and darkness with requests for prayer reveal an understandable need for support. Ideas that are repeated in the writings are often enriched as time went on with a new detail or aspect that indicates a deepening in her understanding or living of a particular facet of her spirituality and mission.

Mother Teresa's writings have been edited as little as possible. Although almost all of them were written in English, it must be kept in mind that English was not Mother Teresa's first language. Her mother tongue was Albanian. Her education and much of her everyday communication while growing up in Skopje was in Serbo-Croatian. The early letters from India to her friends and confessor back in Skopje were written in Serbo-Croatian. The most literal translation has been provided here. For the texts written in English, even if at times the grammar is incorrect or an improvement could have been made, they have been left as she wrote them. Her spelling mistakes have been corrected and the words that she obviously omitted in error have been added in square brackets.

Capitalization is an important part of Mother Teresa's writing style. She had the custom of capitalizing words that would not be capitalized in common English usage. Besides capitalizing "God" and the personal pronouns referring to Him, she also capitalized what was related to the sacred and holy, as well as terms that were important to her, such as "Confession," "our Young Society," "our Poor," "a big Smile," and so on. This was her way of expressing respect for the sacred and emphasizing a particular reality that struck her. However, she was not always consistent in her use of capitals, and most of these have been corrected to standard English usage.

A word about punctuation: Mother Teresa's writings presented here are personal communications to her close associates, not intended for publication. In this "informal writing" the dash is a punctuation mark that characterizes her style. At times, even in her letters, but especially in her journals and notes, the dash replaces every other punctuation mark: it stands for a period, comma, colon, and semicolon, for an exclamation or question mark, and finally for a dash as well. In short, every break of thought was marked with a dash. This particularity of her style is expressive of the dynamism and vivacity of her personality, a certain "haste" to do the next thing and not be busy with the "nonessential." Though the dashes could be a distraction to reading, for the sake of authenticity these have almost always been left in the text as she placed them. In a few instances, however, when a dash would have interfered with the meaning or flow of the text, it was either removed or replaced with the conventional punctuation marks.

Frequent use of uncommon abbreviations is another typical feature of Mother Teresa's writing, another expression of her characteristic hastiness. Some examples of these are "Holy Com." (Communion), "H.G." (His Grace), "Bl." (Blessed) Sacrament, "Cal." (Calcutta), "Nov." (Novices or Novitiate), and so on. The corresponding words have been provided in brackets after the abbreviations.

It is my hope that many will be inspired by Mother Teresa's heroic living of her mission of "[lighting] the light of those in darkness" and will carry it on according to their own call and possibilities. In those parts of our hearts where darkness still abides, may a bright light shine through her example, her love, and now also her intercession from heaven.

ONE

"Put Your Hand in His Hand, and Walk Alone with Him"

MISSIONARY

Jesus, for You and for souls!
—*Mother Teresa*

"Put your hand in His [Jesus'] hand, and walk alone with Him. Walk ahead, because if you look back you will go back."[1] These parting words from her mother were engraved on the heart of eighteen-year-old Gonxha Agnes Bojaxhiu, the future Mother Teresa, as she left her home in Skopje to commence her life as a missionary. On September 26, 1928, she journeyed to Ireland to join the Institute of the Blessed Virgin Mary (the Loreto Sisters), a noncloistered congregation of women religious primarily dedicated to education. She had applied to go to the missions in Bengal. Such a venture demanded abundant faith and courage, for she and her family knew well that "at that time, when missionaries went to the missions, they never returned."[2]

Young though she was, Gonxha had taken six years to decide on her vocation. She had been raised in a family that fostered piety and devotion, and in a fervent parish community that also contributed to her religious upbringing. In this setting, Mother Teresa would later reveal, she first felt called to consecrate her life to God:

I was only twelve years old then. It was then that I first knew I had a vocation to the poor, in 1922. I wanted to be a missionary, I wanted to go out and give the life of Christ to the people in the missionary countries. At the beginning, between twelve and eighteen I didn't want to become a nun. We were a very happy family. But when I was eighteen, I decided to leave my home and become a nun, and since then, this forty years, I've never doubted even for a second that I've done the right thing; it was the will of God. It was His choice.[3]

Thus her decision was not a whim of her youthful years but rather a considered choice, the fruit of her profound relationship with Jesus. Many years later she would disclose, "From childhood the Heart of Jesus has been my first love."[4] She made her determination clear in the application letter to the superior of the Loreto nuns:

Reverend Mother Superior,
   Be so kind to hear my sincere desire. I want to join your Society, so that one day I may become a missionary sister, and work for Jesus who died for us all.
   I have completed the fifth class of high school; of languages I know Albanian, which is my mother tongue and Serbian*, I know

*Here by "Serbian," Gonxha is referring to "Serbo-Croatian," the language that was taught at school.

a little French, English I do not know at all, but I hope in the good God that He will help me to learn the little I need and so I am beginning immediately these [days] to practice it.

I don't have any special conditions, I only want to be in the missions, and for everything else I surrender myself completely to the good God's disposal.

IN SKOPLJE, 28-VI-1928.
Gonđa Bojadijevič[5]

An exceptional grace she had received on the day of her first Holy Communion had fueled her desire to take this daring step into the unknown: "From the age of 5½ years,—when first I received Him [Jesus]—the love for souls has been within—It grew with the years—until I came to India—with the hope of saving many souls."[6]

Sailing across the Mediterranean Sea, the zealous young missionary wrote to her loved ones at home: "Pray for your missionary, that Jesus may help her to save as many immortal souls as possible from the darkness of unbelief."[7] Her hope to bring light to those in darkness would be fulfilled, but in a way she could not have anticipated as she traveled to her chosen mission land.

While at sea, in moments of solitude and silence, as joy and pain mingled in her heart, Sister Teresa (named after Thérèse of Lisieux when she joined the Loreto order)* collected her sentiments in a poem:

FAREWELL[8]

I'm leaving my dear house
And my beloved land
To steamy Bengal go I
To a distant shore.

---

*Carmelite of Lisieux, better known as the "Little Flower," born at Alençon, France, January 2, 1873; died at Lisieux on September 30, 1897. She was Mother Teresa's patron saint.

I'm leaving my old friends
Forsaking family and home
My heart draws me onward
To serve my Christ.

Goodbye, O mother dear
May God be with you all
A Higher Power compels me
Toward torrid India.

The ship moves slowly ahead
Cleaving the ocean waves,
As my eyes take one last look
At Europe's dear shores.

Bravely standing on the deck
Joyful, peaceful of mien,
Christ's happy little one,
His new bride-to-be.

In her hand a cross of iron
On which the Savior hangs,
While her eager soul offers there
Its painful sacrifice.

"Oh God, accept this sacrifice
As a sign of my love,
Help, please, Thy creature
To glorify Thy name!

In return, I only ask of Thee,
O most kind Father of us all:

Let me save at least one soul—
One you already know."

Fine and pure as summer dew
Her soft warm tears begin to flow,
Sealing and sanctifying now
Her painful sacrifice.

On January 6, 1929, after a five-week journey, Sister Teresa arrived in Calcutta. In a letter she sent back home, she shared with her readers her arrival to the city that would become inseparably linked with her name:

On January 6th, in the morning, we sailed from the sea to the river Ganges, also called the "Holy River." Travelling by this route we could take a good look at our new homeland Bengal. The nature is marvellous. In some places there are beautiful small houses but for the rest, only huts lined up under the trees. Seeing all this we desired that we might, as soon as possible, enter among them. We came to know that here are very few Catholics. When our ship landed on the shore we sang in our souls the "Te Deum."[9] Our Indian sisters waited for us there, with whom, with indescribable happiness, we stepped for the first time on Bengal's soil.

In the convent chapel, we first thanked our dear Saviour for this great grace that He had so safely brought us to the goal for which we had been longing. Here we will remain one week and then we are leaving for Darjeeling, where we will remain during our novitiate.

Pray much for us that we may be good and courageous missionaries.[10]

Shortly after her arrival in Calcutta, Sister Teresa was sent to Darjeeling to continue her formation. In May she began the novitiate, a two-year period of initiation into the religious life that precedes the first profession of vows. The first year concentrated on spiritual formation of the candidate, emphasizing prayer and the spirituality of the order, while the second year emphasized the mission of the institute and offered some training in its apostolic works. Having completed her formation, she made her first profession of vows on May 25, 1931,[11] promising to live a life of poverty, chastity, and obedience, and to devote herself with particular care to the instruction of youth. This was an occasion of immense joy, as her longing to consecrate herself to God became a reality. She confided to a friend:

> If you could know how happy I am, as Jesus' little spouse. No one, not even those who are enjoying some happiness which in the world seems perfect, could I envy, because I am enjoying my complete happiness, even when I suffer something for my beloved Spouse.[12]

Following her profession of vows, Sister Teresa was assigned to the Loreto community in Calcutta and appointed to teach at St. Mary's Bengali Medium[13] School for girls. The young nun embarked eagerly on her new mission, one that she would retain (with only one six-month interruption) until 1948, the year she left Loreto to establish the Missionaries of Charity. In a letter to her local Catholic magazine back home she showed how this mission of service, with all its hardships, was a source of genuine joy for her, as it provided the opportunity to imitate Jesus and live in union with Him:

> The heat of India is simply burning. When I walk around, it seems to me that fire is under my feet from which even my whole body is burning. When it is hardest, I console myself with the thought that souls are saved in this way and that dear Jesus has

suffered much more for them. . . . The life of a missionary is not strewn with roses, in fact more with thorns; but with it all, it is a life full of happiness and joy when she thinks that she is doing the same work which Jesus was doing when He was on earth, and that she is fulfilling Jesus' commandment: "Go and teach all nations!"[14]

Many Things *"for Jesus and for Souls"*

After nine years in Loreto, Sister Teresa was approaching a very important moment in her life—she was about to make her profession of perpetual vows. Her superiors and her companions had by now become acquainted with her prayerfulness, compassion, charity, and zeal; they also appreciated her great sense of humor and natural talent for organization and leadership. In all her endeavors she consistently showed unusual presence of mind, common sense, and courage, such as when she chased away a bull on the road in order to protect her girls and when she scared off thieves who broke into the convent one night.

Yet neither her sisters nor her pupils fully realized the remarkable spiritual depths that this hardworking and cheerful nun had reached in the midst of her daily activities. Her profound union with Jesus, the source of her spiritual and apostolic fecundity, was only shared with her confessors. She likewise rarely alluded to her sufferings, while the joy she radiated around her effectively hid her trials. In a letter to Jesuit Father Franjo Jambreković,[15] her former confessor in Skopje, she revealed the secret of God's powerful action in her soul:

Dear Father in Jesus,

Hearty thank you for your letter—I really did not expect it—I am sorry for not writing to you before.

I just received the letter from Reverend Mother General where she gives me the permission to make my final vows. It will be on 24th May 1937. What a great grace! I really cannot thank God enough for all that He has done for me. His for all eternity! Now I rejoice with my whole heart that I have joyfully carried my cross with Jesus.[16] There were sufferings—there were moments when my eyes were filled with tears—but thanks be to God for everything. Jesus and I have been friends up to now, pray that He may give me the grace of perseverance. This month I am starting my three months tertianship.[17] There will be enough and plenty there [to offer] for Jesus and for souls—but I am so happy. Before crosses used to frighten me—I used to get goose bumps at the thought of suffering—but now I embrace suffering even before it actually comes, and like this Jesus and I live in love.

Do not think that my spiritual life is strewn with roses—that is the flower which I hardly ever find on my way. Quite the contrary, I have more often as my companion "darkness." And when the night becomes very thick—and it seems to me as if I will end up in hell—then I simply offer myself to Jesus. If He wants me to go there—I am ready—but only under the condition that it really makes Him happy. I need much grace, much of Christ's strength to persevere in trust, in that blind love which leads only to Jesus Crucified. But I am happy—yes happier than ever. And I would not wish at any price to give up my sufferings. But do not, however, think that I am only suffering. Ah no— I am laughing more than I am suffering—so that some have concluded that I am Jesus' spoiled bride, who lives with Jesus in Nazareth—far away from Calvary.[18] . . . Pray, pray much for me—I really need His love.

I am sorry for chattering so much—but I myself do not know how [this happened]—Jesus surely wanted this—to make you pray a little more for your missionary. . . .

Mama is writing very regularly—truly she is giving me the strength to suffer joyfully. My departure was indeed the beginning of her supernatural life. When she goes to Jesus, surely He will receive her with great joy. My brother and sister are still together—they are having a beautiful life together.

You are surely very busy to think of letter writing. But one thing I beg of you: pray always for me. For that you do not need special time—because our work is our prayer. . . .[19]

A few days ago I had a good laugh—when some incidents from Letnica* came to my mind. Really, how proud I was then. I am not humble even now—but at least I desire to become—and humiliations are my sweetest sweets. . . .

I must go—India is as scorching as is hell—but its souls are beautiful and precious because the Blood of Christ has bedewed them.

I cordially greet you and beg for your blessing and prayers.

> *Yours in Jesus,*
> *Sister M. Teresa, IBVM*
> *[Institute of the Blessed*
> *Virgin Mary]*[20]

"Darkness"—Her Companion

This letter to her confessor back in Skopje is the first instance in her correspondence where Sister Teresa refers to "darkness." It is difficult to grasp precisely what "darkness" meant for her at this time, but in the future the term would come to signify profound interior suffering, lack of sensible consolation, spiritual dryness, an apparent

---

*A town in the vicinity of Skopje where the parish would go on pilgrimage to the shrine of Our Lady of the Black Mountains.

absence of God from her life, and, at the same time, a painful longing for Him.

Her brief description makes clear that most of the time she was not enjoying the light and consolation of God's sensible presence but rather striving to live by faith, surrendering with love and confidence to God's good pleasure. She had so progressed in that love that she could rise above the fear of suffering:[21] "now I embrace the suffering even before it comes, and like this Jesus and I live in love."[22]

Interior darkness is nothing new in the tradition of Catholic mysticism. In fact, it has been a common phenomenon among the numerous saints throughout Church history who have experienced what the Spanish Carmelite mystic St. John of the Cross[23] termed the "dark night." The spiritual master aptly employed this term to designate the painful purifications one undergoes before reaching union with God. They are accomplished in two phases: the "night of the senses" and the "night of the spirit." In the first night one is freed from attachment to sensory satisfactions and drawn into the prayer of contemplation. While God communicates His light and love, the soul, imperfect as it is, is incapable of receiving them, and experiences them as darkness, pain, dryness, and emptiness. Although the emptiness and absence of God are only apparent, they are a great source of suffering. Yet, if this state is the "night of the senses" and not the result of mediocrity, laziness, or illness, one continues performing one's duties faithfully and generously, without despondency, self-concern, or emotional disturbance. Though consolations are no longer felt, there is a notable longing for God, and an increase of love, humility, patience, and other virtues.

Having passed through the first night, one may then be led by God into the "night of the spirit," to be purged from the deepest roots of one's imperfections. A state of extreme aridity accompanies this purification, and one feels rejected and abandoned by God. The experience can become so intense that one feels as if heading toward eternal perdition. It is even more excruciating because one wants only God and loves Him greatly but is unable to recognize one's love for Him. The virtues of faith, hope, and charity are severely tried. Prayer is difficult, almost impossible; spiritual counsel practically of no avail; and various exterior trials may add to this pain. By means of this painful purification, the disciple is led to total detachment from all created things and to a lofty degree of union with Christ, becoming a fit instrument in His hands and serving Him purely and disinterestedly.

It is not surprising that Sister Teresa, already such an exceptional soul, would be purified in the "crucible" of these mystical sufferings. Choosing to face this deep pain with trust, surrender, and unwavering desire to please God, while demonstrating an outstanding fidelity to her religious duties, she was already setting the pattern for her response to the even more demanding interior trial that was to come.

His for All Eternity

After three months of fervent prayer and reflection in tertianship, the long awaited date she had mentioned to Father Jambreković arrived. On May 24, 1937, with a happy and grateful heart, Sister Teresa approached the altar of God to pronounce her final "Yes," committing herself to Jesus in spousal love for the rest of her life. The ceremony took place in the convent chapel in Darjeeling, with Archbishop Ferdinand Périer, S.J.,[24] as celebrant. Following Loreto custom she was now called "Mother Teresa." Other than her obvious joy on the occasion of her final profession, there was nothing so out of the ordinary about her as to attract the attention of the archbishop or anyone else. Thankfully, some of her interior dispositions survived in another letter written to Father Jambreković:

Dear Father in Jesus,

The Christmas feasts are approaching—by the time this letter reaches you—we all will be enjoying the joy of Baby Jesus. That is why I am sending you my heartfelt wishes. May dear God grant that you accomplish much for Him and for souls. Pray for the same also for your missionary.

Surely you know that I have made my final vows. I was thinking also about you on that day; if you would know how happy I was that I could, of my own free will, ignite my own sacrifice. Now His and that for all eternity! You surely cannot imagine former Gonđa, now as the spouse of Jesus. But He has been always so infinitely good towards me—as if He wanted to insure the possession of my heart for Himself. Once again, I sincerely thank you for all that you have done for me.

Sister Gabriela is here. She works beautifully for Jesus—the most important is that she knows how to suffer and at the same time how to laugh. That is the most important—she suffers and she laughs. She is helping me a lot—in many ways—otherwise alone I would surely fail somewhere. She is ever ready to help me and I am so bad that I make use of her goodness.

Sister Bernard is making her vows on 23rd January 1938. Thanks be to God now again everything is all right—Jesus has surely chosen her for something special, since He has given her so much suffering. And she is a real hero, bearing up everything courageously with a smile. . . .

If we want Bengal for Christ we have to pay with many sacrifices.—Now I really rejoice when something does not go as I wish—because I see that He wants our trust—that is why in the loss let us praise God as if we have got everything.

Maybe Mama has written to you. She is now with my brother. They are so happy. One thing only they are missing— and that is their Gonđa. But thanks be to God that Mama again has the church nearby and that she can speak Albanian. How happy she is about it. My sister has become the prefect of the Sodality of Our Lady for the high school girls. I hope that she will do much for Jesus.

Surely you want some news also about me. One thing, pray much for me—I need prayer now more than ever. I want to be only all for Jesus—truly and not only by name and dress. Many times this goes upside-down—so my most reverend "I" gets the most important place.[25] Always the same proud Gonđa. Only one thing is different—my love for Jesus—I would give everything, even life itself, for Him. It sounds nice but in reality it is not so easy. And just that I want, that it not be easy. Do you remember once you told me in Skopje: "Gonđa, you want to drink the chalice[26] to the last drop." I do not know if at that time, I thought as I do now, but now yes, and that joyfully even without a tear. . . . It does not go so easily when a person has to be on one's feet from morning till evening. But still, everything is for Jesus; so like that everything is beautiful, even though it is difficult.

I am terribly sleepy this evening, so please forgive me for writing like this—but if I do not finish this evening, tomorrow will be too late. Please cordially greet Fr. Vizjak—today I have sent him some books.

> *Pray much for me always*
> *Faithfully in Jesus*
> *S. M. Teresa IBVM*[27]

Since Mother Teresa longed for complete union with Christ, who suffered on the Cross, she—His little bride—could not do otherwise than be united to Him in His suffering. If she could not remove His pain, then she would be there, on the Cross as it were, with Him. Choosing to share the lot of her Beloved, she welcomed the crosses that accompanied her constant self-giving.

The daily challenge of striving to overcome her faults was also a part of Mother Teresa's cross. She confided to her former confessor her struggle to conquer pride; yet, though unaware of it, she had already emerged victorious from many battles. While she lamented "the same proud Gonxha," others were impressed by her humility. Sister Gabriela, one of her childhood friends from Skopje, and now her companion in Loreto, wrote to Father Jambreković on the same day:

> I think that Jesus loves Sister Teresa very much. We are in the same house. I notice that every day she tries to please Jesus in everything. She is very busy, but she does not spare herself. She is very humble. It cost her dearly to achieve that, but I think that God has chosen her for great things. Admittedly, her deeds are entirely simple, but the perfection with which she does them, is just what Jesus asks of us.[28]

Mother Teresa was indeed striving to "drink the chalice to the last drop" in living her commitment "to be only all for Jesus." As another sister from her community affirmed: "She was very, very much in love with Almighty God."[29]

"I Go to Give Them Joy"

After her final vows, Mother Teresa returned to her duties at St. Mary's with her characteristic enthusiasm. She went back to teaching and to the ordinary daily activities of a Loreto nun. One of her companions remarked of her: "She was a very hard worker. Very. Up to time on this, up to time on that. She never wanted to shirk anything, she was always ready."[30]

On Sundays, she used to visit the poor in the slums. This apostolate,* which she herself chose, left a deep impression on her:

Every Sunday I visit the poor in Calcutta's slums. I cannot help them, because I do not have anything, but I go to give them joy. Last time about twenty little ones were eagerly expecting their "Ma."[31] When they saw me, they ran to meet me, even skipping on one foot. I entered. In that "para"—that is how a group of houses is called here—twelve families were living. Every family has only one room, two meters long and a meter and a half wide. The door is so narrow that I hardly could enter, and the ceiling is so low that I could not stand upright. . . . Now I do not wonder that my poor little ones love their school so much, and that so many of them suffer from tuberculosis. The poor mother [of the family she visited] did not utter even a word of complaint about her poverty. It was very painful for me, but at the same time I was very happy when I saw that they are happy because I visit them. Finally, the mother said to me: "Oh, Ma, come again! Your smile brought sun into this house!"[32]

To her friends back home in Skopje, she disclosed the prayer she whispered in her heart while returning to the convent: "O God, how easily I make them happy! Give me strength to be always the light of their lives and so lead them to You!"[33] She could not imagine that less than a decade later her prayer would be answered: she would dedicate not just her free time, but her entire life to the poor, becoming a beacon for them through her love and compassion.

---

*Derived from "apostle" (one sent on a mission), this term refers to the work of bringing people to Christ and His work of salvation. It also refers to the specific work done by members of a religious congregation as established by the founder or foundress.

TWO

Something Very Beautiful for Jesus

THE PRIVATE VOW, A FOLLY OF LOVE

Ask Jesus not to allow me to refuse Him anything,
however small. I [would] rather die.
—Mother Teresa

"This Is What Hides Everything in Me"

In the years following her final profession, Mother Teresa's passionate love for Jesus continued to prompt her to seek new and hidden ways of expressing her love. The most striking of these was an exceptional private vow she made in April 1942: "I made a vow to God, binding under [pain of] mortal sin, to give to God anything that He may ask, 'Not to refuse Him anything.'"[1] God had been kindling in her an ever-greater intensity of love that moved her to make this magnanimous offering. Only later did she explain the reason for it: "I wanted to give God something very beautiful"[2] and "without reserve."[3] This vow, truly a folly of love, expressed Mother Teresa's desire to "drink the chalice to the last drop" as she resolved to say "Yes" to God in all circumstances.

This private vow was one of Mother Teresa's greatest secrets. No one except her confessor, whose guidance and permission she sought in this matter, knew about it. Well acquainted with the depth of her spiritual life, he concluded that her daring request to bind herself in this way was not based on mere whim nor aimed at a dangerous or impossible ideal. It was, rather, built on her notable fidelity to commitments and already well-established habit of always seeking to do what was most pleasing to God. That her confessor granted her permission for her to undertake such an obligation confirms his confidence in her human and spiritual maturity.

When Mother Teresa finally referred to her special vow seventeen years later, she revealed its significance: "This is what hides everything in me."[4] The vow was indeed hiding the depth of her love for God, which motivated all her actions, especially her unconditional surrender to His will. Her encounter with the immensity of His love called for her response, as she would later explain:

Why must we give ourselves fully to God? Because God has given Himself to us. If God who owes nothing to us is ready to impart to us no less than Himself, shall we answer with just a fraction of ourselves? To give ourselves fully to God is a means of receiving God Himself. I for God and God for me. I live for God and give up my own self, and in this way induce God to live for me. Therefore to possess God we must allow Him to possess our soul.[5]

Love for Love

In embracing this new obligation, Mother Teresa was yearning to return love for love in a more radical way. One of the paradoxes of genuine love is that the lover freely wishes to bind him or herself irrevocably to the beloved. It was this mysterious feature of love that moved Mother Teresa to seal the total offering of herself by means of a vow and thus tangibly express her longing to be fully united with her Beloved. To the one less advanced on the road of love, this total surrender and complete conformity to God's will might seem a complete loss of freedom. But the one who truly loves seeks to realize the desire of the beloved, to fulfill his expectations even to the least detail. Thus for Mother Teresa the vow was the means of strengthening the bond with the One she loved and so experiencing the true freedom that only love can give.

Mother Teresa would have read about the practice of making private vows in the spiritual literature of her time.

Irish Jesuit Father William Doyle,[6] made numerous private vows, as he found this practice a help in keeping his resolutions. One such vow, which he made in 1911 and renewed from day to day until he could obtain permission from his confessor to make it permanently, was: "I deliberately vow, and bind myself, under pain of mortal sin, to refuse Jesus no sacrifice, which I clearly see He is asking from me."[7]

Sister Benigna Consolata Ferrero[8] also made a number of private vows, for example the vow of doing all for love, the vow of abandonment, the vow of perfection, and the vow of humility. Referring to this last vow, which she first made in 1903, she wrote: "My Jesus wishes that I should make the vow of humility, which consists, He told me, in recognizing that I am nothing without the aid of God, and in desiring to be unknown and despised. He told me to execute without delay or hesitation all that He had asked of me."[9]

An edition of the autobiography of St. Thérèse of Lisieux that circulated at the time included the Bull of Canonization of St. Thérèse of the Child Jesus,[10] by Pope Pius XI, which stated: "Inspired by the Holy Spirit she longed to lead a most holy life and promised earnestly that she would refuse God nothing He should seem to ask of her, a resolution she endeavored to keep until death." Reading about this promise of her patron saint as well as the private vows made by Fr. Doyle and Sr. Benigna Consolata no doubt inspired Mother Teresa and influenced her to do the same.

Mother Teresa's understanding and practice of making vows was also greatly influenced by her cultural background. Having been raised in a family that was strongly rooted in its Albanian traditions, she was acquainted with the highly revered and treasured practice of *besa* (as it is known in her native language) or "word of honor." Because *besa* demands absolute fidelity to one's given word, it has an almost sacred character as an oath or a vow; it cannot be broken, even at the cost of one's life. Mother Teresa would later explain: "They [Albanians] have a word, *besa*, which means even if you have killed my father and the police are after you, if I have given you my word, then even if the police kill me, still I will not disclose your name."[11] In the light of her upbringing, Mother Teresa's private vow took on added gravity: She was determined to be faithful to her word given to God, even at the price of her life.

"Not to Refuse Him Anything"

For almost eleven years, Mother Teresa had faithfully lived her vow of obedience. As a fervent Loreto sister, she believed that her religious superiors took the place of Christ, and therefore in conforming her will and judgment to theirs and submitting to their commands, she was submitting to Christ Himself.[12] Though she endeavored to live the demanding vow of obedience to perfection, her burning desire to prove her love was not yet satisfied. She wanted to give even more! So she bound herself by a vow "to give to God anything that He may ask—'Not to refuse Him anything'"[13]—choosing to be considered accountable "under pain of mortal sin."[14]

She knew well that the consequence of a mortal sin was the death of God's life in the soul and ultimately, if unrepented, the loss of friendship with Him for all eternity. The thought of even a momentary separation from Him by a single offense was for her unbearable. Refusing anything to the One she loved was for her equivalent to the pain of eternal doom. Thus she decided to consider even the smallest voluntary fault, the slightest refusal to submit to His will, as the greatest offense. "Ask Jesus not to allow me to refuse Him anything, however small," she later wrote to her spiritual director. "I [would] rather die."[15] Every new step in her life would be a new opportunity to testify to her fidelity to that promise.

With her vow, Mother Teresa aimed at perfect interior compliance to what was most pleasing to God even in the smallest detail. Hence the vow implied a commitment to discern carefully and obey the slightest manifestations of God's will. This habitual and loving attentiveness to the present moment called for inner silence and recollection. "In the silence of the heart God speaks," Mother Teresa would often say, with a conviction that sprang from being constantly attuned to His voice.

The Blessedness of Submission

Mother Teresa was not afraid to make such a serious commitment, though this implied renouncing her own will at each moment. She knew that God loved her and she trusted that His will for her would always be an expression of that unfailing love, however difficult or even impossible it might be at times to fathom His designs. Consequently, even when she was challenged seemingly beyond her ability, her previous experiences that God had never failed her assured her that she could take the risk once again. Only this certainty that she was loved unconditionally could have given her enough confidence to abandon herself to God so completely and without reserve. "Under pain of mortal sin" was indeed without reserve.

The gravity of her commitment did not make her gloomy or despondent. On the contrary, she was "full of fun" and "enjoyed everything that went on."[16] Her joy was not just a matter of temperament; it was, rather, the fruit of the "blessedness of submission"[17] that she lived. "When I see someone sad," she would say, "I always think, she is refusing something to Jesus."[18] It was in giving Jesus whatever He asked that she found her deepest and lasting joy; in giving Him joy she found her own joy.

> Cheerfulness is a sign of a generous and mortified person who forgetting all things, even herself, tries to please her God in all she does for souls. Cheerfulness is often a cloak which hides a life of sacrifice, continual union with God, fervor and generosity. A person who has this gift of cheerfulness very often reaches a great height of perfection. For God loves a cheerful giver[19] and He takes close to His heart the religious He loves.[20]

The Vow in Daily Life

Mother Teresa's secret vow touched all aspects of her daily life. Ordinary as well as exceptional moments became opportunities to welcome His will and respond by doing "something beautiful for God."

Like her patroness, St. Thérèse of Lisieux, Mother Teresa aimed at "profiting by all the smallest things, and doing them through love."[21] Later she explained to her sisters:

> To the good God nothing is little because He is so great and we so small—that is why He stoops down and takes the trouble to make those little things for us—to give us a chance to prove our love for Him. Because He makes them, they are very great. He cannot make anything small; they are infinite. Yes my dear children, be faithful in little practices of love, of little sacrifices— of the little interior mortification—of little fidelities to Rule, which will build in you the life of holiness—make you Christ-like.[22]

She would again insist: "Don't look for big things, just do small things with great love. . . . The smaller the thing, the greater must be our love."[23] She lived this principle in whatever she was doing throughout each day. Whether it was big or small mattered not to her; everything she did was an opportunity to love.

Prompted by her vow, Mother Teresa also developed the habit of responding immediately to the demands of the present moment. A strong impulse to act without delay—once she was certain that it was God's will for her—was a notable characteristic of all her undertakings. At times this swiftness to act was misinterpreted and taken for impetuousness and lack of prudence. Many years later, in an attempt to clarify one occasion of misunderstanding, she would explain to Archbishop Périer that the private vow she had made many years before was the hidden reason for her urgency.

> I have never told Your Grace the cause of my wanting to act at once.—In 1942—I wanted to give Jesus something without reserve.—With the permission of my confessor, I made a vow to God—binding under mortal sin—to give to God anything that

He may ask—"Not to refuse Him anything." For these 17 years I have tried [to be faithful to that vow]—and this is the reason why I want to act at once.—It is for Your Grace to prevent me—and when you say, "No," I am certain that my vow is alright—for then I don't refuse God my submission— . . . In this point, there has never been a doubt in my soul—because I have always put them before you and Fr. C. Van Exem and each time your "Yes" or "No" has satisfied me as the will of God.[24]

"Extraordinary in Her Sacrifice"

In April 1942, when Mother Teresa made this remarkable vow, the involvement of India in World War II was disrupting the life of her community and school, and her resolve not to refuse God anything would be put to the test. The British Army requisitioned St. Mary's School as a military hospital and, as a result, all nuns and boarders had to leave Calcutta. The English section of the school was moved to Simla, while the Bengali section, with about a hundred boarding girls,[25] was evacuated to Morapai. A few months later, the Bengali section returned to Calcutta and resumed school activities in rented quarters until 1946. One of the boarders remembered the decisive role Mother Teresa played in those difficult years:

At that time our financial condition was very bad. Loreto sisters used to look after us. We were depending on them. Mother used to help us in education. She used to do many things for the girls. When there was no place in 15 Convent Road either to sleep or study, she started looking for places. After that she found a place at 14 Canal Street. The building had four big rooms and a hall. She rented those rooms. Everyday in the morning she used to go with the girls there. They used to stay there the whole day, bathing, studying and spend the whole day there. In the evening, as soon as the classes were over, Mother used to take us back to St. Mary's [school on Convent Road].[26]

As the number of nuns caring for the boarders was reduced, most of the practical concerns for running the house fell on Mother Teresa's shoulders, in addition to her already demanding duties of teaching classes and overseeing the girls. After a few months of bearing these responsibilities she became seriously ill. In September 1942 a Croatian missionary in Bengal reported: "Mother Teresa was very sick, so they did not have much hope that she would survive; but now she is again on her feet and works for ten."[27] One of her pupils enriches this account with some details: "During World War II, there was no teacher from class 4 to class 10. Mother took all the classes and she kept us busy in order to make us forget and overcome our fear."

Added to these hardships was the Bengal famine of 1942–1943, which took the lives of at least two million people. As the sisters and students began to suffer from food shortages, Mother Teresa, who had pledged to refuse nothing to God, in turn trusted that God would not refuse anything to her. One of her former students remembers, "One day, there was no food left. At 8:00 a.m. Mother [Teresa] told us: 'I am going out children, you stay in the chapel and pray.' By 4:00 p.m. the godown[28] was full of different kinds of vegetables. We could not believe our eyes."

In 1944 Mother Teresa was appointed the principal of St. Mary's as well as the de facto superior of the Daughters of St. Anne (the Bengali congregation affiliated with Loreto). She welcomed these new duties as coming from the hand of God. Though efficient and exacting in carrying out her responsibilities, she was not stricter with others than she was with herself. Her example inspired those around her. One of her sisters noted: "She is an utterly selfless creature. She is extraordinary in her sacrifice. She can do anything for the love of God, endure any humiliation or suffering."²⁹

In her readiness to meet every manifestation of God's will with an eager "Yes," Mother Teresa at times ventured into very perilous situations. In August 1946 the Hindu-Muslim conflict broke out in Calcutta, unleashing massive violence. "The Day of Great Killing," as it was later called, left five thousand dead on the streets and at least ten times more wounded. All activities in the city, including the provision of food, were stopped. Compelled by the needs of her pupils, Mother Teresa decided to leave the safety of the convent walls in search of food.

I went out from St. Mary's, Entally. I had three hundred girls in the boarding school and we had nothing to eat. We were not supposed to go out into the streets, but I went anyway. Then I saw the bodies on the streets, stabbed, beaten, lying there in strange positions, in their dried blood. We had been behind our safe walls. We knew that there had been rioting. People had been jumping over our walls, first a Hindu, then a Muslim. . . . We took in each one and helped him to escape safely. When I went out on the street, only then did I see the death that was following them. A lorry full of soldiers stopped me and told me I should not be out on the street. No one should be out, they said. I told them I had to come out and take the risk; I had three hundred students who had nothing to eat. The soldiers had rice and they drove me back to the school and unloaded bags of rice.³⁰

It was not Mother Teresa's superiors who demanded or expected that she put her life at risk. Nor did her responsibility for the girls under her charge oblige her to brave the streets of the blood-bathed city. Rather she chose to go. In the depths of her heart she may have perceived the call of the One to whom she had pledged to give anything that He might ask. And she would not refuse! She entrusted herself to His providential intervention and her trust was rewarded. There may have been many moments when her fidelity to her private vow was challenged, but with each new "Yes" she emerged more intimately united with the Lord to whom she was ready to give "even life itself."

Only with God's Grace

Mother Teresa never lost the keen awareness of her own weakness, limitation, and poverty. Only God's assistance, His constant grace, would make sustained faithfulness possible. As she would later explain, she was all too aware that "we can refuse Christ just as we refuse others: I will not give you my hands to work with, my eyes to see with, my feet to walk with, my mind to study with, my heart to love with. You knock at the door but I will not open. I will not give You the key of my heart."[31] Hence Mother Teresa would always ask others for the support of prayers.

Mother Teresa's vow was a providential preparation for the mission that lay ahead of her. Her pledge "not to refuse Him anything" expressed her firm resolution to set no limit to God's plans for her. Jesus, for His part, took her at her word. Four years later, Mother Teresa would receive a new call from Jesus in which He would echo the very vow she had made to Him.

THREE

"Come, Be My Light"

"THE CALL WITHIN A CALL"

> *Wilt thou refuse?*
> —*Christ to Mother Teresa*

The Day of Inspiration

In September 1946 Mother Teresa, then thirty-six years old, was sent for her annual retreat and a needed rest to the Loreto Convent in Darjeeling, a town nestled in the foothills of the Himalayas some four hundred miles north of Calcutta. During the journey by train, on Tuesday, September 10, 1946, she had a decisive mystical encounter with Christ. Though she would persist in letting the details remain veiled in silence, she later revealed:

[It] was a call within my vocation. It was a second calling. It was a vocation to give up even Loreto where I was very happy and to go out in the streets to serve the poorest of the poor. It was in that train, I heard the call to give up all and follow Him into the slums—to serve Him in the poorest of the poor. . . . I knew it was His will and that I had to follow Him. There was no doubt that it was going to be His work."[1]

Mother Teresa considered this day, celebrated later as "Inspiration Day," to be the real beginning of the Missionaries of Charity. In the entrance register that records the personal data of those who join the congregation,[2] she noted down under her own name: "Entrance into the Society—10 September 1946." As she would tell her sisters late in life:

The strong grace of Divine Light and Love Mother received on the train journey to Darjeeling on 10th September 1946 is where the M.C. [Missionaries of Charity] begins—in the depths of God's infinite longing to love and to be loved.[3]

She further explained:

It was on this day in 1946 in the train to Darjeeling that God gave me the "call within a call" to satiate the thirst of Jesus by serving Him in the poorest of the poor.[4]

"I Thirst"

To the end of her life, Mother Teresa insisted that the single most important reason for the existence of the congregation she

founded was to satiate the thirst of Jesus. In the first draft of the
Rules (written several months after her encounter on the train),
which remain essentially unchanged to this day, she expressed the
aim of the new congregation: "The General End of the Missionaries
of Charity is to satiate the thirst of Jesus Christ on the Cross for
Love and Souls."

That the aim of the congregation is "to satiate the thirst of Jesus
on the Cross" indicates that her mystical experience took place in the
context of Calvary, at the time when Jesus, dying on the Cross, cried
out "I thirst."[5] It was this Scripture quote that stood for her as a
summary and a reminder of her call. While instructing her sisters,
she would explain:

"I thirst," Jesus said on the cross when Jesus was deprived of every
consolation, dying in absolute Poverty, left alone, despised and
broken in body and soul. He spoke of His thirst—not for
water—but for love, for sacrifice.

Jesus is God: therefore, His love, His thirst is infinite. Our
aim is to quench this infinite thirst of a God made man. Just like
the adoring angels in Heaven ceaselessly sing the praises of God,
so the Sisters, using the four vows of Absolute Poverty, Chastity,
Obedience and Charity towards the poor ceaselessly quench the
thirsting God by their love and of the love of the souls they
bring to Him.[6]

There was much more behind this explanation than she ever revealed. But by words and example, her followers would grasp the
meaning of the grace she received that day.

Mother Teresa knew that only by being united with Mary, the
first one to hear Jesus' cry of thirst, could she fulfill her mission.
Thus she exhorted her followers:

✳ Let us always remain with Mary our Mother on Calvary near
the crucified Jesus,[7] with our chalice made of the four vows, and
fill it with the love of self-sacrifice, of pure love, always held up
close to His suffering Heart, so that He may be pleased to accept
our love.[8]

Thirst—a physical need that craves to be satisfied, a painful
longing for what is missing—became synonymous for her with particular aspects of God's love for each person. A few years before her
death, she would remind her followers:

✳ Jesus wants me to tell you again . . . how much is the love He has
for each one of you—beyond all what you can imagine. . . . Not
only He loves you, even more—He longs for you. He misses you
when you don't come close. He thirsts for you. He loves you
always, even when you don't feel worthy. . . .

   For me it is so clear—everything in MC exists only to satiate
Jesus. His words on the wall of every MC chapel,[9] they are not
from [the] past only, but alive here and now, spoken to you. Do
you believe it? . . . Why does Jesus say "I thirst"? What does it
mean? Something so hard to explain in words— . . . "I thirst" is
something much deeper than just Jesus saying "I love you." Until
you know deep inside that Jesus thirsts for you—you can't begin
to know who He wants to be for you. Or who He wants you to
be for Him.[10]

This profound mystery of God's thirst for love and for souls
was engraved on her heart on the journey to Darjeeling, and she
was called to reveal it to the poorest of the poor. In the first Rules
she identified this special mission:

The Particular End is to carry Christ into the homes and streets
of the slums, among the sick, dying, the beggars and the little
street children. The sick will be nursed as far as possible in their
poor homes. The little children will have a school in the slums.
The beggars will be sought and visited in their holes outside the
town or on the streets.

She would later elaborate and broaden the text to read, "Our particular mission is to labour at the salvation and sanctification of the
poorest of the poor, not only in the slums, but also all over the world
wherever they may be."[11] The poor and those who suffer most were
the particular object of her love. She knew that only love, a love that
has God as its origin and end, would give meaning and happiness to
their lives. Like the Good Samaritan,[12] through her immediate and effective service, she was intent on making God's love concrete to the
poor in the desperate situations they encountered in their daily lives.
Through her simple works of love, she wanted to help them live their
lives with dignity and give them the opportunity to know God. The
"salvation and sanctification of the poorest of the poor" or the "salvation of souls" thus meant for her an untiring effort to help everyone
encounter God's infinite love, and having come to know Him, to love
and serve Him in return thereby reaching the blessedness of heaven.

Not only did Mother Teresa bring the light of Christ to the
poorest of the poor; she also met Christ in each one of them. Jesus
chose to identify Himself with the poor and with all those who suffer, and he affirmed this when he said, "As you did it to one of the
least of these my brethren, you did it to me."[13] Mother Teresa grasped
the depth of Jesus' identification with each sufferer and understood
the mystical connection between the sufferings of Christ and the
sufferings of the poor. Through her humble service she endeavored
"to bring souls to God—and God to souls."[14]

The "Voice"

That same September 10, Mother Teresa began to receive a series of interior locutions[15] that continued until the middle of the following year. Mother Teresa was actually hearing Jesus' voice and intimately conversing with Him. She is among those saints to whom Jesus spoke directly, asking them to undertake a special mission among His people. From the beginning of this extraordinary experience Mother Teresa had no doubt that it was Jesus who was speaking to her. Yet she would mostly refer to these communications as the "Voice."

A moving exchange of great beauty went on between Christ and Mother Teresa. With utmost tenderness, He addressed her as *"My own spouse"* or *"My own little one."*[16] "My Jesus" or "My own Jesus," replied Mother Teresa, longing to return love for love. In this sacred dialogue, Jesus was revealing His Heart to her: His pain, His love, His compassion, His thirst for those who suffer most. He also revealed His plan to send her to them as a carrier of His love. This revelation had a deep echo in her soul. Many years earlier, writing back home, she had expressed her desire "to bring joy to the lives"[17] of those to whom she had been sent. She had prayed for "the strength to always be the light of their lives and so lead them to You!"[18] However, the call to leave Loreto and be a sign of Christ's presence, a carrier of His love and compassion to the poorest of the poor in the slums, was not the kind of answer she expected in response to her prayer. Yet the "Voice" kept pleading, "*Come, come, carry Me into the holes of the poor. Come, be My light.*" Jesus' invitation was imbued with trust; He counted on her response.

During her retreat in Darjeeling, Mother Teresa began a record of "what went on between Him and me during the days of much prayer." She later referred to these notes as "the copy of the Voice since September 1946" and used them in her correspondence with the archbishop of Calcutta, quoting the "Voice" she had been hearing. But some months were to pass until that correspondence began.

The First Step

In early October, Mother Teresa returned from Darjeeling to Calcutta to resume her duties at St. Mary's school. As soon as the opportunity presented itself, she related what had happened on the train and during the retreat to her spiritual director, Jesuit Father Céleste Van Exem,* and "showed him the few notes . . . written during the retreat."[19]

Mother Teresa wanted to act immediately upon her inspiration. Yet because she had consecrated her life to God through a vow of obedience, she could proceed only with the approval of her superiors. To her, their blessing was not a mere formality but a protection and assurance that God's hand was in her undertaking. Only their permission would give her the certainty that this call was indeed God's will and not some delusion.

It was the task of her spiritual director, of the superiors of her religious order, and, especially, of the Jesuit archbishop of Calcutta, Ferdinand Périer, to test and discern this call. If they found it inauthentic, they would be obliged to discourage it; if they found it genuine, they would be conscience-bound to help bring it to realization.

Father Van Exem, being a wise spiritual director, took the matter very seriously. He had great admiration for this fervent and humble nun, and a respect for the depth of her spiritual life. He had

*Father Céleste Van Exem was Mother Teresa's spiritual director beginning in 1944. He was born on October 4, 1908, in Elverdinge, Belgium, and entered the Society of Jesus in 1927 and was ordained in 1940, at St. Mary's College, in Kurseong, India. After assisting in the foundation of the Missionairies of Charity, he served for many years as confessor of the sisters in Calcutta. He died on September 20, 1993.

no second thoughts about her sincerity but was aware of the risks of placing too much credence in such experiences should their source prove not to be divine. Knowing Mother Teresa's firm determination to do only God's will, he decided to test the authenticity of the inspirations and counted on her obedience as a confirmation of God's hand in this extraordinary happening.

"He Forbade Me to Even Think About It"

Father Van Exem's first request to Mother Teresa was to stop thinking about the inspiration, to let it rest. In a later letter to her superior general, she wrote:

> [Father Van Exem] put me off—though he saw that it was from God, still he forbade me to even think about it. Often, very often during the four months [between September 1946 and January 1947], I asked him to let me speak to His Grace [the archbishop of Calcutta], [but] each time he refused.[20]

The renunciation that he asked of her was quite a drastic way of testing the genuineness of the call, but nothing less would assure him of its divine origin. So in obedience to her spiritual director, Mother Teresa remained silent and in prayer, not knowing what the outcome would be.

By January of 1947, Father Van Exem had no doubt that Mother Teresa's inspiration was from God and that the time had come for her to pursue the realization of the call. Thus he gave her permission to write to the archbishop. In a simple and straightforward letter she told Archbishop Périer what she believed God was asking of her.

"What Went on Between Him and Me"

Your Grace,

From last Sept. strange thoughts and desires have been filling
my heart. They got stronger and clearer during the 8 days retreat
I made in Darjeeling. On coming here I told Fr. Van Exem
everything—I showed him the few notes I had written during the
retreat.—He told me he thought it was God's inspiration—but
to pray and remain silent over it. I kept on telling him whatever
passed in my soul—in thoughts and desires.—Then yesterday he
wrote this "I cannot prevent you from talking or writing to His
Grace. You will write to His Grace as a daughter to her father, in
perfect trust and sincerity, without any fear or anxiety, telling him
how it all went, adding that you talked to me and that now I
think I cannot in conscience prevent you from exposing
everything to him."

Before I begin I want to tell you that at one word that Your
Grace would say I am ready never to consider again any of those
strange thoughts which have been coming continually.

During the year very often I have been longing to be all for
Jesus and to make other souls—especially Indian, come and love
Him fervently—to identify myself with Indian girls completely,
and so love Him as He has never been loved before. I thought
[it] was one of my many mad desires. I read the life of St. M.
Cabrini.[21]—She did so much for the Americans because she
became one of them. Why can't I do for India what she did for
Amer[America]? She did not wait for souls to come to her—she
went to them with her zealous workers. Why can't I do the same for

Him here? There are so many souls—pure—holy who are longing to give themselves only to God. European orders are too rich for them.—They get more than they give.—*"Wouldst thou not help."* How can I? I have been and am very happy as a Loreto Nun.—To leave that what I love and expose myself to new labours and sufferings which will be great, to be the laughing stock of so many—especially religious—to cling [to] and choose deliberately the hard things of an Indian life—to [cling to and choose] loneliness and ignominy—uncertainty—and all because Jesus wants it—because something is calling me "to leave all and gather the few—to live His life—to do His work in India." These thoughts were a cause of much suffering—but the voice kept on saying *"Wilt thou refuse."* One day at Holy Com.[Communion] I heard the same voice very distinctly—*"I want Indian nuns, victims of My love, who would be Mary & Martha,*[22] *who would be so very united to Me as to radiate My love on souls. I want free nuns covered with My poverty of the Cross.*[23]*—I want obedient nuns covered with My obedience of the Cross.*[24] *I want full of love nuns covered with the Charity of the Cross.*[25] *Wilt thou refuse to do this for Me?"* On another day. *"You have become My Spouse for my Love—you have come to India for Me. The thirst you had for souls brought you so far.— Are you afraid to take one more step for your Spouse—for Me—for souls?—Is your generosity grown cold—am I a second to you? You did not die for souls—that is why you don't care what happens to them.— Your heart was never drowned in sorrow as it was My Mother's. We both gave our all for souls—and you? You are afraid that you will lose your vocation—you will become secular—you will be wanting in perseverance.—Nay—your vocation is to love and suffer and save souls and by taking this step you will fulfil My Heart's desire for you.—That is your vocation.—You will dress in simple Indian clothes or rather like My Mother dressed—simple and poor.—Your present habit is holy because it*

is My symbol—your sarie will become holy because it will be My symbol."
I tried to persuade Our Lord that I would try to become a very
fervent holy Loreto nun, a real victim here in this vocation—but
the answer came very clear again. "*I want Indian Missionary Sisters
of Charity—who would be My fire of love amongst the very poor—the
sick—the dying—the little street children.—The poor I want you to bring
to Me—and the Sisters that would offer their lives as victims of My love—
would bring these souls to Me. You are I know the most incapable
person, weak & sinful, but just because you are that I want to use you,
for My Glory! Wilt thou refuse?*" These words or rather this voice
frightened me. The thought of eating, sleeping—living like the
Indians filled me with fear. I prayed long—I prayed so much—
I asked our Mother Mary to ask Jesus to remove all this from
me. The more I prayed—the clearer grew the voice in my heart
and so I prayed that He would do with me whatever He wanted.
He asked again and again. Then once more the voice was very
clear—"*You have been always saying 'do with me what ever you wish'—
Now I want to act—let Me do it—My little Spouse—My own little one.—
Do not fear—I shall be with you always.—You will suffer and you suffer
now—but if you are My own little Spouse—the Spouse of the Crucified
Jesus—you will have to bear these torments on your heart.—Let Me act.—
Refuse Me not.—Trust Me lovingly—trust Me blindly.*" "*Little one give
Me souls—give Me the souls of the poor little street children.—How it
hurts—if you only knew—to see these poor children soiled with sin. I long
for the purity of their love.—If you would only answer My call—and
bring Me these souls—draw them away from the hands of the evil one.—
If you only knew how many little ones fall into sin everyday. There are
convents with numbers of nuns caring for the rich and able to do people,
but for My very poor there is absolutely none. For them I long—them I
love.—Wilt thou refuse?*" "*Ask His Grace to give Me this in thanksgiving
of the 25 years of grace I have given him.*"

This is what went on between Him and me during the days of much prayer.—Now the whole thing stands clear before my eyes as follows—

"THE CALL"

To be an Indian—to live with them—like them—so as to get at the people's heart. The order would start outside Calcutta—Cossipore—open lonely place or St. John's Sealdah where the Sisters could have a real contemplative life in their noviciate—where they would complete one full year of true interior life—and one in action. The Sisters are to cling to perfect poverty—poverty of the Cross—nothing but God.—So as not to have riches enter their heart, they would have nothing of the outside—but they will keep up themselves with the labour of their hands—Franciscan poverty[26]—Benedict's labour.[27]

In the order girls of any nationality should be taken—but they must become Indian-minded—dress in simple clothes. A long white long-sleeved habit, light blue sarie, and a white veil, sandals—no stockings—a crucifix—girdle[28] and rosary.

The Sisters should get a very full knowledge of the interior life—from holy priests who would help them to become so united to God so as to radiate Him when they join the mission field. They should become true victims—no words—but in every sense of the word, Indian victims for India. Love should be the word, the fire, that will make them live the life to its full. If the nuns are very poor they will be free to love only God—to serve Him only—to be only His. The two years in perfect solitude should make them think of the interior while they will be in the midst of the exterior.

So as to renew and keep up the spirit—the Sisters should spend one day in every week in the house—the Mother house of the city when they are in the mission.

"THE WORK"

The Sisters' work would be to go to the people.—No boarding schools—but plenty of schools—free—up to class II²⁹ only. In each parish two sisters would go—one for the sick and the dying—one for the school. If the number requires the pairs can increase. The Sisters would teach the little ones—help them have pure recreations and so keep them from the street and sin. The school should be only in the very poor places of the parish, to get the children from the streets, to keep them for the poor parents who have to work. The one who will take care of the sick—she will assist the dying—do all the work for the sick—just as much if not more, what a person gets in a hospital—wash them and prepare the place for His coming. At the appointed time the sisters will all meet at the same place from the different parishes and go home—where they would have this complete separation from the world.—This in the cities where the number of the poor is great.—In the villages—the same thing—only there they could leave the said village—once their work of instruction and service ends. To move about with great ease and fast each nun should learn how to ride a bicycle, some how to drive a bus. This is a little too up to date—but souls are dying for want of care—for want of love. These Sisters—these true victims should do the work that is wanting in Christ's apostolate in India. They should also have a hospital for little children with bad diseases. The nuns of this order will be Missionaries of Charity or Missionary Sisters of Charity.

God is calling me—unworthy and sinful that I am. I am longing to give all for souls. They will all think me mad—after so many years—to begin a thing which will bring me for the most part only suffering—but He calls me also to join the few to start the work, to fight the devil and deprive him of the thousand little souls which he is destroying every day.

This is rather long—but I have told you everything as I would have told my Mother.—I long to be really only His—to burn myself completely for Him and souls.—I want Him to be loved tenderly by many.—So if you think, if you wish—I am ready to do His Will. Count not my feelings—count not the cost I would have to pay—I am ready—for I have already given my all to Him. And if you think all this a deception—that too I would accept—and sacrifice myself completely.—I am sending this through Fr. Van Exem. I have given him full permission to use anything I have told him which is in connection with me and Him in this work.— My change to Asansol seems to me a part of His plan—there I will have more time to pray and prepare myself for His coming. In this matter I leave myself completely in your hands.

Pray for me. That I would become a religious according to His heart.

Your devoted child in J.C. [Jesus Christ],
Mary Teresa.[30]

"Wilt Thou Refuse?"

At the time she wrote this letter, Mother Teresa was already a person of considerable holiness. Still, as self-sacrificing and courageous, as generous and compassionate to the poor as she was, on her own initiative she would never have considered leaving Loreto to found a new religious community. But the inspiration was so compelling that she could fail to heed the "Voice" only at the steep price of being unfaithful to her deepest love.

Initially she found herself intimidated by these extraordinary experiences; troubling thoughts arose in her heart. Questioning her own capacity to meet the demands of this new call, she exposed with absolute honesty her fear, her confusion, her reluctance to embrace the hardships and suffer the derision of others that were sure to follow. Not everyone in the Church or city would approve of a European nun living outside the convent walls in a desire to identify with the poor in their local culture and conditions. She grieved as well at the prospect of leaving Loreto, even offering to be "a real victim of [His] love" where she was. In all this, she showed herself to be so ordinary, so real, and even skeptical of her ability to carry out such an important mission.

Yet Mother Teresa, passionately in love with Jesus, could not ignore His "Voice" that kept insisting: *"Wilt thou refuse?"* This piercing question had a particularly compelling effect on her heart because it echoed the secret vow she had made four years earlier. Jesus' plea, like no other, had the power of stirring her inmost being. God was honoring the magnanimity of her soul—and His call evoked at one and the same time joy, because she was being taken at her word, and pain because she felt challenged seemingly beyond her capacity.

After the initial struggle, Mother Teresa remained resolute in her conviction that God was calling her to this new life. By the time she wrote to Archbishop Périer in January, she was clear about what she intended to do. She was innovative in her proposals, ready to "burn myself completely for Him and souls," giving her whole being in response to His call.

FOUR

"To Bring Joy to the Suffering Heart of Jesus"

LONGING TO GIVE ALL

If only one little unhappy child is made happy
with the love of Jesus, . . . will it not be worth . . .
giving all for that?
—Mother Teresa

A Change to Asansol

Shortly before writing her first letter to Archbishop Périer, Mother Teresa's provincial[1] had notified her of her imminent transfer from Calcutta to the Loreto community in Asansol, a town about 140 miles to the northwest. Some sisters of her community had noticed Mother Teresa's frequent and long conversations in confession with Father Van Exem in the months following her retreat in Darjeeling. From this simple fact, suspicion arose concerning the nature of their relationship. Obviously, the sisters had no clue about the reason for these prolonged meetings. Nonetheless, they deemed them inappropriate and brought them to the notice of her religious superiors. On the basis of these "uncharitable suggestions and remarks,"[2] the decision was made to transfer Mother Teresa to the Asansol community.

For St. Mary's school, her leaving was "obviously a blow,"[3] and her absence was keenly felt. As for herself, though she admitted missing St. Mary's and the girls she had under her charge, she accepted the change serenely. Despite the sacrifice of leaving so much she loved, she saw God's hand in these happenings and believed the move ultimately came from Him. This faith-filled response to difficulties was typical of Mother Teresa. The archbishop later affirmed, "In spite of her trials she has experienced from time to time in religious life, she is very loyal to the Institute of the Blessed Virgin Mary and I have never heard her complaining of superiors, or sisters, even when I knew she had been misunderstood."[4] In fact, even in the midst of this unjust situation she remained impressively charitable toward all.

Before leaving Calcutta, Mother Teresa had learned from Father Van Exem about Archbishop Périer's initial reaction to her proposal. Though Father Van Exem expected that with his endorsement of Mother Teresa's plans, the archbishop would give her his consent to move ahead quickly, the archbishop remained cautious and told her he needed time to pray, reflect, and consult.

This unexpected reply became a fresh source of suffering for Mother Teresa, even greater than all her previous fear and confusion. Convinced of the genuineness of the call, and accustomed to act at once as soon as God's will became clear, she felt she must begin immediately. Yet, as convinced as she was, she would not begin without the permission of her religious superiors, for she believed that through her obedience to God's representatives His will would ultimately and securely be made known. Therefore, in spite of her longing to start her new mission and her distress at not being able to do so, she could do nothing but wait.

Upon her arrival at Asansol in mid-January 1947, Mother Teresa, with her characteristic wholeheartedness, took up her new role of teaching. One benefit of the transfer was that she had fewer responsibilities than in Calcutta, and thus more time to spend in prayer. This was a providential opportunity to prepare herself for her new mission.

Her longing to begin the work among the poorest of the poor of Calcutta was becoming ever stronger. As a result, Mother Teresa engaged in a spirited exchange of letters with Archbishop Périer over the next several months. She tried to convince him to let her begin; he, with all due prudence, insisted on the need to wait.

"The Longing to Give All to Our Lord"

The archbishop had expressed to Father Van Exem his three concerns: first, he questioned how much of Mother Teresa's self-will and self-interest were involved; second, he considered the reported request of Jesus that Archbishop Périer approve the project in thanksgiving for his being a bishop for twenty-five years as too sentimental;[5] and lastly, he wondered if the change to Asansol might have provoked her request to leave the Loreto order and start a new congregation.

Father Van Exem had informed Mother Teresa to expect the archbishop's written response to her letter. By January 25 she had not received a reply. The time of waiting already seemed very long, so she decided to write again and address the archbishop's preliminary reservations.

Your Grace,

Fr. Van Exem told me that you had written—but up to now no letter has come.—I believe the post is very bad this side. Any way I thank you for all you told him.

Re—the "work" I have been praying so much to see and understand how much of self is in it, how much of sentimentality is in it. Here in Asansol I have more time to spend with Our Lord and often, very often, I have prayed to see—so as not to deceive or to be deceived—and yet the "work" remains as clear as before—the longing to give all to Our Lord and make many souls do the same remains the same.

I find that if the work begins—there will be plenty of humiliations, loneliness and suffering for me.—As I am, I am very happy and here especially—but Our Lord does not stop calling.—I have tried to stop these thoughts—but without any fruit. I don't see what the self can get from it—I know everybody will speak against.—No, Your Grace, forgive me for saying—in the work there will be complete surrender of all I have and all I am—there will be nothing absolutely left.—Now, I am His, only His—I have given Him everything—I have not been seeking self for sometime now. I know you love the truth—and this is the truth. If I said the contrary I would tell a lie. God has done everything. He simply took everything.—Now I am His. You know, you have been told everything.—So if you say give up all thoughts, I shall try to obey.—We[6] have both done our parts—now it rests with you.

As for the sentimentality—you cannot deny that Our Lord has done wonders for you in these 25 years.—So what He asks is just as natural as it is supernatural.—It is for you to say yes or no.

I leave the whole thing in your hands.—Whatever You wish, that I shall do most happily.

The change to Asansol has absolutely nothing to do with it—what [is] more, I take it as one more proof that He wants the work.

From the age of 5½ years—when first I received Him [in Holy Communion]—the love for souls has been within.—It grew with the years—until I came to India—with the hope of saving many souls. In those 18 years I have tried to live up to His desires.—I have been burning with longing to love Him as He has never been loved before.—I have been praying. In St. Mary's He did use me—it was His doing. I made many mistakes—but these were my doings.—I loved St. Mary's just only for this one thing—the continual touch of Jesus on souls. I worked with Him in them. But when M. [Mother] Provincial told me that I was to come here—I was terribly happy in my heart—that I could give something I love to Jesus, and this is what made me keep smiling during those days and even now. I took the change as a God Send—to get stronger to prepare my body and soul for His coming. Here I have nothing to think about—except how to live for others. The work I have to do is just the one that will teach me this lesson. And then these thoughts—the voice in my heart only started last Sept.—from the day the difficulties against faith stopped.—If I had remained in St. Mary's I would have done the same thing—write to you—as soon as Father gave me the permission.—We both tried everything before the thing came before you.

I write to you—simply—and without any worry.—I leave myself completely in your hands about this.

Pray for me—for I am really unworthy of all He is doing for me and in me. I have asked Father to tell you all my many great sins—so that you will ask Our Lord—if the work is to be done—to give you a more worthy person.

Please excuse this paper—as I have no other kind.—I am trying a little the Franciscan poverty. It is lovely to be poor and free from so many things.

Pray for me.

Your devoted child in Jesus Christ.
Mary Teresa[7]

Besides addressing Archbishop Périer's concerns, Mother Teresa made, almost in passing, two revelations: that she had "not been seeking self for sometime now" and that a singular grace of "love for souls" had captivated her heart from her first Holy Communion. This exceptional favor had urged her to leave her beloved Skopje and take the first daring step into the unknown. The same "love for souls"—an endeavor to bring others to the knowledge and love of God—was now moving her to reach out to those most in need. With these disclosures and the admission that the difficulties against faith had stopped once the locutions started (one important indicator that their source was indeed divine), the archbishop could grasp that he was in the presence of an exceptional soul.

The archbishop, like Father Van Exem, appreciated the significance of Mother Teresa's objective yet was unwilling to rush into a quick decision. Now, however, with another pressing letter in his hand, he was prompted to reply and justify his lengthy decision process.

CALCUTTA,
19TH FEBRUARY 1947.

Dear Mother M. Teresa,
P.X. [Pax Christi—Peace of Christ]
The main point are your two letters of the 13th and 25th January. As I have explained to Fr. Van Exem when he came to see me with your letter this is far too important a question to be solved or to be assessed on the spot or in a day or month. It will require

much prayer on your part and on my side, much reflection, much forethought before we can be sure of our path presently and in the future. . . . I cannot even and I will not say anything about the scheme before the Holy Ghost [Spirit] enlightens me. This is not a man's work it is God's work and to be certain that it is God's work we must use both the intellectual faculties and the spiritual help of prayer, meditation. . . .

In June I shall be in Rome and without giving any name, I shall submit the case to the authorities there and await an encouragement or otherwise.

I hope to be back in September or October. So continue praying in calmness and peace.

In union of hh.CC. [Holy Communions] and prayers, I am

Yours devotedly in Xt. [Christ]

† F. Périer, SJ [8]

"*Longing to Be All Things to All Men*"

If Archbishop Périer hoped that reference to his "[submitting] the case to the authorities" in Rome (where such requests would undergo careful and lengthy examination) would dampen Mother Teresa's enthusiasm, he was mistaken. On the contrary, she saw his trip to Rome as a perfect opportunity to bring God's plan to completion. Writing once more, she pleaded with the archbishop to bring the case directly to the notice of the pope. She was sure that with the pope's intervention, her hope of moving ahead could soon be realized.

LORETO CONVENT

ASANSOL

Your Grace,

Many thanks for your letter. I am not surprised that you will not act—and that you are taking your time over your answer.—

Some day it [the permission] is sure to come—and then you will, I am sure, be the first to give the young institute all the help it will need.

You say in your letter that you will submit the case to the authorities in Rome—where the question will be examined carefully.—I would be grateful if you spoke to our Holy Father about it. He will understand. It will depend on you, Your Grace to tell Holy Father everything. Tell him that the Institute will be especially for the unity and happiness of family life—the life of which he has so much at heart. Tell him of the countless broken homes, here in India, in Calcutta, in everywhere.—It is to make these unhappy homes happy—to bring Jesus into their dark homes that Our Lord wants me and the Sisters to give our lives as victims for homes.—By our poverty, labour and zeal we shall enter every home—gather the little children from these unhappy homes. Tell our Holy Father that the Pastoral letter you wrote a few weeks back, will get its answer in the Missionary Sisters of Charity. We shall be perfectly free in the Poverty we intend—or rather God wants from us. There are Indian, Anglo-Indian & European girls who are longing to give just like this everything to God—and get at the heart of the people—in whatever country they be. Tell our Holy Father of my longing to be all things to all men.[9] Bring him the first letter I wrote to you. I have no proof—but I know it is God who wants this from us.—What if all be failure—I have no fear.—If only one family—if only one little unhappy child is made happy with the love of Jesus, tell me, will it not be worth all of us giving all for that—for you having all the trouble? Your Grace, I know not how to ask you—I leave it to Him to tell you what to tell our Holy Father—but tell him everything you know.—He is our missionary Holy Father. His suffering on account of so many unhappy homes is a continual torture to his fatherly heart. Ask him that we, the Sisters and I—

be his daughters who would bring joy to his heart—by bringing happiness into these unhappy homes.

Amongst the very poor—what suffering the mothers undergo—on account of their children—on account of their husbands.—My Sisters will care for their children—will nurse the sick, the old, & the dying in their homes.—They will teach the young wives how to make their homes happy. There are many places where the priest even cannot get at—but a Missionary of Charity will by her work enter every hole—wherever there is human life, wherever there is a soul for Jesus.

You tell me to pray—pray much.—Yes, I do—and I am asking other people do the same.—You also pray. Ask St. Francis Xavier[10] during this novena of grace—to let us have the grace of doing the most pleasing thing.

I shall wait—wait as long as Holy Father wants me to, but I am also ready to leave all—at one word from him—and go to begin the life of complete poverty so as to be able to give all to Jesus.

You will say where are the Sisters who will join.—I know the mind of many a girl—and what they are longing to do for Christ. This does not trouble me. He will provide everything.—The more we trust Him—the more He will do.

Kindly tell Fr. Van Exem, that I won't be able to write to him, in the way my Superior cannot read it.—I used to write to him everything—but now I shall keep till I see him in confession.—

Thank God, in St. Mary's all is very well. I knew God would give His best for that place. M.M. [Mother Mary] Columba is one of our best Nuns. The Sisters will learn much from her. I am so glad to know that you received such good reports about them. I do hope Asansol will see them soon—for here nothing is done for the natives—they seem to know very, very little. The sisters would be a great, great grace. I am praying that they come soon.

I am teaching Hindi & Bengali, Hygiene & Geography.
The children are very good & simple.—I miss very much the
open simplicity of my St. Mary's girls and their generous love for
Our Lord.

Pray for me—that I become a humble, generous religious—so
that He will use me according to His pleasure.

Your devoted child in J.C. [Jesus Christ],
Mary Teresa.[11]

The Loreto rule of the time permitted Mother Teresa's superiors
to examine her correspondence if deemed "expedient in the Lord";
because she had been unjustly suspected of having an unhealthy
relationship with Father Van Exem, Mother Teresa reasonably expected that any correspondence between them would be examined.
Since she did not want anyone, not even her superiors, to know as
yet about her inspiration, she avoided writing to Father Van Exem.

Seeking the Will of God

Jesus was calling; how could she be indifferent and do nothing? If
God's love would be made present to even one soul, she thought,
her call would be fulfilled and worth all the sacrifice. She could not
understand why the archbishop was not acting more quickly.

For his part, as the one responsible for the archdiocese and its
people, Archbishop Périer had to make sure that Mother Teresa's
proposal would be a positive and fruitful endeavor. He was still
weighing whether she was leaving "a certain good for an uncertain
gain."[12] Perhaps if he had been aware of her private vow he would
have understood her apparent hastiness. Somewhat annoyed by
her insistence, he attempted anew to explain his measured course
of action:

My dear Mother M. Teresa,

P. X. [Pax Christi—Peace of Christ]

On my return from pastoral tour in the Santal Parganas I found your letter, for which I thank you sincerely. I have the impression from what you write that you believe me opposed to your proposals and that you are praying hard for my conversion of heart. I should like to change your mind about these dispositions which you appear to take for granted. I am neither opposed nor in favour of your project and as Archbishop I cannot be anything but neutral at this stage. It is not a question of personal conviction, nor enthusiasm, or feeling that must carry me. . . . The question is too important for the Church to decide all at once. It may take months, it may take years. . . .

In the meantime, please take off your imagination the idea that I am opposed to your scheme. As I said, I have no right to be opposed or in favour. Almighty God will show me the line to be followed and when I am morally certain of where my duty lies, rest assured that I shall not shrink from it, cost what it may. My motto is to "seek God in everyone and in everything." It is not at the end of my career, that I shall give up that guiding principle of the whole of my religious life. It would be foolish. I shall do the will of God; but that must be clear to me. You may think that it is all very easy, when there is somebody to endorse the responsibility, but for the one who has to be responsible it requires discretion, prayer, constant and fervent prayer and readiness to abide by the will of God, as manifested to him.

In union of hh.SS. [Holy Sacrifices] I am
Yours devotedly in Xt. [Christ]
† F. Périer, SJ [13]

"To Please Him Only Is the Joy I Seek"

Though completely willing to obey, Mother Teresa could not ignore Jesus' insistent pleading: *"Wilt thou refuse to do this for Me?"* So when the archbishop's scheduled trip to Europe was delayed, she took advantage of the situation to beg him once more:

LORETO CONVENT

ASANSOL

30TH MARCH '47.

Your Grace,

This will bring you my best wishes for a very happy Easter. I also thank you for your last letter, which I received some time ago. I do hope you will not get tired of me and of my many long letters, but as you are the one on whom so much depends, I have to tell you everything in detail. I wish I could tell you personally everything, but this does not seem possible.

You were to have gone on the 26th and yet everything seems to have turned. I think God has kept you back to be able to work out His desire of starting the work.—I am ready to do whatever I am told—at any cost. Ready to go now or to wait years. It is for you to use me, to offer me to God for the poor. People call you the father of the poor. Your Grace, let me go, and give myself for them, let me offer myself and those who will join me for those unwanted poor, the little street children, the sick, the dying, the beggars, let me go into their very holes and bring in their broken homes the joy and peace of Christ. I know you are afraid for me. You are afraid that the whole thing will be a failure.—What about it? Is it not worth going through every possible suffering just for one single soul? Did not Our Lord do the same: what a failure was His Cross on Calvary—and all for me, a sinner.

I can tell you sincerely from my heart, I will lose nothing. From my Superiors down, I know they will laugh at me. They will think me a fool, proud, mad etc. What if the good God wants my name? I am His and His only.—The rest has no hold on me. I can do without all the rest if I have Him. Fear not for me—nor for those who will join me—He will look after us all. He will be with us.—If for a glass of water, He has promised so much,[14] what would He not do for victim hearts given to the poor? He will do all. I, I am only a little instrument in His hands, and because I am just nothing, He wants to use me.

Your Grace, don't let me be unfaithful to Him now. I would not like for anything, not even for a second of a second to do the less pleasing. I want Him to have all the pleasure. His longing, His suffering on account of these little children, on account of the poor dying in sin, of the unhappiness of so many broken families is great. I feel so terribly helpless in front of all.—I, little nothing, long to take away all that from His Heart.

Day after day, hour after hour, He asks the same question: *"Wilt thou refuse to do this for Me?"* I tell Him that the answer is with you.

You might think that I am looking only at the joy of giving up all, and bringing joy into the Heart of Jesus. Yes, I look at these most, but I see also what suffering the fulfillment of these two will bring. By nature I am sensitive, love beautiful and nice things, comfort and all the comfort can give—to be loved and love.—I know that the life of a Missionary of Charity—will be minus all these. The complete poverty, the Indian life, the life of the poorest will mean a hard toil against my great self love. Yet, Your Grace, I am longing with a true, sincere heart to begin to lead this kind of life—so as to bring joy to the suffering Heart of Jesus.—Let me go, Your Grace—let us trust Him blindly.— He will see to it that our faith in Him will not be lost.

While you are still in Calcutta, could you not do the needful—through the Apostolic Del. [Delegate] and then when the little Institute is in its feet apply to Rome for recognition? I don't know what the Canon Law says in these matters—but what I have heard and read in the little booklet about M. [Mother] Mary of the Passion,[15] the Franciscan foundress, which I read lately, there does not seem to have been much trouble.—Overnight 20 Nuns free to lead the Franciscan life.—But in their case the Bishop was the acting factor. Or do you think I should apply myself through you?—This is why personal explanation would be easier.—I am going to Darjeeling on 8th May—but you will be gone by that time.

Don't delay, Your Grace, don't put it off. Souls are being lost for want of care, for want of love. Without giving any names, if you ask your Parish Priests, they will tell you of the need of such nuns. Look at the appeal of the Holy Father for the children of Europe.[16] What would he say, if he saw your poor, the poor of the slums of Calcutta? Do something about this before you leave, and let us take away from the Heart of Jesus His continual suffering.

I feel sometimes afraid, for I have nothing, no brains, no learning, no qualities required for such a work, and yet I tell Him that my heart is free from everything and so it belongs completely to Him, and Him alone. He can use me just as it will please Him best. To please Him only is the joy I seek.

India is going through days of hatred.[17] Here now again I hear in Calcutta there is trouble. Would that the Missionaries of Charity were there to overrule this hatred by their love. You will say, what could you and your few Indian girls do? We could do nothing, but Jesus and we few victims can do wonders. Let me go and begin this work, which will be an answer to your burning appeal for apostles.

Whenever you think it best, I would like myself to tell Mother General or Mother Provincial everything. I rather they knew it from me.

Your Grace, forgive me for being so tiresome with my continual appeal, but I have to act in this way. Let us bring joy to the Heart of Jesus, and remove from His Heart those terrible sufferings. Think of what Jesus will gain and not what little me will lose.—He has done so much for you—and now at the end of so much grace and love you fear to offer one of your little missionaries to be His victim for the poorest of your flock.— Let me go to Cossipore at "the Boys own home"[18] instead of Darjeeling. By the time you come back—we would have started our solitude after which the mission work would begin.—There are girls in Europe even, who would be only too happy to give all, and follow Christ in perfect poverty and sacrifice.

I don't know if the Holy Ghost [Spirit] has filled your soul with those desires and thoughts, for I am praying that He should do so.

During these days of prayer and penance, pray for me, pray often, that I may love Him more.

Once more I wish you a very happy Easter.

Your devoted child in J.C. [Jesus Christ]
Mary Teresa[19]

The "little nothing," as she called herself, was longing to "bring joy to the suffering Heart of Jesus"—her first love since childhood. For this, she would have embraced any hardship; her preferences or the sacrifices involved did not count. All she desired was to please Him. She insisted on moving ahead because she was convinced that Jesus wanted it. Yet she remained open to the archbishop's decision as the very will of God.

"My God . . . Supply for
What Is Wanting in Me"

Archbishop Périer was taken aback by Mother Teresa's long and exhortative letter.

ARCHBISHOP'S HOUSE

32, PARK STREET

CALCUTTA 7TH APRIL 1947.

My dear Mother M. Teresa,

P. X. [Pax Christi—Peace of Christ]

I was rather astonished to read in your letter a good many reasons for which I was not moving in the matter you had laid before me. I thought I had explained previously in a clear manner, the motives which oblige me to move very slowly in such an important matter.

If I saw after fervent prayers and mature reflection that the will of God was to move in the direction you wish me to move at once, I would not hesitate; I would not give a moment's consideration for difficulties, means or anything else. For me the will of God is supreme and all the rest disappears. But to know the will of God for those who have the authority and to act in His Name requires consultation, prayer and reflection. I am quite convinced that you are ready for everything. But my dear Mother, you must also take my side now and then. By representing your request and defending it before the Holy See, I assume a great responsibility. Not only can I be the cause of the ruin of many vocations, but I may also be the cause of leading souls in the darkness by rashness. Your example of the foundress of the Franciscan Missionaries of Mary is not an argument. First of all I know for sure, from personal contact with people who lived at the time, v.gr. [*verbi gratia*—e.g.] the former Delegate Apostolic in India, Mgr. Zaleski, that things did not go smoothly at all and I know that even now that the life of the Foundress is being discussed for her beatification, many points have to be cleared up. Moreover Canon Law at that time was not yet codified as it is now. A good many new decrees for religious have been issued from that time also.

Another motive which should make you reflect when you press me to start at once, is that I have absolutely no power to let you start this kind of work. Your Mother General has no more power than I have in this respect: the matter must necessarily go to Rome and we must be ready to answer the questions which we shall be asked. To answer these questions I must have acquired a personal conviction, a kind of moral certitude which allows me in conscience to answer favourably or otherwise I must be able to say later on that even if I was mistaken in my views pro or con, I was mistaken in good faith that I did not rush madly in a question on which depends so much for others.

Your object in theory may have my hearty approbation, that doesn't yet suffice to allow you to start or to suggest that you might be allowed to start. If I am not mistaken I suggested in one of my previous letters that you should sit down quietly and write down what exactly and in detail you (1) wanted to do, (2) the means by which you desire to bring it about, (3) how would you form your disciples etc. (4) what kind of people you would recruit for this work, (5) where would be the centre of your work, (6) whether it is not possible to obtain this end by [a] congregation already in existence, (7) whether it would not be more conducive toward the end to use a kind of association or sodality[20] and not religious exactly to work out your scheme. There are hundreds of questions that come to the fore and must be examined seriously and satisfactorily. <u>During my absence, set to work at your plan</u>

<u>under the guidance of the Holy Ghost [Spirit]</u>. It is not desired to have a long description of what you fancy you will be able to do. What we want is to know in a few words: <u>the aim, the means, the rules, the recruitment,</u> the <u>possibilities of success.</u> I do not say the glamour nor do I mean the humiliations, hardships, etc. but if we start something it must be able to achieve the object for which it is started—that's what I call the success. If you are ready when I return from Rome sometime in September it will be all right; do not think the period allowed is too long. Such essentials require long meditation, prayer, reflection, consultation. In the meantime I shall see in Europe how such a congregation would work, what has been the experience of others in this line, whether it is better to have a lay association rather than a religious congregation etc. God bless you. I am in union of hh.CC. [holy Communions] and prayers.

Yours devotedly in Xt [Christ],
† F. Périer, SJ [21]

Despite the disappointment she may have felt, Mother Teresa accepted the archbishop's mandate. Turning to God for help, she wrote the following prayer at the margin of the archbishop's letter:

My God—give me your light and your love to be able to write the things to Thy honor and glory. Don't let my ignorance prevent me from doing your Will perfectly. Supply for what is wanting in me. [22]

Since the archbishop had implied that he would consider her response only upon his return in September, she decided to wait until her upcoming retreat and holiday in Darjeeling (between May 8 and June 14, 1947) to formulate her answers.

In May, on her way from Asansol to Darjeeling, Mother Teresa stopped in Calcutta and met Father Van Exem twice. Not knowing about the archbishop's request, he made a similar one of Mother Teresa, as he reported in a letter to the archbishop:

In May I told her it was the will of Our Lord that during her holiday she would set to work out her plan, explain her aim and the means she intended to use to reach her aim, write also the essential rules which would show me the proper spirit of her work. After that, and after I had asked this also for Your Grace, she read to me the letters received from Your Grace and in one of those letters I heard that Your Grace had made exactly the same request which I had just explained. I told her to answer the questions contained in that letter in order to be obedient.[23]

Once she arrived in Darjeeling, she unexpectedly faced a short but very intense struggle. On her way back to Asansol in June, she related it to Father Van Exem, who in turn informed Archbishop Périer:

She passed through awful desolation (5 days in May) whilst in Darjeeling and then the idea of the work seemed to be a stupidity (excuse the word which I think is hers), a treason to her institute and to her superiors; she was in great fear about it all and underwent big temptations. She wrote to me at that time but I could only pray for her. Happily the temptation left her after a few days, and again everything is light, joy, trust and certainty of being on the right path; that is my conviction after seeing her though I did not talk about her consolations in my interview. When in consolation she has no doubts at all except at the surface of her soul, she is fearless and ready to immolate everything for Our Lord; in desolation she did doubt it all, feared a lot but remained ready to immolate herself. Afterwards Our Lord told her that her great fear had hurt Him; she had been a little responsible for what had happened.[24]

The Blueprint of the New Order

After these days of doubt and confusion during her stay at Darjee-ling, Mother Teresa's usual state of consolation and certainty re-turned. She applied herself to answering Archbishop Périer's questions, "translating" into concrete terms the implications of her mystical experiences and adding new details to those she had formu-lated in January. This time she did not make reference to the "Voice" but specifically to "Our Lord" and His requests to her. Her complete focus was Jesus alone: *He* was the reason for her future apostolate, the model for her charity, the standard for her new way of life, the guarantee of her success; He was her "Everything."

LORETO CONVENT

DARJEELING

FEAST OF CORPUS CHRISTI [25] '47

Your Grace,

In your last letter you told me, "During my absence, set to work at your plan under the guidance of the Holy Ghost [Spirit]."

During the Novena of the Holy Ghost, I wrote out the few rules, which might be useful.—Today after much prayer, I shall try with His help to answer your questions.

1. "What exactly and in detail you want to do?"

Our Lord wants Indian Nuns, victims of His love, who would be so united to Him as to radiate His love on souls—who would lead Indian lives, dress like them, and be His light, His fire of love amongst the poor, the sick, the dying, the beggars and the little street children. I want to satisfy this desire of Our Lord, by becoming Indian and leading that life for Him and souls of the poor. To be united to Him completely, we need be poor—free from all—here comes the poverty of the Cross—Absolute Poverty—and to be able to see God in the poor—Angelic Chastity—and to be able to be always at His disposal—Cheerful Obedience. By these three, my sisters and myself desire to bring Christ into the unhappy holes of the slums of the Calcutta poor and later on of the other places.

2. "The means by which you desire to bring it about?"

By going amongst the people—nursing the sick in their homes—helping the dying to make their peace with God, having little free schools in the slums for the little children—visiting the poor in the hospitals—and helping the beggars of the streets to lead respectful lives.—In a word, act the charity of Christ amongst the poorest—and so make them know Him and want Him in their unhappy lives.—If the number of Sisters permits, we would also have a home for the lame, the blind, the outcasts of human society. The Sisters will tour the villages and do the same work there.—So as to be free to do more, the Sisters will not be permanent in any place—but be always ready to do the work that is wanting in the Church in India.

3. "How would you form your disciples?"

By giving them a complete knowledge of the spiritual life—so that in the street or in the holes of the poor, or at home in the convent they would live the life of close union with God.—The interior must become the main power of the exterior.—To arrive at this the Sisters will have the first year of their religious life—one of complete contemplation—and perfect solitude—which will be renewed every six years, after they have taken the vows. They must also get all the possible help from holy priests in their spiritual life—so that religious perfection would become simple and easy—as the life of Mary was at Nazareth. For if they are

not in love with God—they will not be able to lead this life
of continual immolation for souls. Each must understand,
that if she wants to become a Missionary of Charity—she must
be in love with the Crucified and be His Victim for souls of
the poor.

4. "What kind of people you would recruit for this work?"
Girls from the age of 16 upwards.—Strong in body and mind
with plenty of common sense. No special qualification—but must
be able to learn or know the language of the country thoroughly.
Generous and lovers of the poor. They must be able to put their
hands to any kind of work however repugnant to human nature.
They must be of bright, cheerful disposition.—Girls of any
nationality—but for whatever nation they enter that people's
language and ways must be theirs. For example, if a Tamil
enters—she shall be given work amongst the Tamils—a Chinese
amongst the Chinese and so on. If girls with high qualifications
desire to enter—they may come but that will not make them
whatsoever different. They will have to be one of the Sisters. If
rich—them, but not their money. I need missionaries—souls are
not bought.—In the years of contemplation and solitude they
must be ready to do penance and pray much together with that
manual labour—which should naturally lift their minds to God.

5. "Where would be the centre of your work?"
For the present the slums and the streets of Calcutta and as
the Missionaries of Charity increase all the big towns of India.
We shall not wait to be asked to do this or that work by this or
that Bishop or priest. We shall go in search of souls ourselves and
offer our services to the Bishop of the place.—We shall do any
work, except school work—that is, only up to Std II [Standard II]
our slum schools would be.

For the training of the Sisters—Cossipore—being a quiet, lonely place with plenty of grounds has been chosen by Our Lord.—For the second year training, Sealdah—where the Sisters would be able to attend maternity training and other nursing. This too was chosen.—Personally I do not know either of these places—neither have I seen them. But if the Sisters cannot have daily Mass and holy Com. [Communion]. Your Grace you will have to choose then.

6. "Whether it is not possible to obtain this end by congregations already in existence?"

No. First, because they are European. When our Indian girls enter these orders—they are made to live their life—eat, sleep, dress like them. In a word, as the people say—they become "Mems."[26] They have no chance of feeling the holy poverty. Second—as much as those Sisters try to adapt themselves to the country, they remain foreigners for the people—and then there are their rules—which do not allow them so to say, be one of the people. They have their big schools and hospitals—in all these the souls have to come to them or be brought to them. While the Missionaries of Charity will go in search, live their days in the slums and streets. Close to the people's heart—they would do the works of Christ in their very homes—in the dirty and dark holes of the street beggars. As Our Lord himself says, *"There are plenty of nuns to look after the rich and able to do people—but for My very poor, there are absolutely none. For them I long—them I love."* He also asks for Indian Nuns—dressed in Indian clothes—leading the Indian life.—Whoever desires to be a Missionary of Charity will have to become Indian, dress like them, live like them.

7. "Whether it would not be more conducive to use a kind of association or sodality"?

For the life they would have to live, seculars would not be able to do it. For a work of continual self-forgetfulness and immolation for others, you need interior souls—burning with love for God and souls. Pure souls who would see and seek God in the poor.—Free souls—who would be able to sacrifice everything just for this one thing only, to bring a soul to God.—The work will need much deep, fervent prayers and much penance—and all these people of an association will not be able to bring to the work, and the work will not fulfill its aim—"to bring souls to God, and God to souls."

8. "The possibilities of success"
Our Lord says: *"Do not fear. I shall be with you always. . . . trust Me lovingly—trust Me blindly. . . ."*

You know, Your Grace, the number and the need your poor have of a kind hand, how they leave their children to sin and spend their innocent lives in the streets. How many die without God—just because there was nobody to say one word about His mercy.—The sufferings of their body make them forget the terrible sufferings their souls will have for all eternity. Why Our Lord Himself says, *"How it hurts to see these poor children soiled with sin . . . they don't know Me—so they don't want Me . . . how I long to enter their holes—their dark unhappy homes. Come be their victim.—In your immolation—in your love for Me—they will see Me—know Me—want Me. . . ."*

I don't know what the success will be—but if the Missionaries of Charity have brought joy to one unhappy home—made one innocent child from the street keep pure for Jesus—one dying person die in peace with God—don't you think, Your Grace, it would be worth while offering everything—for just that one—because that one would bring great joy to the Heart of Jesus.

<u>9. How would the Sisters support themselves (my question)?</u>

From the farm they should be able to get most of their food—they will sell some and so buy the other things. As for the clothes—they will make toys and pictures and other hand work things—which will be sold—and with that money get what is most necessary. We shall need very little—as we intend with the grace of God to keep absolute poverty in detail, and as we shall not have buildings of our own. We shall never need much cash.—The sisters will also do all the house work—so they will need no servants—for the rest—or rather for all—I trust Him! He will be with us—and when He is there we shall need for nothing.—

One thing I request you, Your Grace, to give us all the spiritual help we need.—If we have Our Lord in the midst of us—with daily Mass and Holy Communion, I fear nothing for the Sisters nor myself.—He will look after us. But without Him I cannot be—I am helpless.

Now I have told you all.

Pray for me.

Your devoted child in J.C. [Jesus Christ]
Mary Teresa[27]

"Drop It for All Eternity"

Mother Teresa sent this long letter, together with the first set of Rules written some days earlier,[28] to Father Van Exem for review and approval. He studied her notes carefully and waited to meet her in Calcutta on her way from Darjeeling back to Asansol. At the end of an extensive discussion on June 14, Father Van Exem gave her an entirely unexpected reply: he ordered her to "drop it [the whole endeavor] for all eternity" if neither he nor the archbishop mentioned it further. To emphasize the seriousness of his request, he put it in writing. Later that day he related to Archbishop Périer in a letter the strategy he had taken:

She is to leave the whole work to me and to Your Grace, and to put the whole affair out of her mind. She "should drop it for all eternity" if she is asked nothing anymore by Your Grace or by me. As to the writings, I did not tell her at all what I would do with them, burn them, tear them up, keep them or send them to Your Grace. I told her she had to live only in the present and not at all in the future and be a perfect Nun. She could develop initiative in her present apostolate but had to increase especially in the virtue of prudence which she needed most. I insisted on obedience, cheerful, prompt, simple and blind. I assured her that she could never make a mistake if she obeyed. I allowed her a little more penance and much more abnegation, but I doubt whether she can practise more than she does. She has not refused anything to Our Lord.[29]

This was not the answer Mother Teresa anticipated. She had been longing to go and "bring joy to the suffering Heart of Jesus," eagerly waiting for the archbishop's "yes." She was now faced with another severe test, and from none other than her trusted spiritual director. Yet, faithful to her commitment not to refuse the Lord anything, she chose to obey.

FIVE

"Delay No Longer. Keep Me Not Back."

LONGING TO BRING THE LIGHT OF CHRIST

The salvation of souls, the satiating of Christ's thirst
for love and souls, is this not grave enough?
—Mother Teresa

Back to Calcutta

In July 1947, Mother Teresa returned to the Entally community in Calcutta. This change took place at the intervention of her superior general, who believed that "Mother Provincial was mistaken . . . in her estimate of Mother M. Teresa."[1] For her part, Mother Teresa simply obeyed, trusting that through all these happenings God was working out His plan. Upon arriving back at St. Mary's, though no longer principal of the school, she resumed most of her previous activities; she began teaching and looking partly after the boarders. Those around her, while continuing to admire her generosity and the influence she had on the girls, still had no idea of her new call.

Shortly after coming back, Mother Teresa met with her spiritual director. It had not occurred to her that the order he had given her in June, "to drive away as temptations all thoughts connected with the work,"[2] was merely one more test of the genuineness of her call. Despite the intense struggle it had caused her, she had obeyed, giving further proof of the supremacy of God's will in her life. She admitted to Father Van Exem:

> You told me not to think of the work.—Whenever the thoughts used to burn with the longing to offer all—to be His victim in every word—I used to do violence to myself—and begged Him not to let those thoughts come because I wanted to obey—and like a Little Lamb, He used to obey, too. How often, how very often He complained of delays—for whenever He asks for something, He says, people get extra careful about many things— but if the world asks the things are done so quickly.[3]

Learning of her heroic effort, Father Van Exem acknowledged to the archbishop: "I know now that she really tried to obey and did obey."[4] He thus decided to alter his directives, telling her to "go on rejecting all thoughts of the work but to admit all that unites her more to Our Lord."[5]

Not only did Mother Teresa's spiritual director exact strict obedience from her; so too did the "Voice," which spoke to her on one occasion after her return from Asansol. She confided to Father Van Exem Jesus' words:

> *People think you were sent here to teach, and you do well and doing the work with the whole of your heart, but this was not the aim of My Heart—*

*I brought you here to be under the immediate care of your spiritual
father who will train you in the ways of My love and so prepare you to do
My will. Trust him completely and without any fear. Obey him in every
detail, you shall not be deceived if you obey for he belongs to Me
completely.—I shall let you know My will through him.*[6]

Continual, Deep, and Violent Union with Our Lord

Before the archbishop's return, Father Van Exem "felt urged to
change [his] decision"[7] once more and allowed her "to dwell on all
thoughts inspired by Our Lord but without thinking on voices or
supernatural phenomena."[8] With this permission, he expected the
"Voice" would return and in fact feared that the case might become
"more spectacular."[9] In explaining to the archbishop the reason for
his concern, he provided precious testimony of Mother Teresa's interior life:

I knew that Our Lord had raised that nun to the state of
higher prayer; ecstasy as such there may not have been but the
immediate state before ecstasy has been reached. That had
been my conviction, vaguely however, last year and perhaps
before. . . . The state of ecstasy may be reached very soon as the
union with Our Lord has been continual and so deep and violent
that rapture does not seem very far. Never do I say a word of
that but that is surely the way things go. I am a little afraid
of this since then things may become more spectacular for her
and for me. She is deadly afraid of anything that draws the
attention to her person and seems to be very solidly established
in humility. . . .[10]

Although there is no record of Mother Teresa experiencing the mystical state of ecstasy,* it is highly probable that she did so. During these months Mother Teresa enjoyed an intense degree of union with Our Lord, including imaginative visions, the awesomeness of which, according to St. Teresa of Avila, "almost always produces ecstasy."[11] Years later she recalled this extraordinary time: "Before the work started [1946–1947] there was so much union—love—faith—trust—prayer—sacrifice."[12] Reminiscing a second time about the special graces received, she expressed her nostalgia for that intimacy: "There [in Asansol] as if Our Lord just gave Himself to me—to the full. The sweetness & consolation & union of those 6 months passed but too soon."[13]

Father Van Exem continued to be impressed with Mother Teresa's ever-growing fervor and desire for closer union with God. So passionate was her love for Him that she kept seeking ways to give expression to it. It was again to Archbishop Périer that her spiritual director revealed her secret yearnings:

She made several requests to me, one to do more penance which she very ardently desires, one to bind herself by a vow to obey me[†] and one to pray at night. She wrote: "The attraction for the Blessed Sacrament at times was so great. I longed for Holy

---

*In the context of the spiritual life, ecstasy is a mystical phenomenon in which the mind is fixed on God or some religious subject and the normal activity of the senses is interrupted; intense joy and visions may accompany the experience. Ecstasy is characteristic of the "unitive" stage of the spiritual life, in which the person reaches union with God, rather than the "purgative" and "illuminative" stages that precede this stage.

[†]As her letter dated August 8, 1947, to Father Van Exem indicates, Mother Teresa's motivation in requesting permission to make such a vow to her confessor was rooted in the locution that she received upon her return to Calcutta: "I brought you here—to be under the immediate care of your spiritual father. . . . Obey him in every detail, you shall not be deceived if you obey for he belongs to Me completely.—I shall let you know My will through him."

Com. [Communion]. Night after night the sleep would disappear—and only to spend those hours in longing for His coming. This began in Asansol in Feb.—and now every night for one hour or two, I have noticed it is from 11 to 1, the same longing breaks into the sleep."[14]

Father Van Exem would not allow her "extravagant" requests. While struggling to restrain her fervor, she had to follow the regular practices of her convent life and find other avenues of expressing her ardent love. And she had to wait. Through this painful waiting, her thirst for Him only increased.

"How Much I Long to Immolate Myself"

At the end of September, Archbishop Périer returned from his long trip to Europe. In the greetings he graciously sent Mother Teresa for her feast day, he advised her: "It will take still a little while before I can conclude the whole thing."[15] In spite of this caution, Mother Teresa seized the opportunity to take up the cause again. Father Van Exem had left her free to ponder the thoughts inspired by our Lord, so she felt at liberty to seek a meeting with the archbishop in the hope of moving her project forward.

ST. MARY'S
LORETO CONVENT, ENTALLY.
1ST OCT. 47

Your Grace,
Many thanks for your good wishes and prayers for my feast.—
The Little Flower[16] is wonderful how she answers prayers. I had asked her to let me have just a few lines from you on her

50th year of her entrance into Heaven, and sure enough it
did come.

I know you have not forgotten the cause, I shall wait for the
"little while" to be over soon—and I pray for the things to come
out in such a way—so as He would have all the pleasure, all the
glory. Think not of me—for I am very sinful and most unworthy
of His love—but just only think of Him and the love He would
receive from the Sisters and the souls under their care.—I have
told Fr. Van Exem to tell you everything, and as I keep no secret
from him, he would be able to tell you all.

From the 13th Jan. '47 I have been praying very much for you,
that these very desires, which God has entrusted to me, His most
unworthy child, may enter your heart with the same force.

I don't think it would be possible for me to see you, for you
must be simply overworked—but whenever you think it fit, I
would be grateful if I could speak to you.

I knew there would be plenty of complications, but my trust
in Him does not shake. The more trouble and suffering there
would be for the cause, the proof will be greater that it is His
Will to have the work started on the 50th year of the entrance of
Little Flower in heaven and yours in the Society of Jesus. Let this
be the first year of the Missionaries of Charity also. If you only
knew how much I long to immolate myself completely in that
absolute Poverty and so bring the light of Christ into the
unhappy homes of the slums' poor.

Pray for me—

> *Your devoted child in J.C. [Jesus Christ]*
> *Mary Teresa.*[17]

The fiftieth anniversary of St. Thérèse's death was on September 30, and the anniversary of Archbishop Périer's entry into the
Society of Jesus was on October 3, the day St. Thérèse's feast was

celebrated at that time. The "Voice" had been calling her "with so much love and force"[18] and her longing to answer it was growing stronger as the months passed. She therefore wanted to begin the work within this noteworthy year.

"His Grace Is Not Interested in the 'Voices and Visions'"

Mother Teresa's entreaties did not have the desired effect; Archbishop Périer was not ready to meet with her. Instead he expressed a number of reservations to her spiritual director and wanted further clarification on some issues. Father Van Exem reported directly to Mother Teresa all the points the archbishop had raised. For each one she set out to furnish a response:

19-10-47

Father,

As we shall begin work tomorrow I give you my answer to your letter.—You may if you think it good send this to His Grace.

1. The work in Calcutta is so great—that there will never be enough nuns to do all that—still there are at least some to do it while for the *slum* poor—nobody.

2. His [Archbishop Périer's] "Yes" is not sufficient to start the work—it is true—but it is required to begin my action with Rome. Our Lord will do everything, but for the material working of His plan, according to rules and regulations of Canon Law of which I am perfectly ignorant—His Grace's "Yes" is necessary.— It will start the work with Rome.

3. I have never seen Cossipore. I have heard it is a big, open, quiet place. From the very beginning Cossipore and Sealdah have been on the list. I have heard that Mr. Animananda R.I.P. [rest

in peace] left "Boys' own home" to H.G. [His Grace] in his will.
How far this is true I do not know.—In my letter of Corpus
Christi—I wrote that choosing of the place I leave to H.G. as we
cannot be without the Bl. [Blessed] Sacrament.—

4. The Church does not take "chance" but she often uses
means, human means to fulfill her Divine Mission. What those
people meant was this.

5. The life I want to live with my sisters, I know, will be a
difficult one—both for European & Indian sisters.—But nothing
is difficult to one who loves. Who can outdo God in His
generosity—if we poor human beings give Him everything and
surrender our whole being to His service?—No—He is sure to
stand by us, and with us, as everything in us will be His.

6. When I give up the life in the I.B.V.M. [Institute of the
Blessed Virgin Mary], in my poverty and chastity I shall be
bound to God wholly—in Obedience.—I shall, for the present
obey His Grace in all things—until Rome thinks otherwise.
Nobody can unbind me from God—I am consecrated to Him
and as such I desire to die.—I don't know what the Canon Law
has to say in this matter—but I know Our Lord will never
allow Himself to be separated from me.—Neither will He allow
anyone to separate me from Him.—H.G. needs a "grave reason"
to support me in Rome.—The salvation of souls, the satiating of
Christ's thirst for love and souls—is this not grave enough?

7. You must pray much—when the time comes to speaking.—
I trust this also to the Holy Spirit—who is sure to help my
ignorance and show His strength.—Naturally I am not a bit
afraid of H.G. so this will help to speak more freely.

8. I am glad H.G. is not interested in the "voices & visions."
They came unasked—and they have gone. They have not changed
my life. They have helped me to be more trustful and draw closer
to God.—They have increased my desire to be more and more

His little child. I have obeyed you to the letter in regard of them—so I do not fear. I attach no importance to them as regard the call because my desires to immolate myself were just as strong before they came. Why they came I do not know—neither do I try to know. I am pleased to let Him do with me just as it pleaseth Him.

9. Re. the letters—keep them—I shall need them.—Tell H.G. all that He wants to know—and if there are any parts which He wishes to have let me copy them or if you can do it—it will be better. Do not destroy any of the letters that are in connection with the work.[19]

10. H.G. is right—anything or rather many things that come from me are all due to my many sins and weakness. You know that just as well as I do. I can only spoil His work, His plans—but I want so much to be very pleasing to Him, and if through my stupidity and sinfulness God's work is spoilt or done less perfectly—He knows what my desires are in His regard.—Yes, do not spare me in anything—let there be less and less of me in everything.

11. Fr. Moyerseon has two candidates, and the two Yugos [Yugoslavs] in Rome and then 3 Indian girls and myself.

12. The exchange will do harm to both sides for the present. We need the Daughters [of Saint Ann] for the future education of our middle class people.—When we all get stronger there will be more unity between the two orders.

13. Reg. Fr. Cre. [Regarding Father Creusen][20] it is perfectly true—is not my concern.

M. Teresa[21]

To each concern of the archbishop, Mother Teresa's answers were confident and bold, especially when she addressed the role of the voices and the visions. Such unusual phenomena did not appeal to the prudent and practical archbishop; he was not interested in them. This did not worry Mother Teresa, for though these extraordinary graces helped her, she did not consider them essential to the call.

As for the "grave reason" that Archbishop Périer needed to endorse her plan, she could not think of one graver than the "salvation of souls, the satiating of Christ's thirst."[22] The thirst of Jesus that was at the heart of her call was the ultimate reason to move ahead.

On one point Mother Teresa and Archbishop Périer could agree: her weakness. Both of them feared that "self might be involved" in the whole matter, although each had a different idea of how the self might be influencing her efforts. While the archbishop feared that the "self" might be unduly pressing the launch of the project, Mother Teresa feared that the "self" might be hindering it.

Rather ingenuously, Father Van Exem handed Mother Teresa's replies to the archbishop together with his own lengthy letter of support. Earlier he had rendered his positive judgment:

In my examen of the voices I found nothing to disturb my faith in them. I am convinced they come from God: there is no item at all which can make me doubt.[23]

Now again he deemed it opportune to defend his favorable position, which rested solely on the fruits of holiness that he had witnessed in her life.

For Your Grace's information, I must make it clear that in my direction given I have never attached much importance to strange happenings. It is not the voices and visions at all which made me believe in the genuineness of the call but the genuineness of the call which prompted me to believe I had to tell you what I thought of the voices and visions. . . . My belief in the reality of the call was never there [in the strange phenomena]; it was based on my knowledge of the exceptional virtue of x [Mother Teresa] and also of x's [Mother Teresa's] natural endowments to answer the call with success, on the terrible trials which prepared the call and accompanied it for a long time and the manifest action of divine grace in that soul. In these four things I know I am not deceived.[24]

When the archbishop realized that Father Van Exem had repeated to Mother Teresa the details of their conversation, he was not pleased; he had intended some of his remarks only for Father Van Exem. Even as he apologized to the archbishop for his indiscretion, Father Van Exem continued to be Mother Teresa's advocate, restating his conviction that "it all came from God and the Immaculate Heart of Mary."[25]

Archbishop Périer was determined to act only when he could do so in good conscience. So far, neither Mother Teresa's pressing letters nor her spiritual director's personal conviction were sufficient grounds for the archbishop to give his assent. An experienced, zealous missionary and a bishop for twenty-five years, he would not decide until he was "able to say before my conscience and before God that I did everything to come to the right decision." "It may be," he added in a letter to Father Van Exem, "that for her [Mother Teresa] everything is as clear as daylight. I cannot claim it is the same for me."[26]

"Let Me Go. . . . Souls Are Being Lost in the Meantime"

Mother Teresa's ardent longing to satiate Jesus' thirst impelled her to keep pressing ahead. She feared that this slow procedure was a sign of indifference to Jesus' pain and a hindrance to the salvation of

souls. Unaware that her persistence was causing some tension between Archbishop Périer and Father Van Exem, she continued to
plead with the archbishop to act more quickly.

LORETO CONVENT

ENTALLY

24TH OCT. 47

Your Grace,

In your last letter for my feast you wrote, "It will take still a little
while before I can conclude the whole thing." I beg of you, Your
Grace, in the Name of Jesus and for the love of Jesus to let me go.
Delay no longer. Keep me not back. I want to begin that life on
the Eve of Christmas. We have very little time, from now till
then, to make all the other preparations. Please let me go.

You are still afraid. If the work be all human, it will die with
me[27], if it be all His it will live for ages to come. Souls are being
lost in the meantime. Let me go with your blessing—with the
blessing of obedience with which I desire to begin all things. Fear
not for me. It does not matter what happens to me.

Your Grace, anything we ask in Jesus' name from the Father
is granted.[28]—In the same name I have asked you—please let
me go.

Pray for me.
Your devoted child in J.C. [Jesus Christ]
Mary Teresa[29]

A few days later, in a letter to Father Van Exem, Mother Teresa
repeated some of the messages received from the "Voice" that she
had earlier reported to Archbishop Périer. In addition she under-
lined the reasons for her leaving Loreto. Her desire to answer the
call mingled with her feelings of inadequacy, yet she was willing to
bravely venture into the world of "absolute poverty."

☀ You know that I don't want to leave Loreto, I have no personal reason whatsoever, absolutely none—but the call, the life, and the work which God wants me to do is so different to the life and work of Loreto, that I would not be doing His Will if I stayed . . .

He has given the call to a little child—who is unable to fulfill it—who is already bound to Him by so many ties of love, by so much weakness of its own, and yet He puts those very great desires in the heart of this little child who is nearly lost in them. I have been always very happy where I am. I came to India solely with the hope of saving many souls and to gain a Martyr's palm; the work I have been doing all these years has helped a lot to fulfill this desire. And now last year He came with another call within a call. It has grown so strong, so bright with every Mass and Holy Communion. I wonder often at His ways . . .

The world is too rich for the poor.—We have to be very very poor in every sense of the word to gain the heart of the poor for Christ.—The poor are bitter and suffering because they have not got the happiness that poverty should bring if borne for Christ . . .

Absolute poverty which Our Lord wants so much would be out of rules here [in Loreto]—that continual service and mixing with the poorest of the poor, will also be against.

His Grace is afraid for me—that this life will be impossible for me and mine. Did not St. Clare have to face so much because she wanted to give herself and her daughters completely to God in absolute poverty?[30]

Mother Teresa was not aware of all the steps Archbishop Périer was taking behind the scenes. Though he was moving toward a positive answer, it seemed to her that her proposal had reached a dead end. At the same time, her desire "to give herself in absolute poverty to Christ in His suffering poor"[31] kept growing. Undeterred by the archbishop's previous refusals, she appealed to him anew just two weeks later:

LORETO CONVENT

CALCUTTA 15

7TH NOV. 47

Your Grace,

Like the woman in the Gospel[32] here I come again—to beg you to let me go. Forgive me if I tire you with so many letters, forgive this child of yours—who is longing with many desires to give up all to God, to give herself in absolute poverty to Christ in His suffering poor.

Your Grace, you take the place of our Holy Father here. You know his desires, you know how much this work would be according to his heart. Still more, you take the place of Our Lord, Remember His love for the suffering poor.—Please, Your Grace, do let me go soon. Nothing will happen to me, but only whatever He has arranged in His great mercy.—My weakness and sinfulness, my inability, my want of many things must cause you fear as it does with me—but I am very sure of God.—I trust His love.—I hope many things or rather everything from Him.— This is what has made me dare so far.—In Him and with Him I can do all that He wants me to do.[33]

Rev. Fr. Van Exem tells me that the life I have chosen is difficult. It is Our Lord who wants this poverty—because of the many riches by which He has been deprived of so much love. The less we have of our own, the more we shall have to give—for love founded on sacrifice is sure to grow. He wants "poor nuns covered with the poverty of the Cross." There on the Cross He had nothing of His own. That is just what we want [to] do—to love God for His own sake and the poor for Him, in Him, with Him.

Your Grace, please entrust the whole thing to the Immaculate Heart of Mary.—She is doing wonders in other lands.—She will do this for your Archdiocese.—She will take special care of your Missionaries of Charity, for in serving the poor, our aim is to bring them through Mary to Jesus, using the family Rosary as the main weapon. What desires she spoke of at Fatima* about the conversion of sinners. We want to do Our Lady's part in the slums.—Let me go in her name and for her glory. With her for Our Mother, and for her greater glory, Our Lord will not allow the work of love and self-sacrifice to be a failure—from His point of view.

I am terribly unworthy of all the many graces He has given me all these years, without any merit of mine, but please tell me, does the good God give these desires and not mean them to come true? It is now well over one year that they came, they have increased with every Holy Mass and Holy Communion. I long, I desire to bring to Him many, many souls—to make each soul love the good God with a burning love—to carry His love into every street and slum, every home and heart.—You will say you can do that as a Loreto, but I cannot live the life He wants me to, I cannot carry Him in the slums where He wants to be.

Once more, I beg of you, Your Grace, please to let me begin the life to which Our Lord is calling me.—Let me offer myself for the work He has chosen for me.

Your Grace, may I ask you to pray much for me, that my unworthiness may not be an obstacle to His work—to His desires.

Begging you for your blessing.

> *Your devoted child in J.C. [Jesus Christ]*
> *Mary Teresa*[34]

---

*In Fatima, the Blessed Virgin Mary appeared to three little children over a six-month period starting in May 1917. Her message was conversion, penance, and devotion to her Immaculate Heart.

Mother Teresa seemed to have an inexhaustible number of reasons why she should go, and go soon. She was sure of the future fruitfulness of the Missionaries of Charity, and she based her confidence solely on her faith in God and the active presence of Mary. This was the solution she offered to the archbishop's many questions and reservations. Hers was a "God-centered logic" of trust and confidence.

No record exists of a response from Archbishop Périer to this letter. Perhaps he gave up trying to explain himself to his zealous supplicant. Less than a month later, Mother Teresa decided to write again. Using the notes she had been keeping, she presented to the archbishop, as she had done in January, the dialogue between the "Voice" and herself: His persistent invitation, His firm demands, even His reproaches, and her responses, objections, and prayers to Him. To the account of the previous year, she added communications from Jesus received sometime during 1947 and the three visions about which the archbishop had heard only from Father Van Exem. She hoped with these details to finally convince the archbishop that the inspiration was from God.

FEAST OF ST. FRANCIS XAVIER[*]

Dear Father,
I would be grateful if you would give these papers to His Grace.

SEPTEMBER 1946.
During the year very often I have had that longing to be all for Jesus and to make other souls—Indian especially, come and love Him fervently, but as I thought this to be one of my desires I put it off again and again. To identify myself so much with Indian girls would be out of the question. After reading the life of St.

[*]The feast of St. Francis Xavier is on December 3.

Cabrini—the thought kept on coming—why can't I do for Him in India what she did for Him in America—why was she able to identify herself so much with the Americans as to become one of them? She did not wait for souls to come to her, she went in search of them and brought with her zealous workers.—Why can't I do the same for Him here? How could I? I have been and am very happy as a Loreto Nun.—To leave that what I love and expose myself to new labours and suffering which will be great, to be the laughing stock of so many—especially religious, to cling [to] and choose deliberately the hard things of an Indian life—to [cling to and choose] loneliness and ignominy—uncertainty—and all because Jesus wants it—because something is calling me to leave all and gather the few—to live His life—to do His work in India. In all my prayers and Holy Communions He is continually asking *"Wilt thou refuse? When there was a question of thy soul I did not think of Myself but gave Myself freely for thee on the Cross and now what about thee? Wilt thou refuse? I want Indian nuns victims of My love, who would be Mary and Martha, who would be so very united to Me as to radiate My love on souls. I want free nuns covered with My poverty of the Cross.—I want obedient nuns covered with My obedience on the Cross. I want full of love nuns covered with My Charity of the Cross.—Wilt thou refuse to do this for Me?"*

My own Jesus—what You ask it is beyond me—I can hardly understand half of the things You want—I am unworthy—I am sinful—I am weak.—Go Jesus and find a more worthy soul, a more generous one.

"You have become My Spouse for My love—you have come to India for Me. The thirst you had for souls brought you so far.—Are you afraid now to take one more step for your Spouse—for Me—for souls? Is your generosity grown cold? Am I a second to you? You did not die for souls—that is why you don't care what happens to them.—Your heart was never

drowned in sorrow as was My Mother's.—We both gave our all for souls—and you? You are afraid, that you will lose your vocation—you will become a secular—you will be wanting in perseverance. No—your vocation is to love and suffer and save souls and by taking the step you will fulfill My Heart's desire for you. You will dress in simple Indian clothes or rather like My Mother dressed—simple and poor. Your present habit is holy because it is My symbol. Your sarie will become holy because it will be My symbol."

Give me light.—Send me Thy own Spirit—which will teach me Thy own Will—which will give me strength to do the things that are pleasing to Thee. Jesus, my Jesus, don't let me be deceived.—If it is You who want this, give proof of it, if not let it leave my soul.—I trust You blindly—will You let my soul be lost? I am so afraid Jesus—I am so terribly afraid—let me not be deceived—I am so afraid.—This fear shows me how much I love myself.—I am afraid of the suffering that will come—through leading that Indian life—clothing like them, eating like them, sleeping like them—living with them and never having anything my way. How much comfort has taken possession of my heart.

"You have been always saying 'do with me whatever you wish.' Now I want to act, let Me do it—My little Spouse, My own little one.—Do not fear—I shall be with you always. You will suffer and you suffer now—but if you are My own little Spouse—the Spouse of the crucified Jesus—you will have to bear these torments in your heart.—Let Me act.—Refuse Me not—Trust Me lovingly—trust Me blindly."

Jesus, my own Jesus—I am only Thine—I am so stupid—I do not know what to say—but do with me whatever You wish—as You wish—as long as You wish. I love you not for what You give, but for what You take Jesus—why can't I be a perfect Loreto Nun—a real victim of Your love—here—why can't I be like everybody else. Look at the hundreds of Loreto Nuns—who have served You perfectly, who are now with You. Why can't I walk the same path and come to You?

"*I want Indian Nuns, Missionaries of Charity, who would be My fire of love amongst the poor, the sick, the dying and the little children. The poor I want you to bring to Me and the Sisters that would offer their lives as victims of My love—will bring these souls to Me. You are I know the most incapable person—weak and sinful, but just because you are that—I want to use you for My glory. Will thou refuse?*

"*Little one, give Me souls—Give Me the souls of the poor little street children.—How it hurts, if you only knew, to see these poor children soiled with sin.—I long for the purity of their love.—If you would only answer and bring Me these souls—draw them away from the hands of the evil one. If you only knew how many little ones fall into sin every day. There are plenty of Nuns to look after the rich and well to do people—but for My very poor, there are absolutely none. For them I long—them I love. Wilt thou refuse?*"

1947
"*My little one—come—come—carry Me into the holes of the poor.—Come be My light.—I cannot go alone—they don't know Me—so they don't want Me. You come—go amongst them, carry Me with you into them.—How I long to enter their holes—their dark unhappy homes. Come be their victim.—In your immolation—in your love for Me—they will see Me, know Me, want Me. Offer more sacrifices—smile more tenderly, pray more fervently and all the difficulties will disappear.*

"*You are afraid. How your fear hurts Me.—Fear not. It is I who am asking you to do this for Me. Fear not.—Even if the whole world is against you, laughs at you, your companions and Superiors look down on you, fear not—it is I in you, with you, for you.*

"*You will suffer—suffer very much—but remember I am with you.—Even if the whole world rejects you—remember you are My own—and I*

*am yours only. Fear not. It is I.—Only obey—obey very cheerfully and
promptly and without any questions—just only obey. I shall never leave
you—if you obey."*

1) I saw a very big crowd—all kinds of people—very poor and
children were there also. They all had their hands lifted towards
me—standing in their midst. They called out "Come, come, save
us—bring us to Jesus."

2) Again that great crowd—I could see great sorrow and
suffering in their faces—I was kneeling near Our Lady, who was
facing them.—I did not see her face but I heard her say "Take
care of them—they are mine.—Bring them to Jesus—carry Jesus
to them.—Fear not. Teach them to say the Rosary—the family
Rosary and all will be well.—Fear not—Jesus and I will be with
you and your children."

3) The same great crowd—they were covered in darkness. Yet
I could see them. Our Lord on the Cross. Our Lady at a little
distance from the Cross—and myself as a little child in front of
her. Her left hand was on my left shoulder—and her right hand
was holding my right arm. We were both facing the Cross. Our
Lord said—*"I have asked you. They have asked you and she, My
Mother has asked you. Will you refuse to do this for Me—to take care of
them, to bring them to Me?"*

I answered—You know, Jesus, I am ready to go at a moment's
notice.

Since [then]—I have heard nothing nor seen anything, but
I know that whatever I have written—*it is true.*—As I told you,
I do not build on this—but I know it is true. If I did not speak of
this—if I tried to kill these desires in my heart—I would be
guilty before Our Lord.—Why has all this come to me—the
most unworthy of His creatures—I do not know—and I have
tried so often, to persuade Our Lord, to go and seek another soul,
a more generous—a stronger one, but He seems to take pleasure

in my confusion, in my weakness.—These desires to satiate the longing of Our Lord for souls of the poor—for pure victims of His love—goes on increasing with every Mass and Holy Com. [Communion]. All my prayers and the whole day, in a word—are full of this desire. Please do not delay longer. Ask Our Lady to give us this grace on her feast day on the 8th.*

If there are any other things which I have told you but I do not remember now, please, tell His Grace that also.—I told him that I wanted only to obey and do God's Holy Will.—Now I do not fear, I leave myself completely in His Hands.—He can dispose of me as He wishes.—

Please tell H.G. [His Grace] about the two Yugoslav girls in Rome. Then there are Six Bengali girls—The Belgium girl in the South—The one also you know in Belgium.—Vocations would come. I do not fear about this—though everybody thinks me very optimistic, but I know how much love and generosity there [is] in Bengali hearts if they are given the means to reach the highest. Self denial and abnegation will be the means to our end.—There will be disappointment—but the good God wants just only our Love and our trust in Him.

Please pray for me during your Holy Mass.

Yours sincerely in O.L. [Our Lord]
M. Teresa[35]

p.s. Please explain to H.G. what I meant when I said I don't build or believe in visions—I meant that even if the things did not come—my desires were just as strong—and the readiness to do His Holy Will just as fervent.

---

*December 8 is the feast of the Immaculate Conception of the Blessed Virgin Mary.

The Visions

This is the only instance in her correspondence where Mother Teresa revealed these or any other visions. Her later descriptions of Jesus on the Cross give a hint of how vivid the scenes had been. The visions were related to one another, each building on the previous one.

In the first vision she found herself in the midst of a crowd of "very poor and children." The voice this time was not that of her beloved Jesus, calling: *"Come—come—carry Me into the holes of the poor.—Come be My light."* Rather it was the voice of a pleading "big crowd," calling: "Come, come, save us—bring us to Jesus." This double invitation from Jesus and the crowd, "Come," would keep echoing in her heart to the end of her life.

In the second vision, she penetrated deeper into the "great sorrow and suffering" of the "great crowd." She was not alone; she was in the company of Our Lady. It was now Mary's turn to plead with her: "bring them to Jesus—carry Jesus to them." Mary was encouraging her to respond to both pleas, giving her a means for all to "be well"—by teaching the poor to say the rosary as a family and by the assurance that Our Lady would be present.

In the third vision, the great crowd's suffering intensified: they were "covered in darkness." Mother Teresa could see them but she could also see Jesus on the Cross. Mary's role was intensified as well: she was a mother behind her "little child," supporting her as they both faced Jesus on the Cross. The voice was that of Jesus, reminding Mother Teresa: *"I have asked you. They have asked you and she, My Mother, has asked you."* He asked again: *"Will you refuse to do this for Me?"*

After this threefold reminder and the question that echoed her secret pledge, she answered: "You know, Jesus, I am ready to go at a moment's notice." Mother Teresa's certitude of being called by God and her desire to do His will gave her the courage to persist. To ignore or deny this call would make her guilty before God. Yet before she could act, she still had to wait for the archbishop's reply.

"You May Go Ahead"

Archbishop Périer had perceived the strength of character and greatness of heart behind Mother Teresa's persistence. Through the "blueprint" and the first rule of the new congregation, he had seen her clear ideas, concrete proposals, and firm determination. With her straightforward responses to all his misgivings, she had proved to be not an idealistic dreamer, but "down to earth" and completely focused on her lofty aim.

Because the archbishop took Mother Teresa and her proposal so seriously, he had remained firm in his resolve to complete his meticulous process of discernment, in spite of her frequent appeals. During his trip to Europe the previous June, he had consulted a highly regarded theologian in Rome. Upon his return to India, he had asked the advice of two more priests familiar with local conditions. These theologians considered the project without referring to the "so called demands of Our Lord"[36] and "apart from voices and visions."[37] They advised the archbishop that he could "give permission without serious imprudence."[38]

After much prayer and deliberation, the archbishop finally felt free to give Mother Teresa permission to pursue her goal. "I am deeply convinced," he later wrote to Loreto Superior General Mother Gertrude, "that by withholding my consent, I would hamper the realisation, through her, of the will of God. I do not think I could do anything more to enlighten myself."[39] His decision was not based on the extraordinary phenomena that Mother Teresa had experienced but rather on the depth of her life of prayer, her obedience and zeal, and his judgment that her blueprint and rules proposed a concrete solution to a critical need in the Church. "You may go ahead," were his long awaited words to Mother Teresa when he met her after Mass in the Loreto convent. It was January 6, 1948, the nineteenth anniversary of her arrival in India.

SIX

To the "Dark Holes"

THE DREAM REALIZED

I go of my free choice with the blessing of obedience.
—Mother Teresa

"For the Glory of His Name"

With the archbishop's consent, Mother Teresa was now free to take the next step toward fulfilling the call. Following the norms of the Church, she needed permission from her Loreto Superior General, Mother Gertrude Kennedy, to seek authorization from the pope to leave Loreto and begin her new mission. In her petition to Mother Gertrude, written just four days after receiving the archbishop's blessing, she made no mention of the locutions and visions, but presented a synopsis of her new call, emphasizing the spiritual aim of the future congregation.

My dearest Mother General,

The matter of this letter is very sacred to me, therefore, I beg you to keep the content of it a secret. I shall send Mother Provincial a copy of this letter, in case you desire to communicate with her on this matter, otherwise I do not desire that any other nun should know of this.

In Sept. 1946 I went to Darjeeling for a holiday and there also I made my eight days retreat. On my return to Calcutta I informed my spiritual Father of the following:

That God wants me to give myself completely to Him in absolute poverty, to identify myself with the Indian girls in their lives of self-sacrifice and immolation by tending the poor in the slums, the sick, the dying, the beggars in their dirty holes and the little street children. In a word—to give myself without any reserve to God in the poor of the slums and the streets.

The spiritual Father put me off.—Though he saw that it was from God, still he forbade me to even think about it. Often, very often during the four months I asked him to let me speak to His Grace, [but] each time he refused, until the 8th Jan. '47 when he gave me permission to put the whole matter before His Grace. I did so in detail. His Grace kept it for a whole year. He prayed much to see the will of God. On the 6th Jan. '48 he came to say Mass here and after which he told me "You may go ahead." He allowed me to write to you and tell you of the call.

Now dear Mother General, I desire to work out the plan in the best way, for the glory of His name. I turn to you, to help me to fulfill His holy Will in my regard.

I want to leave Loreto as soon as it is possible for the Sacred Congregation to grant me the annulment of my vows and the Indult of Secularization,[1] by which act I desire to be made free to live the life of an Indian in India and do the work in the slums. I ask your permission to let me apply to the Sacred Congregation to be freed from my vows. I entered Loreto in Oct. 1928 and took my final vows May 1937.

Dear Mother General, I am sure that it is God's holy Will for me to go and do the work. Why did He call me, me the most unworthy and sinful, one so full of weakness, of misery and sin, I do not know. There is nothing I can answer—but that His way is a mystery to me. I have prayed and prayed much over this, looked at it from every corner and the answer remains the same—to leave all and follow Him deeper still, in that life of complete surrender and immolation for Him and His poor. I know you will be anxious about me—but please do not keep me back from the path where He wants me to go. If you were in India, if you saw what I have seen for so many years, your heart too would long to make Our Lord better known to the poor who suffer most terrible sufferings and then also eternity in darkness, because there are no nuns to give them a helping hand in their own dark holes. Let me go, dear Mother General. I know I am one of your most unworthy children, but I trust you with the gift God has entrusted to me, and I am sure you will help me to do His Will. Please do not prevent me from giving myself to Him and His poor.

I have foreseen many of the hardships and the difficulties which that life will bring me—but I trust the good God blindly and I know He will not let me down, even though I may make a mistake.

As I told you before His Grace, the Archbishop of Calcutta knows all and to prevent any talk I am sending this letter through him.

Pray for me, dear Mother General, please pray for me, and
ask the dear old nuns at the Abbey to do the same for me.

> *Your affectionate child in J.C. [Jesus Christ]*
> *Mary Teresa Bojaxhiu*[2]

"She Is Absolutely Sure"

As Mother Teresa had predicted,[3] from this point onward Archbishop Périer became her earnest advocate and principal guide. His
present task was to help her move through the process of being
freed from her obligations as a Loreto nun.

An important issue was whether or not Mother Teresa would remain a member of the Loreto order once she began living outside
the convent. In her letter to Mother Gertrude, she disclosed her intention to ask for annulment of her vows (secularization). At the
same time, though she was convinced that a complete separation
from Loreto was required, she was determined to remain consecrated to Jesus as a religious, as she had stressed earlier:

> Nobody can unbind me from God—I am consecrated to Him
> and as such I desire to die.—I don't know what the Canon Law
> has to say in this matter—but I know Our Lord will never
> allow Himself to be separated from me.—Neither will He allow
> anyone to separate me from Him.[4]

She sought reassurance from the archbishop that she would remain totally bound to Christ:

> I want also to make sure that the very minute my vows as a
> Loreto nun will be annulled, will you let me bind myself by
> those which will keep me His from that very minute. I do not

desire not even a minute to pass without my whole being not belonging to Him.[5]

Father Van Exem had recommended exclaustration, which would allow her to retain her vows as a Loreto nun and return to her order if the venture did not succeed. Mother Teresa, for her part, insisted on petitioning for secularization. As to leaving the door open to Loreto, she was confident that this safeguard would not be necessary: "[I]f the inspiration comes from God, and I am convinced it does, there could be no question of failure."[6]

Archbishop Périer came to Mother Teresa's defense. He too saw that it might be more prudent to favor exclaustration. Nevertheless, after dealing with her during the previous year, he understood and respected her position: because the inspiration was from God, He would take care of it. He was therefore unwilling to interfere with her preference:

> For the question of choosing between exclaustration and secularisation, you [Father Van Exem] may be right in preferring the former. I must admit however that this good person [Mother Teresa] is logical when sticking to the latter. If she is absolutely sure that Our Lord wants her to do that work for Him, there is no question of failure and therefore no question of returning to her former order. I can understand that well, [and] that is why I do not wish to influence her one way or the other.[7]

For the sake of confidentiality, Archbishop Périer took charge of Mother Teresa's correspondence with her Loreto superiors. Upon receiving from Father Van Exem her letter to Mother Gertrude, the archbishop, with his faith-filled wisdom, observed to his Jesuit confrere: "Our work is at an end now. It was our business to examine whether we could allow her to go ahead. The rest is the work of God entirely and we shall come in only as instruments, and that is our right place in God's works ad extra."[8]

The following day the archbishop sent her letter to Dublin together with his own report. In it he outlined his discernment process over the past year and expressed his high regard for the Loreto nun making this unusual request:

I must now add that all the while I have examined the Sister, listened to the information from the spiritual father and others. I am aware that Mother M. Teresa has not always been understood well and that in the opinion of a few she is not considered very highly, perhaps even not favourably, owing chiefly to her previous education different in many ways from the one imparted in other countries of Europe: she is Yugoslav by nationality.[9] I have known her for several years, even from the time she made her noviciate in India. Without exaggeration and without revealing any conscience matters, I can say that, notwithstanding exterior defects no doubt, she has a very high ideal in her religious life, is intimately united with Our Lord, humble and submissive, obedient and extremely zealous, entirely oblivious of self.[10]

"You Are His Instrument, Nothing More"

Mother Teresa eagerly anticipated a reply from Mother Gertrude, and when it had not come in less than three weeks, she became concerned. That her request would arrive, be considered and responded to so quickly was not a realistic expectation, but she was on fire to move ahead. Having spoken to Mother Provincial (her higher superior in Calcutta) about her inspiration in anticipation of the decision to come, she urged the archbishop to speed up the process.

Your Grace,

I have been wanting to write to you, but could not get the time. I am still longing to keep my word to God. I want it soon to come true. Up to now the delay was necessary in a way—but now that you have seen that the good God wants the work, that the souls are waiting for the Missionaries of Charity, why make me wait so long? My superiors now know all that they had to know. The meeting with Mother Provincial went off very well. She did not scold, she did not try to make me change, she was extremely kind and gentle—the rest Fr. Van Exem must have told you.—It is over three weeks now that I wrote to Mother General.[11] How long must I wait? May I not write again or straight to Rome? There will be enough delays when the matter goes to Rome.— Why delay now? Forgive me for writing as I do, but the longing to offer myself to God in His poor is more and more growing.

The other thing is—if you approve—I wish to keep Fr. Van Exem as my spiritual father in the new circumstances whatever they be.—The reason for doing this is—he knows me well, and also knows everything about the work—but if you wish it to be otherwise, I shall gladly obey.

There are two girls in Rome from Yugoslavia, who were to have entered Loreto, but were told to wait as the Nov. [Novitiate] is closed for the present. They both want to offer themselves completely for Bengal. One is a trained nurse, the other a teacher.—May I [write], or ask Fr. Van Exem to write to them about the work in the slums?[12]

There is another question which I would be grateful if I could know regarding that absolute poverty, how far would you insist on lessening or rather making easy that poverty—which for us has to be the means to reach our end? By absolute poverty I mean

real and complete poverty—not starving—but wanting—just
only what the real poor have—to be really dead to all that the
world claims for its own.—How far will you try to make us
change in this.— ...

How many must we be to have the Blessed Sacrament in our
midst?—The work that we will have to do, will be impossible
without His continual grace from the tabernacle.—He will have
to do everything.—We have just to follow.

Pray for me, please, that I do the things that are pleasing
to Him.

Your devoted child in J.C. [Jesus Christ]
Mary Teresa[13]

Mother Teresa remained steadfast with the archbishop on the
observance of "absolute poverty" in her future community, an observance that because of the new congregation's aim would be much
stricter than in her present order. Jesus had asked for *"nuns covered
with My poverty of the Cross."*[4] Therefore she deftly tried to forestall
any effort by the archbishop to curb the rigorous poverty she envisioned for her sisters.

The archbishop, though supportive, found Mother Teresa too
hurried and encouraged her to be a docile instrument and wait for
God's time.

ARCHBISHOP'S HOUSE
32, PARK STREET
CALCUTTA 29TH JANUARY 1948.

Dear Mother M. Teresa,
P.C. [Pax Christi—Peace of Christ]
I am in receipt of your letter of the 28th instant.[15] Your letter was
sent on the 12th to Ireland, that is why I want you to wait till the
end of that week to give the news in Calcutta. I presume Mother

G. [General] may have received that letter on the 18th or 19th. To have her answer now would suppose that she had nothing else to do but to write to you at once without reflection. Perhaps she was sick or in visitations. Take a little time. If Our Lord wishes to work miracles in this case certainly He can do it, but we have no right to expect them and He does not work miracles without a very good reason. Be patient. By writing yourself now to Rome you might spoil the whole outcome of your petition. Perhaps the V. [Very] Revd. [Reverend] Mother General has written herself already. Just wait for a reply. Do not rush things, and do not expect others to rush them either. I would quite understand Revd. Mother General wanting to pray for light, to reflect before she takes a decision. You have written under your responsibility, I have written under my responsibility, it is natural and we must expect her to do so. Mother General has to take for granted whatever you or I may have written to her. I have been very pleased to read that Revd. Mother Prov.[Provincial] had taken your petition so kindly. She of course will wish also to pray for light, perhaps to consult without naming anybody. In due time the reply will come, remain quiet. <u>Pray much and live intimately with Our Lord J.C. [Jesus Christ] asking for light, strength, decision;</u> but do not anticipate <u>HIS WORK. Try not to put anything of your own in all this. You are His instrument, nothing more.</u> I do pray also, but I would be disappointed if perhaps things went too fast. Let each one do his work conscientiously not hurriedly. It is not necessary to delay unduly, but there is no necessity either to precipitate things unduly. If Our Lord wants it to be done quickly He can arrange that; in the meantime being human creatures we must act according to our means. God bless you. In union of prayers

Your devotedly in Xt. [Christ]
† F. Périer, SJ[16]

The underlining on the letter is Mother Teresa's own, an indication of the impact these words had on her. She had given this letter to Father Van Exem, with her handwritten notes on the margins:

🌿 Please destroy—I have copied the parts I need. The letter is simply beautiful. You must pray for me—to learn how to get rid of self in myself and live intimately with Him. You will teach me how to do this, will you?

Pray for light that I may see and [for] courage to do away with anything of self in the work. I must disappear completely—if I want God to have the whole.[17]

Any possibility of spoiling God's work was intolerable to her, so once again she surrendered, obeyed, and waited for the reply.

"Your Desire . . . Is Most Noble and Praiseworthy"

Just three days after Mother Teresa wrote to the archbishop, he received the response from Dublin. What seemed to Mother Teresa a long time was unusually quick under the circumstances. Mother Gertrude had made the decision the day after receiving her request:

🌿 Realizing as I do, the long consideration and the earnest prayer Your Grace has given to the matter, as well as the views of others well qualified to judge in Mother M. Teresa's case, I feel I cannot do otherwise than acquiesce in the matter, lest I should fail in compliance with the Will of God.[18]

She not only gave permission to Mother Teresa but also lauded the objective for which the Loreto order was to lose a valued member.

25TH JANUARY 1948

My dearest Mother M. Teresa,

Your desire to immolate yourself completely in the service of God's poor, is most noble and praiseworthy, and though I regard your change as a very real loss to our Institute still you give me so many reasons to believe your call is from God I cannot refuse your request.

One thing, it would be wiser to get a decree of exclaustration for the present and then, if all goes well get a dispensation from your vows.

I shall not mention the matter to any one not even to Mother Provincial and you need not do it either. My consent is sufficient.

God guide and protect you always. You will be in my prayers. Please keep me in yours.

Yours very affectionately [in] J.C. [Jesus Christ]
M. Gertrude
(Superior General)[19]

With this approval, one more door opened for Mother Teresa. The final step she needed to take before she could set out for the streets of Calcutta was to petition the Holy See. In a sober letter to the head of the Sacred Congregation for Religious, Mother Teresa explained her plans.

LORETO CONVENT
ENTALLY
CALCUTTA 15
INDIA
7TH FEB. 1948

To His Eminence

The Cardinal Prefect of the S. C. [Sacred Congregation]
of Religious Rome

Your Eminence,

With the permission and consent of the Very Reverend Mother
M. Gertrude, Superior General of the Institute of the Blessed
Virgin Mary (Rathfarnham, Ireland) I humbly beg leave to
address this petition to Y.E. [Your Eminence], namely to obtain
the Indult of secularisation and thereby free me from the vows
which bind me to the said Institute.

Since September 1946 Almighty God is calling me to devote
myself entirely to a complete poverty after the example of the
great Saint of Assisi and to the entire service of the Poor in the
slums and back streets of the city and elsewhere, to take care of
the sick and dying, to draw away the little street children from sin
and evil, to help the beggars and the starving. To enable me to do
this kind of work, a life of prayer and self-sacrifice is necessary: to
approach the poorest among the poor one must become like unto
them, to attract the poor of Christ, complete poverty is essential.

I have exposed these my desires and many others to my
spiritual Father. For a long time he kept me waiting; he prayed
and asked for prayers in order to find out whether such was the
will of God. After several months, being persuaded that I was not
actuated by any human motives, but by the desire to answer a
genuine vocation he allowed me to expose everything to His
Grace the Archbishop of Calcutta. After a full year His Grace
gave me leave to write to our Very Reverend Mother General and
with her consent I am now sending this request to Y. E. I feel that
if I must serve the poorest among the Indians, it is necessary to
live like an Indian with the Indians, and therefore I cannot remain
a member of the Institute of the Blessed Virgin Mary. Our
V. R. [Very Reverend] Mother General in giving her consent
adds that in her opinion it would be wiser for me to ask the S. C.
of Religious for an "exclaustration" so that if things go well a
dispensation might be asked later on for "secularisation." I was

inclined to think that if the inspiration comes from God, and I am convinced it does, there could be no question of failure and therefore I asked immediate secularisation. I may be mistaken in my views and as I have no other wish than to fulfil the Will of God, I submit in anticipation to whatever Your Eminence will decide in this matter.

I entered the Institute of the Bl. [Blessed] Virgin Mary in October 1928, took my first vows in 1931, my final profession in 1937 at Darjeeling. I have worked in India (Bengal) since 1931. I was born Albanian but resided with my parents in Yugoslavia.

In all sincerity I admit that I possess no virtue and have no merit; it is a mystery to me how the Good God wants this from poor me. All these years of my religious life, I have been quite happy as a member of the Institute of the Bl. V. M. [Blessed Virgin Mary] and the thought of leaving it breaks my heart. Why Almighty God calls me now to this new life I do not know, but I want to do only His Holy Will without any reserve, whatever the cost be.

I want to gather other souls around me to do the same work and together to serve the poor in their humblest and most dejected and contempted members. There are millions who live in Indian cities and villages in ignorance of God and of Christ, in abominable sinfulness. We shall bring them to Christ and Christ to them.

Your Eminence, I am but a humble nun, and I do not know how to express myself as I ought. Y. E. will kindly forgive me, I am sure, and whilst considering my petition, pray for and paternally bless.

Your Eminence's
humble servant in Christ,
Sister M. Teresa, IBVM
In the world
(Miss) Gonxha Bojaxhiu[20]

A cover letter from the archbishop accompanied the petition. Besides explaining his lengthy discernment process, Archbishop Périer confirmed his high regard for Mother Teresa.

At the request of Sister Mary Teresa . . . I am addressing to your Excellency the enclosed letter. It does not belong to me to pronounce myself on this delicate matter. All I can say is that when the spiritual Father of this religious (sister) told me of her desire to leave the above mentioned institute in order to consecrate herself exclusively to the care of the poorest of the poor, I did not manifest any haste to give her an answer. I wanted to realize whether that desire was serious. . . .

I have known Sister Mary Teresa personally for several years, actually since her arrival in India. She is very gifted, has always been deeply humble and submissive, and she has given complete satisfaction by the very religious spirit that she has always manifested. She is very attached to the institute to which she belongs and the separation will be very painful for her. I believe her to be very mortified and very generous. As a whole I can say that I find she has good judgment. She is of Slavic origin and consequently I fear that she is sometimes a bit exaggerated, maybe excited. But that is only a personal impression and I would find it difficult to prove the reason of that impression.

So I am submitting the case for the consideration and the decision of your Excellency.[21]

"How Hard It Is for Me to Wait"

Although she understood a quick reply from Rome was not to be expected, the waiting was nonetheless difficult for Mother Teresa, as she admitted to Archbishop Périer:

It will soon be nearly two months that I wrote to Rome, and as you know no answer has yet come.—I do not want in any way to anticipate His will and work, only pray that my unworthiness and sinfulness will not be the cause of His delay.

In your last letter you wrote that you would be disappointed if things went fast, possibly Our Lord to please you is doing this.—But if you only knew how hard it is for me to wait and keep on as if nothing is happening, you would ask Our Lord to come soon and take me away—to the slums and His poor.[22]

As months passed, the archbishop correctly anticipated that Mother Teresa would attempt to hasten matters. In May the expected request arrived:

LORETO CONVENT

ENTALLY

13TH MAY '48

Your Grace,

Don't you think it is time for us to make a more fervent appeal to Rome? It is nearly four months that you sent my letter.—Why are they not answering? Don't you think we are wanting in zeal for His work if I just wait? It is true, I do not want to anticipate His Holy Will, not for a minute, but please, Your Grace, do not let me wait just because we think we have done enough. I wrote so many letters to you before you gave your consent, possibly the same need be done with Rome. They don't know India. They don't know how much Calcutta needs the Missionaries of Charity. Please, Your Grace, write again, and if need be, let it go to the Holy Father. He will understand it clearly, because this is just what he wants. Please, Your Grace, let us make a stronger appeal to Rome, for I must go—and go quickly. Why so much thought for one so little, so sinful, so weak? Please, let us not delay any longer—let me go. Souls are being lost in the slums and in the streets, the Sacred Heart of Jesus is more and more suffering—and here I am waiting—for just only one "Yes" which the Holy Father I am sure would give, if he knew of it.

Please write by air-letter—so that the answer may come during this month of Mary[23] to whom the Missionaries of Charity will belong—body and soul.

Forgive me, I do not know what else to tell you, but please let me go soon. Use every means that the good God has given you, and appeal to Rome with greater zeal—or tell me what I should do.—I am ready to do it, but to wait—don't tell me. With His help and grace I can bear it, but it is so very difficult, when one's mind and heart is captivated by such strong desires, to keep on as if all is the same. Let me go, Your Grace, please.

Kindly pray for my brother, who is very dangerously ill.— . . . Please pray for me.

> *Your devoted child in J. C. [Jesus Christ]*
> *Mary Teresa*[24]

The archbishop promptly corrected Mother Teresa's belief that her persistence had elicited his consent.

I quite understand that you feel somewhat restive owing to the long delay between your letter to the S. C. [Sacred Congregation] of Religious and their reply. First of all let me correct a wrong idea you mention in your letter, viz. [namely] that it is the number of letters you wrote to me that determined my decision allowing you to write to Rome. I am afraid the number of letters did nothing of the kind and more than once I told Fr. v. E. [Father Van Exem] that I wanted time to reflect and nothing more.[25]

Her tenacity had been challenging to his deliberative and meticulous nature, yet it had not affected his decision making. He was thus skeptical that her imploring the Vatican would have any effect with the authorities there either. "I do not think it will advance your case one inch,"[26] he warned her.

He also pointed out that the process takes time, so there was no reason to be concerned. Reassuring her that she was not wanting in zeal by waiting patiently, he still gave her permission to write again. For the time being, Mother Teresa decided not to act. By July, however, they both agreed that the Holy See should be contacted again; hence they sent her petition of February with accompanying letters from each of them.

"I Go of My Free Choice"

On August 8, 1948, Mother Teresa finally received the news from Rome: Pope Pius XII, through the Sacred Congregation for Religious, had granted her permission to leave Loreto and begin her new mission. Instead of the requested indult of secularization, she had been granted an indult of exclaustration authorizing her to stay outside the Loreto convent "for one year or less if a shorter period is sufficient"[27] and to keep her religious vows as a Loreto nun under the authority of Archbishop Périer. The indult had actually been signed on April 12, 1948,[28] but for reasons unknown the document reached Calcutta only in August.

Mother Teresa had been longing for a positive reply; at last she would have "the joy of giving up all, and bringing joy into the Heart of Jesus."[29] Before she received permission from Rome, she had foreseen that the transition would not be without pain: "The thought of leaving breaks my heart,"[30] she had told the Cardinal

Prefect in February. Now the moment had arrived to make that heroic sacrifice, to abandon the security of the convent and plunge into an unpredictable future in the slums. Only to the archbishop did she reveal the cost of the step she was about to take.

LORETO CONVENT

ENTALLY

15TH AUG. '48

Your Grace,

First of all I want to thank you for all you have done for me—to help me to follow this new call. I have been a cause of much extra work and anxiety.—I do hope the good God will repay you in His own way.

On Tuesday evening I am leaving by the Punjab mail[31]—All is very dark—plenty of tears—but I go of my <u>free choice</u> with the blessing of obedience.—Please pray for me that I may have the courage to complete my sacrifice as He has given me the inspiration and grace to begin. . . .

Please pray.—I have very little courage—but I trust Him blindly, in spite of all feelings.

Your devoted child in J. C. [Jesus Christ]

Mary Teresa.

P.S. in Patna I shall be just only "Mary Teresa."[32]

On August 17, 1948, clad in a white sari with a blue border, Mother Teresa—a European nun alone in newly independent India—set out to begin life as a Missionary of Charity. Her lifestyle would be as innovative as the dress she wore. Considering "absolute poverty" essential to her new mission, she chose to leave with just five rupees. That was the entire capital of this "lone woman . . .

wearing only a sari . . . [a] nun yet not looking like a nun."[33] Yet her wealth lay in her heart: unshakable faith in God and absolute confidence in the promise He had made to her two years earlier: *"Do not fear—I shall be with you always. . . . Trust Me lovingly—trust Me blindly."*

SEVEN

"The Dark Night of the Birth of the Society"

THE PLAN OF OUR LORD IS BEING FULFILLED

My God, give me courage now—this moment to persevere in following Your call.
—Mother Teresa

"It Cost a Very Good Deal"

Only God knew the heavy price of Mother Teresa's sacrifice as she walked with steady step out the gate of her beloved Loreto. Her destination was the Holy Family Hospital of the Medical Mission Sisters in Patna, where she was to learn the basics of nursing needed to serve the poor. Determined as she was in the pursuit of her new calling, she still found it "much harder to leave Loreto than to leave my family."[1] After arriving in Patna, Mother Teresa wrote to Archbishop Périer:

The first step towards the slums is over. It cost a very good deal, but I am grateful to God for giving the grace to do it and also for showing me how very weak I am.[2]

Her letter ends with a request that highlights her heart's aspiration: "Please pray for me that I may keep up looking at Him cheerfully."[3]

The prayer she copied on the first page of her medical notebook also reflects her pain at leaving Loreto and adjusting to a new way of life:

O Jesus, only love of my heart, I wish to suffer what I suffer and all Thou wilt have me suffer, for Thy pure love not because of the merits I may acquire, nor for the rewards Thou hast promised me but only to please Thee, to praise Thee, to bless Thee as well in sorrow as in joy.[4]

Friends Forever

Mother Teresa's leaving Loreto had a great impact on all who knew her, especially her sisters. During her twenty years in Loreto, she had built strong and warm relationships with them. From Calcutta and the surrounding cities her former companions wrote encouraging notes and letters. In those days of pain, she greatly appreciated them.

My heartfelt congratulations on your decision and all my good wishes <u>and prayers</u> for the success A.M.D.G. [Ad Majorem Dei Gloriam,[5] For the Greater Glory of God] of your enterprise. I feel sure that you will have full scope for your zeal in this new life you are beginning and I want you to know that you can always rely on us to help you with our prayers. And if there is anything else we can do for you, please never hesitate to call upon us.—

I know God is calling you to this work so you need have no fear for the future and it is really with a certain feeling of joy and confidence that I see you go forth to do Christ's work among the poor and down trodden.[6]

They wished her well, promised prayers, and added witty remarks that friends understand.

My dearest M M [Mother Mary] Teresa—
My little (Appendix![7]) friend ever.
This little note brings you my love & the assurance of my prayers. God be with you in the new work He has in store for you. When I heard of it, I was astonished but not <u>surprised</u>.

God wants the Gifts He has given you used in His own way i.e. Your facility to learn the language of the country—(& not English). Your influence over the people of the soil will help you now to go ahead and win a great harvest of Souls for Heaven.—I wonder if St. Peter looking at us both at the Eternal Gates will say <u>which is which</u>? because I shall have helped you with my prayers all along the way.—Please remember me too—I need prayers—

Always your friend
in Deo—
Mary Joseph
IBVM[8]

Mother Gabrielle, her childhood friend from Skopje, found the separation particularly painful:

My most beloved Sister,
Today is your feast day and I prayed much for you; thank you very much for your letter, it made me very happy. My sister I wrote to you last night when I heard that you have left us. Ah, if

you knew, when I read your letter I cried all day, and I see that it is God's will. Everyday I am praying for you and you will never be missing in my prayers.

If you want to know all the sisters have spoken well about you; not even one has spoken bad about you. Everyone is remembering you. He, the glorious one, wants to show His will in you—

How blessed are you that God has chosen you to make this great sacrifice, because from Him you have always received courage, that is why God has given you for this difficult way; He knows that you can take His Cross— . . .

I hope that you will not change your name—

Much love and greetings and know that I will never forget you.

> *Your little sister*
> *Mary Gabrielle*[9]

"*Do Not Worry for Having Had to Refuse Me*"

Though she was feeling the pain of separation, Mother Teresa wrote to Father Van Exem from Patna, "My soul at present is in perfect peace and joy."[10] Practical as ever, she was already looking for a place to stay upon her return to Calcutta. She had received a suggestion from Jesuit Father Julian Henry[11], the pastor of St. Teresa's Church in Calcutta, to go to Krishnagar[12] as a helper in return for lodging. Her first reaction to this proposal was that "it would be the best medicine to get out of me every drop of pride; it will well kill my natural ways."[13] She was joyful at the thought of living like the poor, "Just only a jhi [servant]—This I would really love—and it would also help me to know the ways and the sorrows of the poor by living with them, doing the same work as them."[14]

While willing to face the humiliation of going there as an exclaustrated Loreto nun and looking forward to doing the work of a servant, she realized that the special treatment she would receive in a place where she was known would not permit her to live in "absolute poverty."

☀ Krishnagar will not be good for this, because I know the Superiors and most of the nuns and the teachers. I had to do something for them some years back, and so they will try to make it easy. You will have to find a place where I am not known at all. What about Gobra?[15] I know nobody there.—Do not tell them anything, just say that a servant is looking for work and would be pleased to get anything.—I would also have a chance to get in touch with lepers, which I am sure to meet amongst the beggars.[16]

Depending completely on divine guidance, she wrote in the same letter to Father Van Exem: "If Gobra does not need a jhi— you ask Our Lady to make them need one.—They will be surprised at the fair face, but tell them I am Indian since last month."[17] As providence ordained, none of these places were available, so she had to continue searching.

From Patna she had also written to ask if she could stay in the Loreto's vacant building in Tengra once she returned to Calcutta. Having received initial positive reactions from her former companions in the order, Mother Teresa was surprised when the newly elected superior general, Mother M. Pauline Dunne, I.B.V.M., refused her request.

☀ LORETO ABBEY,
RATHFARNHAM.
29TH OCTOBER 1948.

Dearest M. M. Teresa,
I am exceedingly sorry that my first letter to you will bring you a disappointment, but I feel you will accept it as God's Will.

You must have forgotten that our Constitutions forbid the alienation of property, and that therefore it was not in Mother Dorothy's power to grant such a permission as you asked in your last letter to her. Therefore she had to refer the matter to the Council-General.

My Consultors and I wish you every blessing and success in the new work for the salvation of souls for which you are now preparing in Patna. We would like you to understand, however, that Loreto is not connected with, or responsible for, the new Order which you hope to found. To have another religious Order living in a house on the grounds of any of our Convents would be quite contrary to the customs and spirit of our Institute. Tengra cannot be given to you. We shall pray earnestly that you may soon find suitable accommodation.

I was one of Rev. Mother Gertrude's consultors, and was under the impression that you intended to live as a native among the poorest of the poor in Calcutta, and by your example there you hoped to attract others to join you.

I hope you keep ever so well, for you must find life in Patna a great change. I remember seeing you here in the Abbey before you went to India. You were here for some weeks, and knew no English, I think.

With love, and every best wish

> *Yours affectionately in J. C. [Jesus Christ],*
> *M. Pauline Dunne*
> *Superior General*[18]

Given the responsibility of the Loreto superiors to protect the members of the order from being affected by this "experimental" enterprise, the decision was understandable. Their response challenged Mother Teresa to be accountable for the step she had taken. Even so, it was a huge disappointment to Mother Teresa. Her response to Mother Pauline once again reveals her prudence and common sense, as well as her trust in God.

HOLY FAMILY HOSPITAL
PATNA CITY
9TH NOV. 1948

Dear and Reverend Mother General,

Many thanks for your letter of the 29th Oct. Please do not worry for having had to refuse me, some good is sure to come from it.

I am afraid I was not clear enough in my letter to Mother Dorothy. I did not ask for the building as a permanent stay—but only until I got a more suitable place, and also I did not mean her to give but to rent.—But as you say it would be against the customs and the spirit of the Institute, I would not like either to have the building.

I never thought nor think for a moment that Loreto would be connected with or be responsible for the new work.—I know I am still a Loreto Nun but that does not mean that the work is bound to Loreto. From my letters, I suppose you get that impression that I want to cling to Loreto—well it is only natural that it should be so. You cannot break a thing you have loved for 20 years. But if you wish that I should not write to any of the Nuns, or keep a keen interest in all Loreto does, you have only to say it and I shall do it.

It is perfectly true that I intend living like an Indian and yet fully religious, with God's grace, but that does not mean that I could bring my young companions and throw them blindly into the hard work, without first giving them the aim of their self sacrificing work. For them I asked the house where they could have been well protected and yet prepare for the work; but it does not matter.—When the King of Kings and His Blessed Mother sought for a dwelling place "There was no room in the inn."[19]

Why should there be place for us? We too shall find a stable and begin the work for souls.

Yes, many years ago I was at the Abbey—those were happy days as all and every day in the 20 years of my life in Loreto have been. I am just as happy now to do God's Holy Will. It cost what it may. I shall most probably stay here with the Sisters until the 13th Dec. and then make my eight days retreat in Calcutta.

I have been able to get much help from the Sisters, who treat me as if I was one of their own. God is sure to bless them for their charity.

All beginnings have their many crosses, but pray for me and for those who join, that we may have the courage to do this work for souls. The way of life and work will I am sure not meet the approval of many, though at present every person I have met has been all for it. But the work is His, not mine and even if I die before it has had [a] chance of starting, still I know I have answered the call and made the step towards His forgotten poor and destitute.—Success or failure whatever be His plan—the first is His—the second be mine.—It will be all for Him.

I would like to keep in touch with you—just for the sake of getting the prayers—but if you do not desire, pray for me all the same.—I pray for you every day.

When I was in Asansol I heard much about you from Mother Concepta. She makes a first class Superior and has a fervent community.

Kindly give my best wishes to dear Mother Gertrude and Mother Rozario.

A very happy Christmas and New Year.

Your affectionate child [in] J. C. [Jesus Christ]
M. Teresa[20]

By December, thanks to the Medical Mission Sisters' competent training, Mother Teresa was prepared to begin her work in the slums. She returned to Calcutta on the ninth and took up lodging with the Little Sisters of the Poor at the convent of St. Joseph's. Before starting her mission, she made an eight-day retreat under the direction of Father Van Exem.

"What Suffering, What Want of God"

At last, on December 21, Mother Teresa went into the slums for the first time as a Missionary of Charity. Through the challenges of the past two years, she had remained faithful to the call and had finally reached her goal: "the dark holes of the poor." One of her first followers later remarked, "Seeing her poorly dressed in a simple, humble sari, with a Rosary in her hand, was like seeing the Gospel come alive, making Jesus present among the poorest. One could say a Light has dawned in the darkness of the slums."[21]

The Calcutta Mother Teresa now faced had been very much affected by the consequences of World War II, the aftermath of the 1943 famine, and the frequent riots in the city. Immediately after India's independence, the influx of people into the capital of Bengal was enormous. The city that was known for its palaces saw its slum areas growing. The poor who could afford to rent tiny shacks (only several square feet of often windowless space jammed with their scant belongings) survived often on a bare minimum of food and with practically no medical help available. Schooling for their children was beyond their means. The number of street dwellers, who lacked even this bare minimum, was growing and they were at the mercy of illness, hunger, and starvation.

Mother Teresa describes the painful reality she encountered on that first day:

At 8 a.m. I left St. Joseph's . . . At St. Teresa's . . . I took Veronica[22] with me and we went out.

We started at Taltala and went to every Catholic family.—The people were pleased—but children were all over the place—and what dirt and misery—what poverty and suffering.—I spoke very, very little, I just did some washing of sores, and dressings, gave medicine to some.—The old man lying on the street—not wanted—all alone just sick and dying—I gave him carborsone and water to drink and the old man was so strangely grateful. . . . Then we went to Taltala Bazaar, and there was a very poor woman dying I think of starvation more than TB. What poverty. What actual suffering. I gave something which will help her to sleep—but the woman is longing to have some care. I wonder how long she will last—she was just 96 degrees at that time. She asked a few times for confession & holy Communion.—I felt my own poverty there too—for I had nothing to give that poor woman.—I did everything I could but if I had been able to give her a hot cup of milk or something like that, her cold body would have got some life.—I must try and be somewhere close to the people where I could easily get at the things.[23]

Every new day in the slums brought new challenges. Besides the poverty, hardships, and insecurity, Mother Teresa had to face the criticisms that she had anticipated. Not all understood her efforts nor saw the benefit of her work among the poor. This did not alarm her. Her confident answer—the harbinger of future ones—shows her determination:

I believe some are saying what use of working among these lowest of the low—that the great—the learned and the rich are ready to come [so] it is better to give full force to them. Yes, let them all do it.—The Kingdom must be preached to all.[24] If the Hindu and Muslim rich people can have the full service and devotion of so many nuns & priests, surely the poorest of the poor and the lowest of the low can have the love and the devotion of us few. "The slum Sister" they call me, and I am glad to be just that for His love and glory.[25]

In time, to remain "the slum sister," Mother Teresa would need an extension of her status as an exclaustrated nun. She realized that remaining a religious, which she had initially considered unnecessary, was providential; being a nun inspired confidence in the people and in the young girls who thought of joining her. Thus, in February 1949, she wrote to Archbishop Périer:

Of my free choice I desire to continue working for the poor in the slums and live the life. Therefore, I beg, Your Grace, to allow me to ask from the Sacred Congregation to prolong the Indult of Exclaustration until the life and Constitutions of the Missionary Sisters of Charity be approved."[26]

Despite sufferings and the nagging temptation to go back to the security of Loreto, Mother Teresa continued to follow the difficult path God had set for her. That the path was indeed formidable is evident from the journal entry of February 16:

Today I learned a good lesson—the poverty of the poor must be often so hard for them. When I went rounding looking for a home—I walked & walked till my legs & my arms ached.—I thought how they must also ache in body and soul looking for home—food—help.—Then the temptation grew strong—the palace buildings of Loreto came rushing into my mind—all the beautiful things & comforts—the people they mix with—in a word everything.—"You have only to say a word and all that will be yours again"—the tempter kept on saying. Of [my] free choice My God and out of love for You—I desire to remain and do what ever be Your Holy Will in my regard.—I did not let a single tear come.—Even if I suffer more than now—I still want to do Your Holy Will.—This is the dark night of the birth of the Society.—My God give me courage now—this moment—to persevere in following Your call.

As Mother Teresa had foreseen, this new life was bringing her "for the most part only suffering."[27] Yet she accepted that it had to be so, for this was "the dark night of the birth of the Society." "The poverty of the poor" was becoming her own. At the same time, God was supplying the courage to persevere, for which she had prayed.

After two long months of searching, God answered her plea for a new home. The Gomes brothers, two of whom lived in Bangladesh, made available to her the third floor of their home at 14 Creek Lane; this was to become "the first home for the Missionaries of Charity."[28] Mother Teresa moved there at the end of February, yet the trials persisted:

Today—my God—what tortures of loneliness.—I wonder how long will my heart suffer this.—Fr. Bauwens, S.J. the Parish Priest of St. Teresa's came to bless the house.—Tears rolled & rolled.—Everyone sees my weakness. My God, give me courage now to fight self & the tempter. Let me not draw back from the sacrifice I have made of my free choice and conviction.— Immaculate Heart of my Mother, have pity on thy poor child. For love of thee I want to live & die an M.C.[29]

It was unusual for Mother Teresa, normally self-possessed, to let others see her suffering. Only two weeks earlier, though pressed by trials and temptation, she had "not let a single tear come."[30] Her ability to bear the pain and loneliness had now reached her limit. Certain that by her own strength she could not cope, she turned to God in prayer.

The Growth of the "Little Seed"

With only volunteer help, Mother Teresa was ministering to a large number of poor in various parts of Calcutta. Seeing the enormity of the need and wanting to do more, she implored the Virgin Mary to send her followers to further her work:

I keep on telling her "I have no children"—just as many years ago she told Jesus "They have no wine"[31]—I put all my trust in her Heart. She is sure to give me in her own way.[32]

Her prayer was soon answered. Some of her former students from St. Mary's were interested in her new mission. She had already made an impact on them as their teacher, and now, in the example she was providing in this new life of Gospel service to the neediest they saw an ideal worth leaving everything to follow. On March 19, 1949, Shubashini Das, the future Sister Agnes, came to join her.[33] During the following months more candidates arrived. By June 1950, the community numbered twelve.

In June 1949, Mother Teresa confided to Archbishop Périer:

The more the work is spreading the more clear it becomes [it is] His Will. Soon it will be one year [since she had left Loreto]—

though there has been plenty of suffering and tears, there has not been one moment of regret. I am happy to do God's will.[34]

The authorities in Rome so far had not responded to the request she had sent in March for the renewal of her status as an exclaustrated religious. Although she believed that she was where God wanted her to be, her uncertainty about the future was real. "The poor sister M. Teresa does not understand why no answer is given to her petition and she wonders with anguish whether she has to abandon all this wonderful work and return to her Institute,"[35] Archbishop Périer wrote to the Holy See, as the one-year indult was about to expire. Relief and gratitude came when, just a few days after the archbishop's letter had been sent, she received permission from the Holy See to continue for three more years.

Mother Teresa's accomplishments in little more than a year were remarkable. When in March 1950 she wrote to Pope Pius XII asking for the approval of the new congregation as a diocesan institute, she submitted an impressive report on the activities carried out by her community:

On my return from Patna I made an 8 days retreat and then on the 21st Dec. '48 I started the work. I went visiting and nursing the people in their dark homes and holes. So many neglected poor children surrounded me everywhere. Slowly with some lay helpers I gathered the children in two slums. Then in March the first Bengali girl joined. Now we are seven. We work in five different centres. We have the dispensaries where the poor get free treatment and medicine from generous Catholic and Hindu doctors—who have generously offered their services free. We visit the families from street to street. On Sundays we take the poor children from the slums to Sunday Mass. We started the Sunday

School with 26 children last May. Now we have over 350. . . .
The abandoned whom we often find in the streets we take to the
different hospitals.[36]

In July 1950 Mother Teresa wrote to Archbishop Périer, hinting at
the hidden price of her achievements: "Your Grace please pray for me
that I may do God's Holy Will in all things at any cost."[37]

Misunderstanding with Loreto Nuns

In the Loreto convent, meanwhile, unrest and tension had arisen because of the students from St. Mary's school who had decided to join
Mother Teresa. The support she initially enjoyed from her Loreto
companions was curtailed by a warning from the superior general.
Mother Teresa confided to the archbishop:

> Mother General is afraid that I am a great danger to the Loreto
> Nuns—so she has forbidden everyone to have anything to do
> with me.—Every means has been used not to render any help
> to me—every time a new comer comes there is anxiety felt at the
> Entally Convent.—That is why I have made provisions for the
> Sisters to study at home for the Matric & even Senior
> Training.—With all they do to prevent them from joining there
> are more & more girls wanting to join.—I say nothing to anyone
> about Loreto so even M. Prov. [Mother Provincial] could not find
> any such thing to make a remark.[38]

These misunderstandings, occasioned by this alleged pilfering
of vocations, added to the heaviness of her sacrifice, yet she remained upright and charitable toward the Loreto nuns.

The Birth of the New Society

With the permission of the Holy See, Archbishop Périer officially established the Society of the Missionaries of Charity in the arch-diocese of Calcutta on October 7, 1950, the feast of Our Lady of the Holy Rosary. In the presence of those assembled in the tiny chapel, the archbishop, now responsible for the new community, solemnly proclaimed the decree:

For more than two years now, a little group of young women, under the guidance of Sister M. Teresa, a lawfully uncloistered religious of the Institute of the Blessed Virgin Mary, have devoted themselves with generous heart and very great profit for the souls, to helping the poor—the children, grown-ups, the aged ones and also the sick, in this Our Metropolitan City.

As they begged from Us the favour that We should now erect their Group into a religious Congregation, We have with great care scrutinised their way of living and of working, and given diligent consideration to the purpose they have in view. This earnest examination led Us to the conclusion that no other Congregation already in existence answers the purpose which this new Institute is intending; and that, consequently, its erection into a religious Congregation, for the relief of so many and such dire needs, will redound to the greater Glory of God and the advantage of the Catholic Faith in Our Archdiocese.

In consequence, We do, by the present Decree, to the greater Glory of God and for the promotion in these parts of the Kingdom of Truth, Justice, Charity and Peace of Christ the Saviour, institute and erect the religious Congregation that shall have for:—

its Name or Title: The Congregation of the Missionary Sisters of Charity *its Holy Patron*: The Immaculate Heart of the Blessed Virgin Mary

its Purpose: To quench the thirst of Our Lord Jesus Christ for the salvation of souls by the observance of the three Vows of Poverty, Chastity and Obedience, and of an additional fourth Vow to devote themselves with abnegation to the care of the poor and needy who, crushed by want and destitution, live in conditions unworthy of the human dignity. Those who join this Institute, therefore, are resolved to spend themselves unremittingly in seeking out, in towns and villages, even amid squalid surroundings, the poorer, the abandoned, the sick, the infirm, the dying; in taking care of them, rendering help to them, visiting them assiduously and instructing them in the Christian Doctrine, in endeavouring to the utmost to bring about their conversion and sanctification . . . AND in performing any other similar apostolic works and services, however lowly and mean they may appear.[39]

Jesus' call that Mother Teresa heard on September 10, 1946, was now recognized and confirmed by the Church. She felt humbled, seeing all that God had done, as she told the archbishop in a letter:

The thought of my unworthiness for all His gifts to me and to my children gets deeper and clearer. In my meditations & prayers, which are so full of distractions nowadays—there stands one thing very clear—my weakness & His Greatness. I fear all things from my weakness—but I trust blindly His Greatness.[40]

In addition to the stability assured to her religious community by the official approval of the Church, there was another reason for Mother Teresa's joy that day: the long desired permission to have the Blessed Sacrament present in the convent chapel. She had written to the archbishop: "Soon Our Lord will be with us.—Everything will be easy then—He will be there personally."[41] The consolation of

Jesus' Eucharistic presence in her tiny convent was now hers. Thus she decided to have Eucharistic adoration the whole day in thanksgiving for this singular event in the life of the new congregation.

Paying the Price for Souls

The outstanding work they accomplished was not without cost for Mother Teresa and her young companions. The work in the slums was demanding: They had to walk long distances; their food was poor, and at times they had to beg for it. At the same time, many of them had to continue with their studies. "We have to pay the price for souls,"[42] the foundress kept repeating to her young sisters.

In her Explanation of the Original Constitutions she wrote:

> Jesus says, "Amen, I say to you, unless the grain of wheat falling into the ground die, itself remaineth alone. But if it die it bringeth forth much fruit."[43] The missionary must die daily, if she wants to bring souls to God. She must be ready to pay the price He paid for souls, to walk in the way He walked in search for souls.[44]

The aim of the new institute was being realized not in spite of the difficulties and sufferings but precisely through them. Mother Teresa did not want to avoid sacrifice or eliminate it from her life or the lives of her followers. "Grab the chance to offer something to Jesus," she would insistently counsel her sisters. She knew their suffering would bear fruit. When Archbishop Périer objected that the life would be too hard for non-Indian candidates she replied:

> I would very much like a few [non-Indian candidates] because it will be hard for them, and the more sacrifices there will be in the

Society, our aim of quenching His thirst will be sooner fulfilled. Our work for souls is great, but without penance and much sacrifice it will be impossible.—We have to do much more penance than even the Carmelites because of closeness of sin.[45]

Challenges did not dishearten Mother Teresa. On the contrary, she impressed those around her by her cheerful disposition. It was a conscious choice; she wanted "to keep on smiling in spite of everything"[46] and to "give Our Lord always all with a cheerful smile."[47] Overlooking her pain, she chose to spread joy, confirming the resolve of her youth to "drink the chalice to the last drop."[48] Now she expressed her determination more radically in a letter to the archbishop:

I want to become a real slave of Our Lady[49]—to drink only from His chalice of pain and to give Mother Church real saints. I know what I want is above my strength—but He who has given me the desire will also give me strength to do the impossible. . . . Your Grace, please pray for me, that I may give to Our Lord all that He asks without a thought of self.[50]

Our Lady was her indispensable companion and the rosary the simple but powerful means to remain united to her:

We are taught to love and say the Rosary with great devotion; let us be very faithful to this our first love—for it will bring us closer to our Heavenly Mother. Our rule asks of us never to go to the slums without first having recited the Mother's praises; that is why we have to say the Rosary in the streets & dark holes of the slums. Cling to the Rosary as the creeper clings to the tree—for without Our Lady we cannot stand.[51]

On April 11, 1951, the first group of sisters began their novitiate as Missionaries of Charity. This important step, along with their spiritual progress, gave Mother Teresa great satisfaction, as she told the archbishop a few months later:

The Sisters are keeping up their good spirit.—There is great competition in virtue. Their only aim seems to be what means & ways to find to satiate the burning thirst of Jesus.—When I see them, I feel that the plan of Our Lord is being fulfilled.—But there is one part still left and that is that I would have to suffer much.—In spite of everything that has happened these last years, there has always been perfect peace & joy in my heart.—Our Lord knows I am at His service. He can do with me just whatever He wishes.[52]

Surprising as it may seem, Mother Teresa feared that the many and varied sufferings she was experiencing were not yet corresponding to the "promise" she received at the time of the inspiration—that she would suffer much. Archbishop Périer once again provided wise advice.

For sufferings you have not to look for them. Almighty God provides for them daily: they are not always what we imagined, bodily sufferings and the sort, but interior sufferings, contradictions, failures of our plan, anxieties for the community, for the work, misunderstandings in our relations with other religious, or families; oppositions unexpected at times, etc.[53]

In the meantime, accusations and rumors continued to spread among the Loreto nuns and the Daughters of St. Ann[54] because of her. Mother Teresa confided to the archbishop this new wave of suffering:

There has been a storm in Entally.—The Daughters [of St. Ann] have been very upset with M. M. [Mother Mary] Bernard's coming here.—I have become something terrible for Loreto. I am well compared to the devil & the work as his work & so on. Someday all will be clear. I am grateful to God for all.—I love Loreto just as much if not more, now as I did for so many years.— I pray for them often, & their "persecution" makes me love my new vocation more.[55]

The remarks from a few of the nuns were upsetting to Mother Teresa not only because they were coming from former companions, but even more so because attributing the work of her fledgling congregation to the devil was a direct attack on the divine origin of her call. It undermined her whole endeavor and God's tender love for His poor. The conviction that she was doing "God's work" was the anchor that enabled her to weather this storm.

To respond to these falsehoods, Mother Teresa decided to write to the Loreto provincial, Mother Francis Xavier Stapleton, "purely out of duty to our own Society."[56] Realizing the seriousness of the situation and the hurt caused by some of her nuns, the provincial responded immediately, assuring Mother Teresa that she would take action: "You already know my opinion of your work which God is visibly blessing. . . . I am sorry if you have been shown any ill-feeling and shall do my utmost to correct it."[57] A mutual understanding and collaboration eventually developed between the two congregations.

To Become and to Give Saints

The needs of the sisters and of the poor were becoming more demanding. Mother Teresa confided to the archbishop in February 1952 that she had "not a minute"[58] to herself. Yet in the midst of all these occupations, she neither lost her focus nor forgot the purpose of the little society. A letter she wrote in April 1952 reveals the motivation that sustained her:

> I want to become a saint, by satiating the thirst of Jesus for love and souls.—And there is another big desire—to give the Mother Church many a saint from our Society.—These two are the only thing I pray for, work and suffer. Please pray for me, that I may fulfill His desire as regards our Society & myself.[59]

The aim of the Missionaries of Charity and the pursuit of holiness were foremost in her mind and heart. Her pursuit of sanctity was not for self-glorification; rather it was the expression of the depth of her relationship with God. She strove to instill these same desires in her sisters. The means to achieve these ends was wholehearted and free service to the poorest of the poor: "It is wonderful to see in our young Sisters this desire to satiate the thirst of Jesus for souls," she wrote to the archbishop. "They count nothing as too hard or impossible, when there is a question of souls."[60] The amount of work done by some twenty sisters indeed reflected an outstanding zeal.

The "Treasure House" of the Congregation

While going about the city to meet the needs of the poor, Mother Teresa often encountered people dying in the streets. Because these people were considered "hopeless cases," the hospitals would not accept them; they were destined to face the end of their life alone, unwanted and abandoned by all. Mother Teresa sought a home where they would be received with love and treated with dignity at least in the last moments of their lives. The city government of Calcutta provided her one of the shelters for pilgrims at the Kali Temple, which she named Nirmal Hriday, Bengali for "pure heart," in honor of Mary's Immaculate Heart.[61] There she and her sisters would bring the dying off the streets and offer them accommodation, basic medical care and above all, tender love.

Two months after its opening on August 22, 1952, the feast of the Immaculate Heart of Mary, Archbishop Périer paid a visit to the home. Usually reserved in his judgments, he expressed his esteem for the dedicated service he witnessed there:

> I was extremely pleased to have come yesterday to visit your hospital for destitutes and dying people. I do not hide that I was deeply impressed and moved at the sight of so much misery but also of so much generosity on the part of your little band of religious ladies. Almighty God must look on them with love and pleasure. Great, exceedingly great will be the reward of the good nuns in heaven. Our Lord inspired you when asking for this hospital and your nuns have been inspired when accepting it so generously. Let us hope this is a standing lesson of charity for all to see. The lay people who help you are also admirable. God bless them abundantly! That's all I can say, for no reward on earth will repay them.[62]

Mother Teresa was not indifferent to his opinion. Because he was her superior, thus God's representative, his approval and praise was one more sign of God's blessing on the work. She could not deny the satisfaction she felt, while giving all the credit to her sisters rather than herself:

> I read your letter to our Sisters and they have got a new push to love Our Lord with a more generous love.
>
> Yes, Our Lord has given me tremendous graces in giving me these spiritual children. . . . Some put me to shame when I see how in a short time they have been in the service of the good

Master and what progress in spiritual life they have made—and here I am with my 24 years in religion.[63]

Mother Teresa regarded Nirmal Hriday as the "treasure house" of her congregation. The neglected, the rejected, the unwanted that she sheltered there closely resembled the suffering Christ—"Christ in distressing disguise"[64]—and gave her the opportunity to "put her love into living action." Their acute sufferings, especially the interior ones, were becoming her own, uniting her with Christ in His Passion and with the poorest of the poor in their pain.

"Second Self"

In her apostolate Mother Teresa was full of initiative. The difficulties and challenges in the work often provided her with opportunities for innovation. Such was the case with Jacqueline de Decker, a Belgian nurse and social worker who wished to join the Missionaries of Charity but could not because of poor health. Mother Teresa came up with the solution: since Jacqueline could not work with the poor in Calcutta, she would share in the apostolate by becoming Mother Teresa's "second self"[65]—a spiritual twin who would offer to God her prayers and suffering for Mother Teresa and the fruitfulness of her work. Mother Teresa in turn would offer her prayers and good works for Jacqueline. Jacqueline and others who could not join directly in the work ("the sick and suffering co-workers," as they were later called) would join efforts with the sisters in fulfilling the common aim of satiating the thirst of Jesus. Mother Teresa believed that finding a purpose in their sufferings would give them a new incentive to carry on: "Love demands sacrifice. But if we love until it hurts, God will give us His peace and joy. . . . Suffering in itself is nothing; but suffering shared with Christ's Passion is a wonderful gift."[66]

This hope of expanding the work of her mission of love to those who at first seemed incapable of sharing in it was a source of joy and consolation for Mother Teresa. She explained to Jacqueline her understanding of the vocation of the Missionaries of Charity:

I am very happy that you are willing to join the suffering members of the Missionaries of Charity.—You see what I mean—you and the others who will join will share in all our prayers, works and whatever we do for souls—& you do the same with us with your prayers & sufferings. You see, the aim of our Society is to satiate the thirst of Jesus on the Cross for love of souls by working for the salvation and sanctification of the poor in the slums.—Who could do this better than you & the others who suffer like you? Your suffering & prayers will be the chalice in which we the working members will pour in the love of souls we gather round. Therefore you are just as important & necessary for the fulfillment of our aim.—To satiate His Thirst we must have a chalice—& you & the others—men, women, children, old & young, poor & rich—are all welcome to make the chalice. In reality, you can do much more while on your bed of pain than I running on my feet, but you & I together can do all things in Him who strengthens us.[67]

... One thing we must have in common, the spirit of our Society—total surrender to God, loving trust and perfect cheerfulness.—By this you will be known as Missionaries of Charity.

Everyone and anyone who wishes to become a Missionary of Charity—a carrier of God's love—is welcome, but I want specially the paralysed, the crippled, the incurables to join, for I know they will bring to the feet of Jesus many souls. In our turn, the sisters will each one have a sister who prays, suffers, thinks, writes to her & so on—a second self. You see, my dear sister, our

work is a most difficult one. If you are with us—praying &
suffering for us & the work—we shall be able to do great things
for love of Him—because of you.

. . . Personally I feel very happy & a new strength has come
in my soul at the thought of you & others joining the Society
spiritually. Now with you & others doing the work with us,
what would we not do, what can't we not do for Him? As for
you, your life is like a burning light which is being consumed
for souls. . . .[68]

The spiritual assistance of her sick and suffering "co-workers"
proved to be a heartening support in time of trial: "When things are
difficult, my soul is encouraged with the thought of having you to
pray & suffer for me," she wrote to Jacqueline. "Then I find it easy
& the smile for the good God comes much quicker."[69]

The Flourishing Mission and Its Price

By the end of 1952, the third floor of the Gomes' family house had
become too small for the community of twenty-six members.
Mother Teresa was obliged to look for a larger home to accommo-
date the increasing number of sisters. After storming heaven with
prayer, she found a house on Lower Circular Road that is still today
the motherhouse of the Missionaries of Charity. The community
moved there in February 1953.

The inspiration of 1946 was now a "living reality"[70]—a flourishing community serving the poorest of the poor of Calcutta. The
challenges and sufferings involved had been worth it. But they were
not over. There was one particular trial for which Mother Teresa repeatedly sought spiritual support. After some time she finally revealed this painful interior ordeal, by now deeply settled in her soul.

EIGHT

The Thirst of
Jesus Crucified

A TERRIBLE DARKNESS WITHIN

*I want to smile even at Jesus & so hide if possible the
pain and the darkness of my soul even from Him.*
—*Mother Teresa*

Darkness Disclosed

18TH. 3. 53

Your Grace,
... Please pray specially for me that I may not
spoil His work and that Our Lord may show
Himself—for there is such terrible darkness
within me, as if everything was dead. It has
been like this more or less from the time I
started "the work." Ask Our Lord to give me
courage.

Please give us Your blessing,
Your devoted child in J. C. [Jesus Christ].
M. Teresa, M.C.[1]

After several years of suffering in silence and with only occasional and vague references to her interior state, Mother Teresa at last revealed to Archbishop Périer the great pain that had been tormenting her soul from the beginning of her mission with the poor. The archbishop, though, did not appear to understand what she was experiencing, since her honest but brief description gave little insight. He assumed that she was referring to the challenges of guiding the new congregation. Suspecting that her inclination for "hastiness"—a permanent cause of tension between the two of them—was a possible reason for it, he advised moderation.

God guides you, dear Mother; you are not so much in the dark as you think. The path to be followed may not always be clear at once. Pray for light; do not decide too quickly, listen to what others have to say, consider their reasons. You will always find something to help you. You have exterior facts enough to see that God blesses your work. Therefore He is satisfied. Guided by faith by prayer and by reason with a right intention you have enough. Feelings are not required and often may be misleading.[2]

"I Have Tried to Refuse Nothing to God"

A month after revealing her interior ordeal to the archbishop, Mother Teresa professed her final vows as a Missionary of Charity and the first ten sisters made their first vows. This joyous occasion moved her to gratitude and humility. To Archbishop Périer she wrote:

When I think of the 10th Sept. '46—I only thank God from my heart for all He has done. I hold no claim to the "work" as it was, it is, and will always remain His. I beg you, to point out to me my defects so that they may not spoil His work. I know there have been things which could have been better, but in all sincerity I have tried to refuse nothing to God to answer His every call.

Our Lord had asked "for nuns covered with the poverty of His Cross." . . . There are the first ten. They have lived that life generously and cheerfully. . . . If I had known, that this is what Our Lord would give me, I would have been afraid to answer the call, because of my unworthiness to be their Mother. My heart is very full today with gratitude to God and to you, for all you have done for our Society, especially for taking up "the work" under your own personal care and love. The only way, we can show you our gratitude, [is] by becoming true Missionaries of Charity . . .

Your Grace, please pray for me that I may give myself completely to Our Lord.[3]

The archbishop, touched by the witness of this group of young fervent religious, replied to Mother Teresa on the day of profession, expressing his energetic support of the new community:

That long aspiration and call of God, after a few years had become a reality, not only a start, but a tested and confirmed institution declared capable of life, endowed with a strong vitality and a capacity for a lasting and fruitful apostolate. . . . I wholeheartedly shared in your joy this morning. Alleluiah.[4]

He would later admit, "I am profoundly grateful to God who has allowed me to be His instrument in initiating this great work through you and your sisters."[5]

"Many a Soul Has Been Brought Back to God"

The accomplishments of her community began to attract admiration and praise as articles describing her work began to appear locally and internationally. Mother Teresa shared her concern with the archbishop:

I am afraid we are getting too much publicity.—A few things I heard this evening have made me feel cold with fear. God preserve us. Please pray for me—that I be nothing to the world and let the world be nothing to me.[6]

In the face of this danger, her well-established humility, the persistent darkness and the numerous demands of the expanding work helped to prevent pride and a worldly spirit from entering her heart. The fact that she and her sisters were at times in real physical danger served to keep their "feet on the ground":

We had again trouble in Kalighat [Nirmal Hriday]—they very coolly told me I must thank God that up to now I have not received a shot or a beating from them, since all those who worked for them death has been their reward. Very peacefully I told them, that I was ready to die for God. Hard times are coming, let us pray that our Society will stand the test of Charity.[7]

In the midst of all these trials, Mother Teresa was bolstered by the fervor of her sisters, as she wrote to the archbishop:

Today our little Sister Maria Goretti went to Our Lord. The greatest joy of her life was to be a Missionary of Charity,[8] such a real one was she—that often when I saw her or spoke to her I was glad to have made the sacrifice of Loreto—to become the Mother of such a child. Now she is with Jesus—the first M.C. in heaven. . . . Now with Sister in heaven we shall get many vocations.[9]

Though not without struggles, Mother Teresa's work among the poor continued with remarkable results. She was aware that it was "God's work"; she was but an instrument in bringing "souls to God—and God to souls."[10] For such a mission, prayer and sacrifice were essential: united to Jesus' redemptive suffering, prayer and sacrifice leavened the work for the poor. This vision of faith guided her in the establishment of her "sick and suffering co-workers," as she explained to Archbishop Périer:

I don't know if I have told Your Grace, but I have started with the sick a spiritual relationship. Every Sister has a second self—to pray & suffer for her—& the Sisters will share her good works & prayers with her.—Spiritually they are children of the Society—so I have some in England, Brussels, Antwerp, Switzerland, Calcutta who have joined, men, women, children.—They would like some short prayers to say in union with us. Miss de Decker & Nicholas Gomes are my second self. There are now 18 on the list. Please will you give your blessing to this work?—It is their prayers & sufferings that [are] blessing our apostolate. It makes them so happy to have to suffer for somebody—to be a Missionary of Charity— though they be blind, lame, TB [tuberculosis patients], crippled, having cancer. Often when I find the work very difficult, I offer the suffering of these my children and I find help comes at once.—I think many of our sick & suffering would be sanctified much quicker if they suffered to satiate the thirst of Jesus. When Your Grace comes I shall explain myself better.

. . . I am 25 years in Religion—please thank God for all He has done for me.[11]

As her interior darkness became harder to bear, anniversaries of significant dates stood as reminders of God's "interventions" in the little group's short history. On such occasions, Mother Teresa could not help but recognize the results of her "yes" to God and express her deep gratitude:

☀️ On the 21st Dec. will be five years that the work in the slums started, and I want to thank your Grace for all your personal interest and fatherly love you have shown the young Society. Many a soul has been brought back to God. Many a dying person has been sent to God, many a child has been taught to love God, many a sick person has been comforted and taught to suffer for love of God, and above all the generous and self-sacrificing lives of our young Sisters must have given much reparation to the Sacred Heart.—And for all these, I beg you to thank God with me.[12]

"My Own Soul Remains in Deep Darkness"

In the midst of this evident fruitfulness, almost a year after her first disclosure to the archbishop, Mother Teresa again reported to him that "my own soul remains in deep darkness & desolation. No I don't complain—let Him do with me whatever He wants."[13] Surrendering anew, she sacrificed willingly the consolation of felt union with Jesus for the challenge of living by pure faith. This experience made her even more understanding and compassionate toward others, enabling her to offer encouragement and practical advice:

☀️ When it is very hard for you—just hide yourself in the Sacred Heart, & there my heart with you will find all the strength &

love. You want to suffer in pure love—rather say in the love that He chooses for you.—You have to be a "spotless host."[14]

Despite the night within, Jesus was Mother Teresa's sole focus; she loved Him and wanted to be united with Him, especially in His Passion. A true portrait of her soul—not swayed by feelings but steadfast in faith—emerges from the explanation she gave to Jacqueline de Decker of the call of a Missionary of Charity:

17TH OCT. 1954

L.D.M. (LAUS DEO MARIAEQUE— GLORY TO GOD THROUGH MARY)*

My Sister Jacqueline Theresa,[15]

Your very welcome letter of the 11th was most gladly received. I have been longing to get news from you.

How the good God loves you, my own dear little sister, when He draws you so much to His Cross.—If you were not my second self I think I would envy you, but like that I rejoice because you are my own second self. You suffer much and your soul is crucified with pain—but is [it] not that He is living His life in His Jacqueline? What a beautiful vocation is yours—a Missionary of Charity—a carrier of God's love.—We carry on our body and soul the love of an infinite thirsty God—and we, you and I, and all our dear Sisters and the second selves will satiate that burning thirst—you with your untold suffering, we with hard labour. But are we not all the same?—one?—"as you Father in me & I in you" said Jesus.[16]

You have learned much. You have tasted the chalice of His agony—and what will be your reward my dear sister? More

*In several places Mother Teresa mistakenly translated this phrase as "Glory to God through Mary" instead of "Glory to God and Mary."

suffering and a deeper likeness to Him on the Cross. I feel unworthy to be your sister, so when you pray ask Jesus to draw me closer to Himself on the Cross that there the two of us may be one. . . .

Dear Marguerite—how hard she must find it to be totally blind—but she can see Jesus better—& this [is] the one thing that matters. . . .

Please tell our dear Brother Clement that he can be a real John [the] Baptist[17]—for our work is just that to prepare the way—after us other nuns & friends enter the field of souls—

I am really very proud of you—a real Missionary of Charity.—Be brave and keep smiling.—You know He loves you with a tender, eternal love. . . .

Pray for me—I have much to do.

Much love from your Sister in Jesus,
M. Teresa[18]

"A carrier of God's love," "the love of an infinite thirsty God"— this was Mother Teresa's lofty concept of a Missionary of Charity. The sisters engaged in arduous work and their co-workers who suffered illness and disability, united in the common aim of satiating the burning thirst of Jesus on the Cross.

"Spouse of Jesus Crucified"

Interior darkness was Mother Teresa's privileged way of entering into the mystery of the Cross of Christ. Knowing that suffering should be expected as a part of the calling of a Missionary of Charity, she instructed one of her sisters:

My dearest Child,
Thanks for the lovely consoling letter of the 14th. Keep looking

at the Sacred Heart.—Why worry if it be TB or not?—You are His and it is His gift to you, His spouse. Was it not Mother who taught you to say for the profession "I desire to become the Spouse of Jesus Crucified?—— It is not Jesus glorified or in the crib, but on the Cross—alone—naked—bleeding—suffering— dying on the Cross. So if you are the first one in the Society whom He chooses to be alone on the bed of the Cross, why my child, we must thank God for all—for this His special love for you, for me and the Society. You are but a child still, and life is beautiful—but the way He has chosen for you is the true way.— So smile—smile at the Hand that strikes you—kiss the Hand that is nailing you to the Cross.—I don't believe just as you that you have TB—but let them do all that they want with you.— Be like a little lamb—smile at everyone. Don't worry, I shall beg the money & will come to see you as soon as I hear more definite news from Sister.

"Let them look up & see only Jesus."[19] I have promised Our Lady 25000 Memorares[20] for your cure & we shall say it within these 9 days. Please thank M. Rose for her kindness to you. I am very happy with whatever God does with you all—you are all His.

Love Jesus & keep a smiling heart for Him.—All these disturbing thoughts come from the devil—ignore them all. God bless you my child.

Mother [21]

"A Deep Loneliness in My Heart"

In January 1955, a little less than a year since she had last mentioned the darkness to Archbishop Périer, Mother Teresa noted a new element in her experience: deep loneliness. This loneliness, her "traveling companion" from this point forward, resulted from her apparent separation from God and those she trusted most. This sense of alienation made her cross harder to bear.

> Your Grace,
>
>   I am very grateful to Your Grace for coming—I always feel the burden a little lighter after you have been.—I don't know, but there is such a deep loneliness in my heart that I cannot express it.—For months I have not been able to speak to Fr. Van Exem and I find it harder and harder to speak. How long will Our Lord stay away?
>
>   Please pray for me.
>
> *Your grateful child in J.C. [Jesus Christ]*
M. Teresa, M.C.[22]

In this distress, she was longing for Jesus to return, but it seemed as if He had turned away from her.

The archbishop replied with a lengthy letter, encouraging her and offering possible reasons for her inner condition. He suggested that the experience might be a temporary trial: "God seems to hide Himself for a while. That may be painful and if it lasts long it becomes a martyrdom. The Little Flower passed through that like the great S. Teresa* did and we may say most if not all the saints."[23] He warned her, too, that it could be a temptation of the evil one to discourage her in the good work she was doing. Not failing to strike his typical note of caution and prudence, he hinted once more at what he considered "hastiness" on her part. Not grasping the depth of her affliction, the archbishop even suggested that her condition could be a result of being overworked or physically fatigued. Though she

---

*Saint Teresa of Avila (1515–1582). Doctor of the Church, Spanish Carmelite reformer, mystic, writer.

said that she found them "most helpful,"[24] his counsels did not really address the roots of her difficulty.

"Offer Each Other to Christ for Souls"

Mother Teresa continued to be cheerful and enthusiastic. Hers was no mere superficial joy but a deeply spiritual one. She explained the reasons behind it in an encouraging letter to her sick and suffering coworkers:

> My very dear Sisters & Brothers,[25]
> For a long time I have been wanting to write & each time the post goes without my having written. But be assured that every one of us claim your love before the throne of God & there every day we offer you or rather offer each other to Christ for souls. We the Missionaries of Charity how grateful we must be—you to suffer & we to work.—We finish in each other what is wanting in Christ.[26] What a beautiful vocation is ours, to be the carriers of Christ's love in the slums.—Your life of sacrifice is the chalice or rather our vows are the chalice & your suffering & our work are the wine—the spotless host. We stand together holding the same chalice & so with the adoring Angels satiate His burning Thirst for souls.
> My very dear children—let us love Jesus with our whole heart & soul. Let us bring Him many souls.—Keep smiling. Smile at Jesus in your suffering—for to be a real M.C. you must be a cheerful victim.—How happy I am to have [you] all.—You belong to me as much as every Sister belongs to me here & often when the work is very hard I think of each one of you—& tell God—look at my suffering children & for their love bless this

work, & it works immediately. So you see you are our treasure house—the power house of the M.C. . . .

Pray for me dear second selves & keep smiling for Jesus & for me.[27]

Mother Teresa's inner pain did not diminish. She longed to unburden her soul to someone she trusted, yet she did not. She found it harder to communicate with her spiritual director, Father Van Exem. Her great reverence for God's action in her soul, especially the mystical experiences related to her call, made her reluctant to open her soul to anyone else. So she chose to suffer this ordeal in silence rather than disclose the secret of "my love for Jesus—and His tender love for me."[28] All that was left was to write to Archbishop Périer.

Today we have finished our sixth day.[29] The more I pray the clearer it grows the desire of Christ to "intimate likeness to Him"—and this to do by more motherly love, affection and attachment to every individual Sister—and by sweetness & kindness even in the tone of voice with all—especially when I make a remark or have to refuse the poor.

This year I have often been impatient & even sometimes harsh in my remarks—& I have noticed each time I have done the Sisters less good—I always got more from them when I am kind.—One thing is worrying me—sometimes when faced with difficulty about some Sisters I have had to speak to Fr. Van Exem or Fr. Cordeiro. How far is this against charity? Can I keep silence? If I have spoken to Fr. Van Exem [it is] because he takes your place—if to Fr. Cordeiro, for help through the instruction & also his advice has always been very wise—& I have great need of learning. Each time I have done it to either of them, I have been to confession.—What should I do? To me this is uncharitable &

yet I have to find the answer to the difficulty that sometimes comes from the Sisters' different characters, etc. Yet, Your Grace, how we have to thank God for our good Sisters—in spite of all their shortcomings they are very fervent & generous.—God must be very pleased with the great amount of sacrifices these young Sisters make everyday. God keep them so.

... Before I used to get such help & consolation from spiritual direction—from the time the work has started—nothing.—Even myself have nothing to say—so it seems. I would very much want to have once a good talk—but the thought of having to tell all that is connected with the Call keeps me back—and so I speak to no one.—Please forgive me for writing all this—you have so much to do.—

Please pray for me, that I answer Him generously....[30]

"Only that Blind Faith that Carries Me Through"

Because Archbishop Périer was her superior, Mother Teresa was expected to write a report to him at least once a month about her spiritual life, the concerns of her community, and their apostolate. She also sought his counsel or permission on certain points. In this correspondence with him, she shared, for the most part, the ordinary details of daily life, but occasionally she remarked on her darkness. These seemingly casual references give a glimpse of the depth of her interior trial and the magnanimity of her response.

15TH DEC. '55

Your Grace,
In 1956 will be the 1st ten years since Jesus spoke of the "work." May we have the coming year as a "Eucharistic Year" for our

Society. We will try to spread through the slums the love and the true devotion to the Blessed Sacrament in thanksgiving for our Society.

On the 12th it was beautiful.—Thank you for coming.—130 little ones—really the words of Our Lord are being fulfilled "the blind—the lame—the sick—the poor I want them.[31]" From Shishu Bhavan [home for children] we had 12.—

I am enclosing the work of the Sisters for 1956. I have written down all that they do—so that it will give you a better look into their work.

God has been very wonderful to use the poor instruments for His work. With the whole of my heart I can say—I claim absolutely nothing in all this, only that the Sisters & I have let God use us to the full.—

I would be very happy if you wrote a letter to all the Sisters. They would be so very much helped. We have more than any other Congregations [a] right on your love and care because we are your very own. It is because of you that we are.

Next year there seems to be about 10 or 12 vocations.—When they will write officially I shall write to you.

The Sisters are all doing very well.—Even Sister M. . . . has changed completely. I have really much to thank God.

I am writing long before Christmas because during those days you have plenty to do.

Will you be able to come for Holy Mass on the 28th? May I take the Sisters to Bandel on the 31st Dec.?

We are having our Christmas treat at St. Laurence.— We shall have plenty to do to prepare for 2400 and to find conveyance for all of them. God has provided, He will provide again. The Marian Society ladies have bought new clothes for 1212 slum Catholic children. To the Hindus we shall give in Sept. during the Pujas & the Muslim children for Idd.[32]

We have got a new harmonium.—May I send you our old one—for some mission station?—It was in good order but Rev. Fr. Bouwens kept it in St. Teresa's for a long time—now it is not so good.

There is a wonderful spirit of sacrifice among the Sisters—the crib is nearly full with straw. For Christmas we shall send you some for your crib.[33]

Capt. [Captain] Cheshire gave me a first class relic of the Little Flower given to him by Celine. In return I gave him my Rosary. His work and our work will complete each other. He was very much impressed by Nirmal Hriday.

Pray for me—for within me everything is icy cold.—It is only that blind faith that carries me through for in reality to me all is darkness. As long as Our Lord has all the pleasure—I really do not count.

I beg a renewal of my general permissions—to give—to receive—to spend—for the Sisters & the Society—for our poor & all those who need our help and are dependent on us. May I also have the permission to give the required permissions to the Sisters—and I beg to be admonished for all my faults.

> *Your devoted child in J. C. [Jesus Christ].*
> *M. Teresa, M.C.*[34]

"I Will Satiate Thy Thirst for Souls"

Only in February 1956 did Mother Teresa offer Archbishop Périer a more detailed description of her spiritual experience, providing a fuller picture of an interior affliction for which it seemed human help could offer no remedy.

Your Grace,

I want to say to you something—but I do not know how to express it. I am longing—with a painful longing to be all for God—to be holy in such a way that Jesus can live His life to the full in me. The more I want Him—the less I am wanted.—I want to love Him as He has not been loved—and yet there is that separation—that terrible emptiness, that feeling of absence of God.—For more than four years I find no help in the direction of Rev. Fr. C. Van Exem. Yet I obey him blindly. Often I have gone to the confessional with the hope of speaking and yet nothing comes.—Sometime last year I told Father about this— and he told me that this should be put before you.—I am not complaining—I only want to go all the way with Christ. I am not writing to you as to His Grace—but to the father of my soul— for to you & from you I have not kept hidden anything. Tell me what your child should do—I want to obey at any cost—and if you tell me to continue like this till the end of my life I am ready to obey cheerfully. . . .

Please Your Grace pray for me—that I may draw very close to God.

Your devoted child in J. C. [Jesus Christ].
M. Teresa, M.C.[35]

To this baring of her soul, the archbishop answered with a short summary of the teaching of St. John of the Cross on the "dark night," without directly referring to it:

In what you reveal there is nothing which is not known in the mystical life. It is a grace God grants you, the longing to be His entirely without return on self or creatures, to live by Him and in Him but that longing which comes from God can never be satisfied in this world, simply because He is infinite and we finite.[36]

He again pointed to the great success of the mission as a sign of God's presence. "God's blessing is on your work, thank Him for it,"[37] he wrote, recommending her to pray, "'DO with me what Thou wilt' . . . and refuse Him nothing."[38]

Without knowing it, the archbishop was echoing the private vow she had made fourteen years earlier not to refuse God anything under the pain of mortal sin. He was touching that secret bond that was hiding everything within her. Did she perceive in this exhortation God's hand encouraging her to continue in the way He had chosen for her?

As the excruciating inner pain persisted, she hoped for a few days of respite during the upcoming retreat. In her response to the archbishop she showed her determination to give Jesus a free hand and accept anything He would permit in order to satiate His thirst for souls:

> Please pray for me, that it may please God to lift this darkness from my soul for only a few days. For sometimes the agony of desolation is so great and at the same time the longing for the Absent One so deep, that the only prayer which I can still say is—Sacred Heart of Jesus I trust in Thee—I will satiate Thy thirst for souls.[39]

"To Smile at God"

The retreat preached by Jesuit Father Lawrence Trevor Picachy[40] in April 1956 did not impart the hoped for relief, but it was the occasion of a decisive meeting. Only later did Mother Teresa reveal to Father Picachy its significance:

> Some years back when you gave the retreat to the novices—& I made it with them—Our Lord forced me to speak to you & open

myself, and then as if to approve my sacrifice he made you our confessor.[41]

Although it would have been legitimate under the circumstances to seek help or relief, Mother Teresa stressed at various times that it was solely at God's insistence that she had made known her spiritual state to Father Picachy. "I don't know why," she wrote later, "He wants me to open my soul to you—I do it because I can't 'refuse.'"[42]

To the archbishop she reported the comfort the retreat had afforded her: "I was happy to be one of the postulants once more so I had many hours of prayer."[43] The resolutions she made during these days of prayer covered important aspects of her life: her attitude when humiliated, her charity toward others, and her "smile"—as an expression of her loving disposition toward God—in spite of her feelings.

My resolution—1st is to follow Jesus more closely in humiliations

With the Sisters—kind—very kind—but firm in obedience

With the poor—gentle & considerate

With the sick—extremely kind

2nd To smile at God.

Pray for me that in the first & second resolution I give glory to God.[44]

Rather than hardening her, her correspondence shows that suffering rendered her more kindhearted. She encouraged others to smile in suffering as she herself did.

My dear Jacqueline Teresa,

I wonder how disappointed you must be with my silence—but please forgive me—as I am kept going the whole day.—Please

thank in my name . . . all those who [have] given so generously.—
I used the money for the convent.

You will be glad to hear we have got a new house for the
Professed.—It was a miserable looking building—now it looks
really beautiful. Our chapel is there also.—I hope someday you
will come to India & see our lovely chapel. The priests love
coming here for Holy Mass. . . .

How are you my little sister? You don't know how much I
rely on you, on your love for Jesus and souls. It seems as if I
neglect you—but I don't think a day passes without me uniting
myself to you.—So what does it matter whether I write or not—
you know in the Sacred Heart of Jesus we are one.—So smile
and have that total surrender, loving trust & perfect cheerful[ness]
which is the spirit of our Society—and so bring many, many
souls to Christ.

Love Jesus—live with Jesus that you may live for Jesus.

M. Teresa[45]

Archbishop Périer continued to counsel Mother Teresa concerning the darkness. At this time, he interpreted it as purification
and protection against pride in the face of the remarkable fruitfulness of her work.

With regard to the feeling of loneliness, of abandonment, of not
being wanted, of darkness of the soul, it is a state well known by
spiritual writers and directors of conscience. This is willed by God
in order to attach us to Him alone, an antidote to our external
activities, and also, like any temptation, a way of keeping us
humble in the midst of applauses, publicity, praises, appreciation,
etc. and success. To feel that we are nothing, that we can do
nothing is the realisation of a fact. We know it, we say it, some
feel it. That is why stick to God and like the little Bernadette[46] at

the end of her last retreat wrote: God alone, God everywhere, God in everybody and in everything, God always.

With St. Ignatius[47] you may add: My only wish and desire, the one thing I humbly crave to have is the grace to love God, to love Him alone. Beyond that I ask for nothing more.

I wish you all a happy feast of St. Ignatius. God bless you one and all.[48]

Mother Teresa took his advice seriously, yet grasped a further purpose to her suffering: It was the price she was paying for others to come closer to God. A couple of months later she asked the archbishop: "Please pray for me for now more than ever I understand how close I must come to God if I wish to bring souls to Him."[49]

"The Dark Holes—There Our Lord Is Always Really Present"

From the time the darkness had set in and thwarted the feeling of Jesus' presence, Mother Teresa had nonetheless been recognizing Him in the distressing disguise of the poor: "[W]hen I walk through the slums or enter the dark holes—there Our Lord is always really present."[50] The "dark holes" had become the privileged meeting place with Him. There she wanted to love Him to the end:

As for myself—there is but one desire—to love God as He has never been loved—with deep personal love.—In my heart there seems to be no other thing but He—no other love but His: the streets, Kalighat, slums & Sisters have become places where He lives His own life of love to the full. Pray for me, Your Grace, that there be really "only Jesus" in me.[51]

Two months later, in her first letter to Father Picachy, Mother Teresa tried to convey what she was enduring:

Today—we the professed had a beautiful day of prayer. It did me good to see my children pray so fervently.—We have much to thank God for these young hearts. If you only knew what I am going through—He is destroying everything in me.—But as I hold no claim on myself—He is free to do anything. Pray for me that I keep smiling at Him.[52]

Aware that God, whose presence she did not feel, was "responsible" for her pain, she surrendered to His work within her soul. Yet she appreciated this new opportunity of sharing her innermost thoughts with someone she trusted; it provided a sense of release.

"Happy to Be Nobody Even to God"

Though Father Picachy was now Mother Teresa's confessor, she continued to confide in Archbishop Périer with impressive transparency.

Your Grace,
Why is it that everybody is so good to us?—I have no answer but one deep gratitude. . . .
There is so much contradiction in my soul.—Such deep longing for God—so deep that it is painful—a suffering continual—and yet not wanted by God—repulsed—empty—no faith—no love—no zeal.—Souls hold no attraction—Heaven means nothing—to me it looks like an empty place—the thought of it means nothing to me and yet this torturing longing for

God.—Pray for me please that I keep smiling at Him in spite of everything. For I am only His—so He has every right over me. I am perfectly happy to be nobody even to God. . . .

Your devoted child in J. C. [Jesus Christ]
M. Teresa, M.C.[53]

Feeling that the very pillars of her life—faith, hope, love— had disappeared must have been agony. The darkness had dimmed the certainty of God's love for her and the reality of heaven. The burning zeal for the salvation of souls that had led her to India had apparently vanished. At the same time, paradoxically, she clung steadfastly to the faith she professed, and without a drop of consolation, labored wholeheartedly in her daily service of the poorest of the poor.

Mother Teresa professed to be "perfectly happy to be nobody even to God." In 1947 she had written to Archbishop Périer, "By nature I am sensitive, love beautiful and nice things, comfort and all the comfort can give—to be loved and love."[54] She normally remained silent about any lack of love, though she felt it keenly.[55] How much more sensitive must she have been to signs of God's love—or their apparent absence. Her longing to sense His closeness made the darkness all the more excruciating. Yet she had attained a spiritual maturity that helped her humbly and ungrudgingly assume the last place and happily be "nobody even to God."

"To Become an Apostle of Joy"

During her yearly retreats, Mother Teresa would review her life and renew her commitment to strive after holiness—and she was very demanding of herself. In April 1957 she made known to Archbishop Périer her determination to uproot the defects of her strong personality. Following through on her resolution of the previous year, she set herself to overcome her shortcomings by meekness and humility.

I speak my faults—Sometimes I have been rather quick and harsh in voice when correcting the Sisters. Even with the people I have been impatient a few times—for these and all my other faults I humbly ask pardon and penance—and I beg a renewal of my general permissions (of giving, receiving, buying, selling, borrowing, lending, destroying, of giving of these permissions to the Sisters in kind & in money) for the Sisters and all the works of the Society, and I beg you to admonish me for all my faults.* I want to be a saint according to His Heart meek and humble,[56] therefore at these two virtues of Jesus I will try my best.

My second resolution is to become an apostle of Joy—to console the Sacred Heart of Jesus through joy.

Please ask Our Lady to give me her heart—so that I may with greater ease fulfill His desire in me. I want to smile even at Jesus & so hide if possible the pain and the darkness of my soul even from Him.

The Sisters are making a very fervent retreat.—We have much to thank God, for giving us such generous Sisters.[57]

To commit herself to becoming "an apostle of Joy" when humanly speaking she might have felt at the brink of despair, was heroic indeed. She could do so because her joy was rooted in the certitude of the ultimate goodness of God's loving plan for her. And though her faith in this truth did not touch her soul with consolation, she ventured to meet the challenges of life with a smile. Her one lever was her blind trust in God.

---

*Refers to a practice of religious life in which a sister spoke her faults and renewed general permissions with her superior once a month.

Her magnanimous desire to hide her pain even from Jesus was an expression of her great and delicate love. She did all she could not to burden others with her sufferings; even less would she wish her sufferings to be a burden to her spouse, Jesus. Compared to His sufferings and to those of His poor, she did not consider her pain worth calling attention to. She aspired instead to console His Heart through joy. For this she counted on Mary's support.

"I Offered . . . to Pass Even Eternity in This Terrible Suffering"

In her letters to Archbishop Périer, Mother Teresa had reached the point where she could describe her interior pain in greater depth. It was to the tortures of hell that she now compared the total separation from God she was feeling:

> Pray for me, pray that I may have the courage to keep on smiling at Jesus.—I understand a little the tortures of hell—without God. I have no words to express what I want to say, and yet last First Friday[58]—knowingly and willingly I offered to the Sacred Heart to pass even eternity in this terrible suffering, if this would give Him now a little more pleasure—or the love of a single soul. I want to speak—yet nothing comes—I find no words to express the depths of the darkness. In spite of it all—I am His little one—& I love Him—not for what He gives—but for what He takes. . . .[59]

About ten years earlier, when seeking permission to leave Loreto and begin her mission in the slums, Mother Teresa had written about "the poor who suffer most terrible sufferings and then also eternity in darkness, because there are no nuns to give them a helping hand in their own dark holes."[60] She had insisted that it would be "worth going through every possible suffering just for one single soul"[61] and "offering everything—for just that one—because that one would bring great joy to the Heart of Jesus."[62] Now that she was bearing "the tortures of hell," her willingness to go further in her love confirmed that her earlier assertions had not been made in a momentary excess of zeal. "Knowingly and willingly" she offered to spend even eternity in this terribly painful darkness if it would please Jesus and make just a single person love Him. Her love for God went hand in hand with her love for neighbor.

In the same letter she had unveiled another profound suffering of her heart:

> I had a long letter from my old mother. At last they received news of me—& it is only now that she knows about the Missionaries of Charity. In 1948 she heard I was leaving Loreto—& then nothing—so she thought I was dead.
>
> Please pray for me.[63]

Upon hearing of her daughter's intention to commence her new mission among the poor, Mother Teresa's mother, Drana, had offered her full support and encouragement. Eleven years had passed before any further exchange of letters took place because of the political situation in Albania. This had been an excruciating suffering for both, but Mother Teresa kept silent about it.

"The Darkness Is Becoming Greater"

Mother Teresa's efforts at helping the neediest continued to attract attention and recognition in the local press:

Mother Teresa needs no introduction to Calcutta. Her zeal and compassion have touched every remote corner of the city. She has met opposition and the maddening disregard for our vast problem of human distress with a defiance belying her frailty. Mother to innumerable abandoned children, companion to the dying and destitute, succour to the diseased she has carried the battle against suffering to fields never before considered and hardly known.[64]

At the same time, she shared with Archbishop Périer her increasing inner struggle:

Please pray for me—the longing for God is terribly painful and yet the darkness is becoming greater. What contradiction there is in my soul.—The pain within is so great—that I really don't feel anything for all the publicity and the talk of the people. Please ask Our Lady to be my Mother in this darkness.[65]

While in darkness, Mother Teresa was still able to promptly recognize and appreciate the graces she received, sharing them at times with her confessors:

When I went to your chapel to thank Jesus—there I received a tremendous grace. I shall tell you next Thursday. Please thank Jesus for what He gave.[66]

In June 1958, in a letter to Father Picachy, she acknowledged one more grace:

You must have prayed much for me—I have found real happiness in suffering, but the pain is sometimes unbearable.—You don't know how miserable & nothing I am."[67]

Mother Teresa did not enjoy suffering for the sake of suffering; in fact, she found it almost unbearable. But she treasured the opportunity of being united to Jesus on the Cross and showing Him her love. The "mad desires" she had had when she was at the peak of consolation in the months following the inspiration in 1946 still burned within her heart: "Pray that I may love God with a love with which He has never been loved before.—What a foolish desire."[68]

"*The Smile Is a Big Cloak*"

These "mad desires," along with the conviction that the "work is His," gave Mother Teresa the strength to move forward. For nearly ten years she had been observing God's action in her young congregation. Grateful for all that God was doing through her, she used every opportunity to advance "His work" among the poor. In 1958 she was hoping to open a center for lepers called Shanti Nagar— "City of Peace." Immersed in the pain of rejection, she was extremely sympathetic to the lepers' experience of being rejected, unwanted, and unloved.

Your Grace,

Knowing how very overworked you are I have not written.— . . .

The other day I sent the Sacred Returns[69] to Rev. Mgr. Barber. I could not but just kneel and thank God for all. Ten years ago "the call" was but a longing—today it is a real living reality. The Society lives with His life—works with His power.—I love the Society with all the powers of my soul—yet the conviction that it is wholly His own keeps me in the spirit & feelings that I am His little instrument—His little nothing. That it is He and not I that works.

The conditions under which the leper families live are terrible.—I would like to give them better homes—uplift them close to the Sacred Heart—make them know that they too are the loved children of God & so give them something to live for . . . I want slowly to build like a little town of their own where our lepers could live normal lives. . . .

If Our Lady really wants it—she will see to it.—I would like to call it "Shanti Nagar" (City of peace). All this only if Your Grace approves.

If you only knew what goes on within my heart.—Sometimes the pain is so great that I feel as if everything will break. The smile is a big cloak which covers a multitude of pains.

Pray for me, please.

Yours in Jesus,
M. Teresa, M.C.[70]

The smile that covered "a multitude of pains" was no hypocritical mask. She was trying to hide her sufferings—even from God!—so as not to make others, especially the poor, suffer because of them. When she promised to do "a little extra praying & smiling"[71] for one of her friends, she was alluding to an acutely painful and costly sacrifice: to pray when prayer was so difficult and to smile when her interior pain was agonizing.

While her interior trial continued, her sisters were giving her added strength. "The new Sisters are just blooming into saints.—All of them are such a joy to me.—Looking at them I can do double the amount of work,"[72] she wrote to a friend.

An Oasis in the Desert

In October 1958 Mother Teresa unexpectedly received a major grace on the occasion of the requiem Mass for Pope Pius XII,[73] as she reported to Archbishop Périer:

☀ You will be very happy to hear the day you offered your Holy
Mass for our Holy Father's soul in Cathedral—I prayed to him
for a proof that God is pleased with the Society. There & then
disappeared that long darkness, that pain of loss—of loneliness—
of that strange suffering of ten years. Today my soul is filled with
love with joy untold—with an unbroken union of love. Please
thank God with me & for me.[74]

This experience was like an oasis in the desert. Not only was it a
tangible confirmation "that God was pleased with the Society" but
it was also a refreshment for her weary soul. It reaffirmed her belief
that God was ultimately responsible for her interior condition, and
thus encouraged her to even greater trust.

This consolation, however, lasted but a short time, as she reported to the archbishop:

☀ Our Lord thought it better for me to be in the tunnel—so He is
gone again—leaving me alone.—I am grateful to Him for the
month of love He gave me. Please ask Our Lady to keep me close
to herself that I may not miss the way in the darkness.[75]

As Mother Teresa had entered fully into the core of her vocation—the mystery of the thirst of Jesus Crucified—she willingly
accepted being in the "tunnel" once again, enwrapped in pitch-black
darkness. What mattered to her was that she loved God, whether or
not He granted her the consolation and joy of His felt presence. And
Christ preferred to unite her, as He did His sorrowful Mother, to
His "terrible thirst" on the Cross. She was to embody that thirsting
love of Jesus for the poor and suffering whom she served. Not
knowing when the light would appear again, she clung to Mary,
trusting that with her help she would not lose the way.

NINE

"My God, How Painful Is This Unknown Pain"

AN IMPRINT OF THE PASSION

What are You doing My God to one so small?
—*Mother Teresa*

"My Deepest Secret"

Mother Teresa had revealed her spiritual state to Father Picachy during the retreat he preached to her community in April 1956. In addition to the striking openness that marked her dealings with all her spiritual directors, a notable spontaneity in sharing her pain marked her relationship and correspondence with Father Picachy. She was pouring out her soul to someone she trusted not only as a spiritual director but also as a friend.

Dear Father,

I want to express my thanks—not for what you gave but the way it was given. . . .

Forgive me for asking you—Does Our Lord not wish you to speak to my soul? Your encouragements in confessions have been a help—but I am ready most willingly to give up even this—for souls.

No priest[1] except Fr. Van Exem & you have known the darkness in me.—If you think silence will please Him more, I am most happy to keep it for the rest of my life.

Pray for me.

Yours in Jesus,
M. Teresa M.C.[2]

To Father Picachy she had entrusted her "deepest secret," while insisting that its sacredness should be protected:

You hold my deepest secret—please for His sake, keep everything you read as a matter of conscience. I have trusted you blindly. I wanted to give you something beautiful today—so this was my gift to you. Keep it for Jesus.[3]

Despite her confidence in Father Picachy, there remained a gap in communication that she apparently could not bridge. When he realized this, he advised her to write about her inner experience. He aimed not just to get acquainted with her spiritual state and be in a better position to guide her but above all to help her cope with this terrible suffering. Thanks to the preservation of the correspondence that followed, the intensity of Mother Teresa's suffering is better grasped:

Here are the three letters.[4] Please read them—& if you find them
stupid—destroy them. Please forgive me—that I could not tell
what I wanted you to know. I am just full—I did not know that
love could make one suffer so much.—That was suffering of
loss—this is of longing—of pain human but caused by the divine.
Pray for me—more now than ever.[5]

Mother Teresa was aware that it was love that made her suffering so acute. The absence of her Beloved had turned into a torturing
longing for Him. She was torn between the feeling of having lost
God and the unquenchable desire to reach Him. It was a veritable
martyrdom of desire.

Though bewildered, she was not disoriented by her inner darkness. Rather she turned it into a blessing by offering her pain for the
poor she served.

Our friend the Punjabi[6] girl is in terrible pain.—When I saw her
she was crying loudly. I left when her mother came. Let us pray
much for her. I wish I could suffer more spiritually—if this would
give her relief.—What a contrast between the rich & the poor.—
My people in Kalighat are living martyrs & yet not a word.—A
young boy who suffered horrible pain—at last he said—he was
sorry to die—because he had just learned to suffer for the love
of God. [7]

Only by possessing a firm and ardent love—the very love she
felt she had lost—could she choose to suffer for those she loved, the
poor. Her dedication to them spurred her on to greater generosity in
offering up her own suffering. Like them, she accepted her interior
"martyrdom" in silence, hiding it even from those who were closest
to her, and offering it for the love of God and of the people she
claimed as her own.

"God Will Fill What He Had Emptied"

For ten years, except for the interlude of a month, the darkness had not weakened its grip on her soul. At times a short phrase from her reading rekindled the hope that the darkness would end, as she confided to Father Picachy: "I read something beautiful in Br. Benito S.J. life—'There would come a time when God will fill what He had emptied.'"[8] The state of Brother Benito's soul at the final stage of his life—total desolation and hopelessness—as described in a biography of Brother Benito, must have appeared to Mother Teresa much like her own:

Even God seemed to elude him. Like before, in his novitiate days, when God hid behind His gift of frustration, and emptiness. Was God hostile too? . . . Impossible. God was just, whatever His designs for desolate souls. There would be a time when He would fill what He had emptied, of this Benito was certain even though he couldn't see the hope of it. When the time came, the darkness of night would be dispelled by flashes of God's mercy.[9]

This was her hope as well.

Realizing that her responsibility toward the rapidly growing community and its apostolate was placing heavy demands on her, and knowing her inner sufferings, Father Picachy advised a long retreat, hoping it would provide some rest and respite. Initially, she refused this potential source of consolation, charity toward her sisters taking precedence over her own comfort.

I have prayed & thought well.—Though it would be a real pleasure for me to make the long retreat—still I don't think it would be right for me to do it.—My place is with the novices.—

I always make my retreat with them—they need me much
more than the 3rd year.[10] As I always do—I shall go for most
of the instructions & meditations so as to be able to help the
Sisters— . . . Pray for me much & often.[11]

Open to welcome new sacrifice, she did not hesitate to forgo the
comfort that the advice and support of Father Picachy was giving
her, in order to obtain grace for others: "You seem to be following
the policy of Jesus.—I am very happy that, that little human consolation has gone also—China needs every drop. . . ."[12]

"I Can Take a Part from His Suffering"

The long retreat given by Father Picachy for the tertians took place
from March 29 to April 12, 1959. Changing her mind, Mother
Teresa decided to make the retreat. She feared, however, that it
would only be a time of greater loneliness and deeper pain, as God's
apparent absence would be more keenly felt and the longing for the
"Absent One" more hurtful:

> My heart is so empty.—I am afraid the retreat will be one long
> suffering—but we better not think of this.—I want to make a
> fervent retreat. . . ."[13]

Just a few days before the retreat she wrote to Archbishop Périer,
"I think Fr. T. Picachy will give the Sisters a very fervent retreat."
And she added: "Please pray for me during this Holy time[14]—my
heart is so full of darkness and of loneliness and a continual pain."[15]

Each day of the retreat Father Picachy gave the sisters a typed
handout to help them with meditations and examination of con-

science. On these papers Mother Teresa jotted down her answers.[16] They present a vivid and honest picture of her soul and highlight her humility and holiness. Her straightforward and unpretentious replies also portray how she perceived her spiritual life. They constitute a striking profession of faith from one who felt she had lost sight of her faith.

Several days into the retreat, Mother Teresa wrote to Archbishop Périer: "The retreat Rev. Fr. T. Picachy is preaching to the Sisters in preparation for final vows—is the most practical one I have ever heard in 30 years of my religious life. and yet he strictly keeps to the spiritual exercises of St. Ignatius."[17]

Though it was a great sacrifice for her, she handed her notes to Father Picachy. On the third day of retreat she wrote, "To give you these papers it is one of the greatest sacrifices of the retreat, my gift for the Sisters." Yet this was one more opportunity to "grab the chance," as she used to say to her sisters, and to offer this costly sacrifice for the spiritual benefit of her followers.

"Absolute Surrender to God's Holy Will"

This retreat culminated in the final profession ceremony of the first group of sisters, on April 12, 1959. Moved to tears of joy at the blessings she had witnessed, Mother Teresa wrote to Archbishop Périer after the ceremony:

> My heart is full of gratitude to Almighty God for calling me and the Sisters to this work—to the Church for accepting our final offering and to you our Father and friend for all you have done, are doing and are ready to do. . . . I just had a good cry for God has done so much for us.—My thoughts and my heart are full of gratitude.[18]

During the retreat, she had written to the archbishop, concerned that his successor might not understand and respect the charism of the Missionaries of Charity as he had. She suggested that, because of his advanced age and delicate health, the congregation be allowed the independent governance envisioned in the constitutions, while remaining under his guidance. The archbishop agreed and appointed Mother Teresa to be the superior general. She humbly accepted this new responsibility:

Through you oh Mother of God I make my absolute surrender to God's Holy Will now in accepting this nomination with faith and love and cheerfulness.—Do with me whatever you will—I am at your disposal—your willing instrument.[19]

The archbishop had also approved Mother Teresa's proposal to begin foundations outside of Calcutta. As a result, two new missions were opened in Ranchi and Delhi later that year. With these foundations, "the little seed" was growing into a fruitful tree. Mother Teresa's desire to spread the fire of God's love amongst the poor, the sick, the dying, and the little children was being realized. With gratitude and wonder she acknowledged this remarkable growth and her desire to do even more:

This will bring you the best wishes and prayers of every one—the 85 Sisters & 15 to come, people & children, sick & dying and our lepers in our 52 centres in Calcutta.

What we owe Your Grace—only in Heaven we can pay.— Ten years ago at this time we were just 3 of us. It was you who trusted the little seed so blindly.—Today when our Sisters are going—in my heart there is blind trust in the Sacred Heart.—I offer each one of them to Him alone.—I hope one day He will help us to light the fire of charity in all the cities of India—where there are poor living in the slums.

A charitable person took all our things to Ranchi by lorry. The railway gave us 50% concession.—To make sure I come back they gave me for return also. How very wonderful is God in His simple—infinite love. I shall get all the papers as you have told Rev. Fr. V.E. [Reverend Father Van Exem].[20]

Instead of stifling her missionary impulse, the darkness seemed to invigorate it. Mother Teresa understood the anguish of the human soul that felt the absence of God, and she yearned to light the light of Christ's love in the "dark hole" of every heart buried in destitution, loneliness, or rejection. She recognized that whatever her interior state, God's tender care was always there, manifested through the small favors others did for her or unexpected conveniences that accompanied her undertakings.

One of the fruits of her retreat with Father Picachy was a greater acceptance of her mysterious interior suffering. Surrender was becoming one of the key virtues in her life.

Please Father pray very much for me, that I may not spoil His work.
Pray for me that I may forget myself completely in that absolute surrender to God's Holy Will.—I use the retreat resolution as a prayer.—I do not know how deeper will this trial go—how much pain & suffering it will bring to me.—This does not worry me any more. I leave this to Him as I leave everything else. I want to become a saint according to the Heart of Jesus—meek & humble. This is all that really matters to me now.
SM. [Sister Mary] Agnes does very well—and they have all taken the appointment beautifully.[21] Thank God. She is a holy child. God will do great things through her.
The Sisters made a real fervent retreat—now the fruit is coming.—One virtue that is coming very much forward—since the retreat—is humility. Thank you Father, for all you did.—

The only way I have to show you my gratitude is by offering everything in me for your intentions. The darkness—the loneliness & pain—the loss & the emptiness—of faith—love—trust—these are all I have and in all simplicity I offer them to God for your intention as a token of gratitude.

Pray for me—that I may not "refuse God"—to accept anything & everything in absolute surrender to God's Holy Will—now—and for life.

Please destroy any letters or anything I have written.—God wants me to open my heart to you.—I have not refused. I am not trying to find the reason—only I beg you destroy everything.

Don't take the trouble to write—[22]

"Who Am I That You Should Forsake Me?"

In her letter to Father Picachy of July 3, 1959, Mother Teresa again stressed that it was in obedience to God's direction that she was revealing her interior state to him:

I also enclose this paper. Thoughts put on paper give a short relief. Why He wants me to tell you all these I don't know.—I wish I could refuse to do it.—I would refuse Him gladly.[23]

The paper she refers to here,[24] written as a prayer and sent to Father Picachy, is one of the most detailed and longest descriptions of her experience of darkness:

Matter of confession
    In the darkness . . .
    Lord, my God, who am I that You should forsake me? The child of your love—and now become as the most hated one—

the one You have thrown away as unwanted—unloved. I call, I
cling, I want—and there is no One to answer—no One on
Whom I can cling—no, No One.—Alone. The darkness is so
dark—and I am alone.—Unwanted, forsaken.—The loneliness
of the heart that wants love is unbearable.—Where is my
faith?—Even deep down, right in, there is nothing but emptiness
& darkness.—My God—how painful is this unknown pain. It
pains without ceasing.—I have no faith.—I dare not utter the
words & thoughts that crowd in my heart—& make me suffer
untold agony. So many unanswered questions live within me—I
am afraid to uncover them—because of the blasphemy.—If there
be God, please forgive me.—Trust that all will end in Heaven
with Jesus.—When I try to raise my thoughts to Heaven—there
is such convicting emptiness that those very thoughts return like
sharp knives & hurt my very soul.—Love—the word—it brings
nothing.—I am told God loves me—and yet the reality of
darkness & coldness & emptiness is so great that nothing touches
my soul. Before the work started—there was so much union—
love—faith—trust—prayer—sacrifice.—Did I make the mistake
in surrendering blindly to the call of the Sacred Heart? The work
is not a doubt—because I am convinced that it is His not mine.—
I don't feel—not even a single simple thought or temptation
enters my heart to claim anything in the work.

The whole time smiling.—Sisters & people pass such
remarks.—They think my faith, trust & love are filling my very
being & that the intimacy with God and union to His will must
be absorbing my heart.—Could they but know—and how my
cheerfulness is the cloak by which I cover the emptiness & misery.

In spite of all—this darkness & emptiness is not as painful as
the longing for God.—The contradiction I fear will unbalance
me.—What are You doing my God to one so small? When You
asked to imprint Your Passion on my heart—is this the answer?

If this brings You glory, if You get a drop of joy from this—if souls are brought to You—if my suffering satiates Your Thirst—here I am Lord, with joy I accept all to the end of life—& I will smile at Your Hidden Face—always.[25]

Mother Teresa's fear that this interior suffering would unbalance her was not realized. According to one of her first followers, "Mother was a very balanced person and Mother was joyful when things went right; but even when things went wrong, she would not show depression or moodiness. In season and out of season she was joyful."[26] After her death, a longtime associate observed, "I think balance was one of Mother's greatest attributes. Also she was so even. . . . She never let the hurts and sufferings interfere with her love of Jesus. That love gave her so much joy. She was able to hold it all."

Her closeness to God, which she herself could not perceive, was at the root of the stable and serene disposition that others admired in her. The vigor, joy and enthusiasm with which she carried out her responsibilities powerfully influenced those who came in contact with her, especially her sisters and the poor she served. Yet her radiant smile hid an abyss of pain; it veiled the Calvary within.

"When You asked to imprint Your Passion on my heart—is this the answer?"[27] Her anguished question to Jesus remained unanswered. She could only accept living silently the mystery of the Cross that Christ was calling her to share.

The "grand finale" of this "confession" was a new magnanimous offering of love and surrender. Taking one more step apparently beyond her own strength, she pledged to smile at His Hidden Face in the midst of this suffering to the end of her life. The faith, hope, and love that she did not perceive within herself were very much at work in her soul. The overwhelming darkness had concealed Him, yet it did not obscure the reality of her identity: she was now, more than ever, "the child of His Love."

Mother Teresa was giving the impression that her relationship with Jesus was filling her with consolation. In reality it was God's sustaining grace and her unrelenting determination and strength of character that gave her the energy to overcome herself and live the joy that she did not feel. She challenged her sisters to face trials in the same way:

My dearest Sister,

I was very sad to see you this morning so down & sad. You know how much Jesus loves you.—You know how He has shown His love to you through Mother—how much & with what care Mother has helped you to love Jesus. Be good, be holy—pull yourself [up]. Don't let the devil have the best from you.—You know what Jesus & Mother expect from you.—Just be cheerful.— Radiate Christ in the hospital.—Please be careful how & what you say to those round you.

I am sending you the Sacred Face—look at the Face of Him who loves you.

God bless you,
Mother [28]

Why?

As resigned to this interior trial as she was, Mother Teresa could not help asking Father Picachy:

Tell me, Father, why is there so much pain and darkness in my soul? Sometimes I find myself saying "I can't bear it any longer" with the same breath I say "I am sorry, do with me what you wish." [29]

As she struggled to continue surrendering to the pervading darkness within her, she had to repeatedly affirm her resolve to move along the way He was tracing for her. Thus the battle continued between the temptation to refuse and the determination to accept. A few weeks later Mother Teresa wrote again, "Pray for me—that I may not refuse God.—It comes to the breaking point & then it does not break.—I wish I could tell or write what I long to tell—but I find no words."[30]

While immersed in darkness, unable to understand why, tempted to refuse, and under the impression that she could not adequately express what she was going through, Mother Teresa made one more strong affirmation of her faith and blind obedience to the will of God. A misunderstanding had arisen between her and Archbishop Périer which he again attributed to her "hastiness." Writing to clarify her stance, Mother Teresa revealed to him the secret vow that motivated her actions. Her questioning of the purpose of her pain and darkness was now silenced in an act of supreme obedience to God's will.

DATE IST SEPT. '59

Your Grace,

Last time when I spoke to Your Grace—I understood—that you think I have been acting on my own.—I sincerely can tell you that my conscience does not blame me—for I know for certain that since 17th Aug. '48 I have tried to obey, not only to obey ordinary, but with my mind and judgment.* If Your Grace has written to me as you spoke to me the other day—I would not have taken a single step. You approved everything.—You blessed everything.—You were pleased with every step I took.—I have your letters which have encouraged me and helped me when the cross was so heavy.

---

*i.e., conforming her mind and judgment to that of her superiors, not just exteriorly performing commands.

I have never told Your Grace the cause of my wanting to act at once.—In 1942—I wanted to give Jesus something without reserve.—With the permission of my Confessor I made a Vow to God—binding under Mortal Sin—to give to God anything that He may ask—"Not to refuse Him anything." For these 17 years I have tried—and this is the reason why I want to act at once.—It is for Your Grace to prevent me—and when you say "No" I am certain that my Vow is alright—for then I don't refuse God my submission.—I have gone and am still going through hard spiritual trials—but in this point—there has never been a doubt in my soul—because I have always put them before you and Fr. C. Van Exem—and each time your—"Yes" or "No" has satisfied me—as the will of God. Our claim on you is much greater—for to the other Congregations—you are their Ordinary—to us you are our father—for God used you for His instrument to bring to life this His least Society.—The exterior change that was made last April by Your Grace—has made no change in my attitude of action nor feelings.—To me and I think to every Sister in the Society, Your Grace remains the head—[the] father of the Society—as it has been since 10th Sept. '46.—All these years I have only wanted one thing—to know and do the Will of God. And now even in this hard and deep darkness—I keep on wanting only that. The rest He has taken all—and I think, He has destroyed everything in me.— The only thing that keeps me on the surface—is obedience.—

Please, Your Grace, don't be displeased with me, the mistakes I make are not willful—they are due to my ignorance.—I have to learn many things and this takes time.—From my childhood I have always been guided by my mother or confessor—now I have so many to guide. . . .

On the 10th Sept. please pray for me.—

Your devoted child in J.C. [Jesus Christ]
M. Teresa, MC[31]

"Don't Mind My Feelings"

Besides the constant struggle to remain faithful to her vow, she was haunted by her inability to express herself even to those she trusted most. This contributed to her sense of alienation, yet she accepted it as part of the suffering that God wanted from her. She wrote to Father Picachy in September 1959:

> You have told me to write.—I just can't express anything.—I don't know why [it] is like this—I want to tell—and yet I find no words to express my pain. Don't let me deceive you.—Leave me—alone.—God must be wanting this "aloneness" from me. Pray for me.—In spite of everything—I want to love God for what He takes.—He has destroyed everything in me. Pray for me. I will try to speak in confession or after—if you are not afraid of being deceived."[32]

On the other hand, when addressing Jesus—that is, in prayer—she could express herself with ease. Fulfilling her confessor's request, she sent to him a letter addressed to Jesus, enclosing it with her letter dated September 3, 1959:

> Part of my confession of today
> My own Jesus,
> From my childhood you have called me and kept me for Your own—and now when we both have taken the same road—now Jesus—I go the wrong way.
>   They say people in hell suffer eternal pain because of the loss of God—they would go through all that suffering if they had just a little hope of possessing God.—In my soul I feel just that terrible pain of loss—of God not wanting me—of God not being

God—of God not really existing (Jesus, please forgive my blasphemies—I have been told to write everything). That darkness that surrounds me on all sides—I can't lift my soul to God—no light or inspiration enters my soul.—I speak of love for souls—of tender love for God—words pass through my words [*sic,* lips]—and I long with a deep longing to believe in them.—What do I labour for? If there be no God—there can be no soul.—If there is no soul then Jesus—You also are not true.—Heaven, what emptiness—not a single thought of Heaven enters my mind—for there is no hope.—I am afraid to write all those terrible things that pass in my soul.—They must hurt You.

In my heart there is no faith—no love—no trust—there is so much pain—the pain of longing, the pain of not being wanted.—I want God with all the powers of my soul—and yet there between us—there is terrible separation.—I don't pray any longer—I utter words of community prayers—and try my utmost to get out of every word the sweetness it has to give.—But my prayer of union is not there any longer.—I no longer pray.—My soul is not one with You—and yet when alone in the streets—I talk to You for hours—of my longing for You.—How intimate are those words—and yet so empty, for they leave me far from You.—

The work holds no joy, no attraction, no zeal. I remember, I told Mother Provincial, that I was leaving Loreto—for souls—for a single soul—and she could not understand my words.—I do my best.—I spend myself—but I am more than convinced that the work is not mine. I do not doubt that it was You who called me, with so much love and force.—It was You—I know. That is why the work is Yours and it is You even now—but I have no faith—I don't believe.—Jesus, don't let my soul be deceived—nor let me deceive anyone.

In the call You said that I would have to suffer much.—Ten years—my Jesus, You have done to me according to Your will—

and Jesus hear my prayer—if this pleases You—if my pain and suffering—my darkness and separation gives You a drop of consolation—my own Jesus, do with me as You wish—as long as You wish, without a single glance at my feelings and pain. I am Your own.—Imprint on my soul and life the sufferings of Your Heart. Don't mind my feelings.—Don't mind even, my pain. If my separation from You—brings others to You and in their love and company You find joy and pleasure—why Jesus, I am willing with all my heart to suffer all that I suffer—not only now—but for all eternity—if this was possible. Your happiness is all that I want.—For the rest—please do not take the trouble—even if you see me faint with pain.—All this is my will—I want to satiate Your Thirst with every single drop of blood that You can find in me.—Don't allow me to do You wrong in any way—take from me the power of hurting You.—Heart and soul I will work for the Sisters—because they are Yours. Each and every one—are Yours.

I beg of You only one thing—please do not take the trouble to return soon.—I am ready to wait for You for all eternity.—

Your little one. [33]

Along with this letter to Jesus, she sent a note seeking Father Picachy's guidance about what she had written:

I am sending you what you told me. . . . You can either write or talk to me about it if you wish. . . .

It was not so hard to write.—If you wish to explain things to me—I am in the house the whole afternoon.—

. . . Don't forget to pray for me on the 10th Sept. [34]

The depth of Mother Teresa's love for Jesus is highlighted in this contrast between the pain she was feeling and the way she chose to act, guided by pure faith. She felt reluctant to speak about her darkness—which she compared to the pain of hell—because she was afraid that whatever she thought or wrote would hurt Jesus.[35] Paradoxically, the more she felt stripped of faith, the more her reverence and love for God grew.

Mother Teresa had always kept hidden the deepest working of God's grace in her life—her private vow, the details of the inspiration, and now her interior darkness—because of her delicate respect for her relationship with God and His work in her soul, which she treated as something sacred and revealed only to her trusted guides.

Her letter to Jesus is a prayer full of tenderness, of transparency and childlike simplicity. She addressed Jesus in the same way as she had at the time of inspiration, when she was at the peak of consolation: "My own Jesus"; and instead of her name, she signed her letter: "Your little one." The intimacy of the relationship had only deepened, though aridity instead of sweetness now accompanied her prayer. All she yearned for was His happiness; she wanted to satiate His thirst with every drop of her blood. And she would wait, if need be, even for all eternity for the One she believed in but felt did not exist, for the One she loved but whose love she perceived not.

In April 1959, during the retreat, she had stated with total frankness:

I have loved Him blindly, totally, only.

I use every power in me—in spite of my feelings to make Him loved personally by the Sisters & people.

I will let Him have a free Hand with and in me.[36]

Written at a time when the darkness was so thick that she could not pierce through to "lift" her soul to God—and even felt there was no God—these declarations constitute an extraordinary act of faith.

Only by such faith could Mother Teresa know that Jesus was there but keeping silent. Yet this faith took away neither the feeling of unremitting aloneness nor the overwhelming darkness that she was plunged into. In this spiritual agony and missing a word of encouragement from her spiritual director, she did not hesitate to admit to him: "I was expecting a few lines from you.—You too like Him keep on the silent road."[37]

Better "Mistakes in Kindness" Than "Miracles in Unkindness"

A few weeks after handing these revealing papers to her spiritual director, in her first general letter to her sisters, Mother Teresa exhorted her sisters to grow in the virtues to which the darkness had made her more attentive.

> Be kind to each other.—I prefer you make mistakes in kindness—than that you work miracles in unkindness. Be kind in words.—See what the kindness of Our Lady brought to her, see how she spoke.—She could have easily told St. Joseph of the Angel's message[38]—yet she never uttered a word.—And then God Himself interfered.[39] She kept all these [things] in her heart.[40]—Would that we could keep all our words in her heart. So much suffering—so much misunderstanding, for what? Just for one word—one look—one quick action—and darkness fills the heart of your Sister. Ask Our Lady during this novena to fill your heart with sweetness.[41]

Refusing to allow her inner suffering to be an excuse for failing in charity, Mother Teresa was striving to have a ready smile, a kind word, a welcoming gesture for each one. She expected the same from her sisters.

The second virtue she insisted on was silence. To envelop in silence God's work within her soul, as Mary had at the Annunciation, was for Mother Teresa an expression of reverence and trust. Mary, who "kept all these things in her heart,"[42] was her model and, as in Mary's case, she hoped that God would intervene in His own time and way.

Not only had Mother Teresa kept a sacred silence to conceal her inner sufferings, but she felt that God was doing the same. She believed that His showering so many graces on her work was His way of disguising *her* secret! "I am much better & will leave for Delhi on Friday—on 3/—ticket[43] with a nice place to sleep all the way up," she wrote to Father Picachy. "You see God spoils me exteriorly and so the eyes of the people are held."[44]

Afraid of Refusing God

While she continued guiding her sisters with strength and wisdom, she was seeking help from her spiritual father, remaining, however, willing to renounce even that support, despite the pain that might result:

> May I ask you to do just one thing for me.—Please put on paper all the things you tell me—so that I can read it over.—Write as I wrote—to Jesus—& you need not sign either. I think it will help me—but if you think He won't like it—don't do it. I know you pray for me.[45]

She appreciated greatly the assistance Father Picachy provided:

> I am grateful to you for all the kindness & help you give to my Sisters & me. My prayer though miserably dry & frozen is often offered for you & your work for souls. The conflict in my soul is increasing—what unspoken pain.—Pray for me— . . .[46]

Part of the reason for the conflict was the fear that the inner pain might condition her response to God, and that in a moment of weakness, without really wanting it, she might turn from her pledge never to refuse Him anything. She wrote to Father Picachy:

Pray for me, Father—inside of me there is so much of suffering.— Pray for me that I may not refuse God in this hour.—I don't want to do it, but I am afraid I may do it.[47]

Mother Teresa continued to carry out her apostolate with great interest and zeal, and while she did not get any consolation from it, she rejoiced in others' joy as she wrote to Father Picachy:

Thank God all went well yesterday, Sisters, children, the lepers, the sick and our poor families have all been so happy and contented this year. A real Christmas.—Yet within me—nothing but darkness, conflict, loneliness so terrible. I am perfectly happy to be like this to the end of life—[48]

"He Has Cut Off One More Human Help"

In April 1960, Father Picachy was transferred from St. Xavier's College in Calcutta to Basanti,[49] so Mother Teresa was to lose him as her spiritual director. As she had recognized God urging her to open her heart to Father Picachy, so now she recognized Him challenging her to give up this important support. In her parting letter to her confessor, she admitted that Father Picachy's transfer was a real sacrifice. Nonetheless, she accepted it with graciousness, serenity, and gratitude for all his help.

Dear Rev. Father,

Some years back when you gave the retreat to the novices—& I made it with them Our Lord forced me to speak to you & open myself, and then as if to approve my sacrifice he made you our confessor.—I have opened my soul with all its trials & darkness—and the working of God as you say—to you. Each confession & writing or speaking to you has been a great sacrifice—only that I knew for certain that I could not refuse.—I spoke to you—and now I just want to thank you for all your kindness to me—and your patience—for you put up with all my trials—repeating myself each time—yet you never seemed tired of it all.

Keep my soul with all its darkness & loneliness, its longing and the torturing pain close to the altar.—Pray for me—much & often—for now it seems He has cut off one more human help, and left me alone—to walk alone in darkness. Pray for me—that I may keep up the smile of giving without reserve.—Pray that I may find courage to walk bravely and with a smile. Ask Jesus not to allow me to refuse Him anything however small—I [would] rather die.

I beg one favour of you, please destroy everything that I have written to you.—I wrote all these because I had to—but now they are not necessary any longer. Please Father, destroy them.

To ask you to come—I think that I will not do but if Jesus asks you to come—please come I will be grateful.

Thank you for all the good you have done to the Sisters—and the wonderful way you have guided them always with your eyes fixed on Jesus & our rules.

My prayer for you will be a daily one that you may become more and more like Jesus—and bring many souls to Him.

God bless you, Father.

Yours in Jesus.
M. Teresa M.C.[50]

"*Sacrifices Are Only a Means to Prove Your Love*"

Before leaving for his new mission, Father Picachy became ill; for that reason his departure was delayed. This gave Mother Teresa an opportunity to write once again.

Dear Rev. Father,

How happy you must be with the gift of St. Ignatius. Yet, Basanti will have many a sacrifice ready for you.—But for you—who love Jesus and souls—sacrifices are only a means to prove your love.

You begin well your missionary life, by being first a patient. I do hope you are better—and they will soon find the means to make you well. In all the houses the Sisters are praying for you & I only keep "smiling" for you.—Your feast day[51] will be soon—the Sisters & I send you our best wishes & prayers & may St. Laurence* obtain for you the graces you ask for yourself.

With me the sunshine of darkness is bright. Pray for me.

If you are able—the Sisters would be glad if you come for the 13th. On that day we begin the novena for our Society—please join with us.—

I looked for a picture for your feast—and this is the only one I have here.—He has helped me much—he will do the same for you.—The words on the top—was my program for 1960. Cut them off.

*Deacon of Rome in the third century, martyr.

Pray for the Sisters often—they are still very young—in spiritual life and otherwise.—Pray for me that I may help them to seek and find only Jesus.

I hope you will soon be better.

God be with you,
Yours in Jesus,
M. Teresa M.C.[52]

Not unlike Father Picachy, Mother Teresa too had "many a sacrifice ready" for her in the decades to come. She was fifty years old and was about to begin a new phase in spreading her mission of love that would take her on numerous journeys around the world. "Love is proved by deeds; the more they cost us, the greater the proof of our love."[53] These trips would exact their price in time, fatigue and public speaking and serve as further proof of her love.

First Trip Abroad

In July 1960 the Catholic Relief Services of New York invited Mother Teresa on behalf of the National Council of Catholic Women to their national convention in Las Vegas. At first she declined the invitation:

I am sorry to have to say—"Thank you, I won't be able to come." I am not meant for meetings and conventions. Speaking in public and I don't agree.—My friend Miss E. Egan will do the needful much better—in my place.[54]

Some days later, having receiving a second and then a third invitation, she consulted Archbishop Périer for direction. She was "praying that he would say no,"[55] but she had to change her position, as she told her friend Eileen Egan*:

🌺 I asked His Grace—and he told me that I should go—
therefore . . . I will come for the Convention. Thank God I have
plenty to do—otherwise from now I would be terrified of that
big public.[56]

"*I Have Been on the Verge of Saying—No*"

A few days before leaving for Las Vegas, Mother Teresa wrote to
Father Picachy:

🌺 I am leaving alone with Jesus and for Jesus—on the 25th Oct. at
6 a.m. & will be in Los Angeles—on the 26th. Miss Bracken will
be there to meet me. On my way back I will stop in England,
Germany & Italy.

Pray for me— . . .

I had to smile when I read that you make use of my
resolution—Who makes it & who keeps it? How happy you are
to be so much with Jesus—and so close to Him. I have been on
the verge of saying—No. It has been so very hard. That terrible
longing keeps growing—& I feel as if something will break in me
one day—and then that darkness, that loneliness, that feeling of
terrible aloneness. Heaven from every side is closed.—Even the
souls that drew me from home, from Loreto as if they don't

---

*Eileen Egan (1911–2001) first met Mother Teresa during a Catholic Relief Services
mission to Calcutta in 1955. She traveled extensively with Mother Teresa for over
thirty years and became her co-worker in America in 1971. She is the author of *Such a
Vision of the Street: Mother Teresa, the Spirit and the Work.*

exist—gone is the love for anything and anybody—and yet—I long for God. I long to love Him with every drop of life in me—I want to love Him with a deep personal love.—I can't say I am distracted—my mind & heart is habitually with God.—How this thing must sound foolish to you because of its contradiction.—For my meditation I am using the Passion of Jesus.—I am afraid I make no meditation—but only look at Jesus suffer.—and keep repeating—"Let me share with you His pain"![57]

When you go to Jesus—make one fervent act of love for me—since I can't make it myself.—

The words don't come. I have nothing else to write—though I would have liked to write more—but nothing comes.[58]

In the deepest darkness, when the longing for God was almost unbearable and she found herself on the verge of saying "No," Mother Teresa affirmed she was constantly united with God. Without this habitual recollection she would not have been able to live through the years of darkness. Not only was it a precondition for this mystical participation in the Cross of Christ; it was also a confirmation of the true origin of this ordeal.[59]

"The Hardest Act of Obedience"

On October 25, 1960, "alone with Jesus and for Jesus"[60] Mother Teresa left India for the first time since disembarking in Calcutta in January 1929. In Las Vegas, over three thousand women were waiting expectantly to see the "simple little unknown missionary,"[61] this "poor little Missionary, without anything natural to attract,"[62] as Mother Teresa described herself. "Imagine me in U.S. in front of those thousands of great people. I would die of fear & shyness,"[63] she had written before her trip. Yet once there, in a long address she spoke about "her people" and the work in the slums and ended by inviting all to share in the "works of love":

> For me, I have never spoken in public. This is my first time, and to be here with you and to be able to tell you of the love story of God's mercy for the poorest of the poor, it is a grace of God. . . . I am glad to say that with my whole heart I offer you to share in these works of love."[64]

From the United States, Mother Teresa went to England, Germany, Switzerland, and finally to Italy. While in Rome she shared with a friend her longing to see her sisters:

> I am just counting the hours to see their smiling faces—It has been a long journey and very useful but I am glad I can go back to my simple life of a Missionary of Charity.[65]

After her return to Calcutta on December 1, 1960, she confided to Archbishop Périer: "My going to U.S.—was the hardest act of obedience I had ever had to give to God."[66] She also sent a report to her friend Eileen Egan:

> My dear Eileen,
> I had a lively journey. We arrived in Cal. [Calcutta] about 3:30 p.m. Miss Mailey & 3 Sisters were waiting for me.—I can't tell you how happy the Sisters were when I came home.—I think the whole Cal. must have heard their loud voices. Thank God all is well here. . . .
> I hope your cold is really better—& you are taking care of yourself. The Sisters' remarks are many—"fair, younger etc. etc.—but above all their own dear Mother." Can you imagine the things they did—I could not but feel the fullness of their love.—

I told them that in [the] whole great world—though so beautiful and great there is no place like 54A. . . .[67]

I am going to ask you for a big sacrifice.—In the book you are writing—<u>please</u> omit anything about me personally.—You can tell everything about the Sisters and the work.—I want you to leave me and my family out.[68] Begin from 1948—it will be a beautiful story of God's tender love for His children.—Eileen I know this will spoil the book.—I prefer this to having a single soul fix his or her eyes more on me than on God's wonderful work. . . . If you are my Second Self then you must feel for God's work exactly what I feel—deep love and respect—something very holy.

This will be one for His Grace—a very big one.

Best wishes & prayers for all at home & Howard. (Is this the way you spell his name?)

God love you,
M. Teresa, M.C.[69]

Again "on the Verge of Refusing"

As soon as she was back in Calcutta, Mother Teresa resumed her regular visits to her mission houses.[70] At this time she had communities in Delhi, Jhansi, and Ranchi. Numerous responsibilities, fatigue, and sickness added to her already heavy cross. She shared her struggle with Father Picachy who had been in Calcutta while she was away:

Many thanks for your letter of the 12th. I am glad to be back. What an experience.—Thank God it is over—and that every bit was only for Him. . . .

I am sorry to have missed you.—I had to go & see the Sisters in the other houses—and the week to Delhi, Jhansi & Ranchi has taken more from me than the 35 days out.—In Ranchi I got such

a heavy cold—but as the children's Christmas treat is near—I
have to be on the move the whole time. So you can imagine
the rest.

Many times I have been on the verge of "refusing." If you
only knew how hard it is.—I want to write yet I have nothing to
tell.—Pray for me.

Happy Christmas & New Year.[71]

She may have felt like "refusing," but she managed to refuse no
one but herself, placing God and His work, the sisters and the
people, before herself. This total availability to God and His work
among the poor, rather than extraordinary penances, was the spirit she
wanted to instill in her sisters. She asked Father Picachy to help her:

Insist [when instructing the sisters] that in our Society Our Lord
does not want us to use our energy on doing penance—of fasting
etc. for our sins—but rather in spending ourselves in giving
Christ to the poor & for this we need Sisters strong in body &
mind.—If God sends sickness—that is His own look out—but I
don't think we have [the] right on breaking our health—&
feeling miserable through weakness by the time we come to the
poor.—It is better to eat well & have plenty of energy to smile
well at the poor & work for them.[72]

"I Don't Know What Pleasure He Can Draw from This Darkness"

Father Picachy, now in Basanti, occasionally visited Calcutta. Yet
when Mother Teresa had the chance to speak with him, she was unable to. After one such meeting, she wrote asking for prayers to stay
cheerful:

Dear Father Picachy,

I was looking forward to your visit—& then nothing.—Our Lord has taken even the power of speech. I don't know what pleasure He can draw from this darkness—but as you said—I will let Him free.—I can't express—but I want to want it as He wants it. Only pray that I keep up the joy exteriorly. I deceive people with this weapon—even my Sisters. Why I ever spoke to you—it is a mystery to me—but I know that I could not refuse.

You have your difficulties.—I don't want mine to be a burden to you—so only pray much for me—and when you come the next time I hope I will be able to tell you more—and not just say nothing. . . .

My table is full of letters to be answered.—Pray for me—that I may be Jesus to souls. . . .

Pray for me much & often. If you have time, write—otherwise please do not take the trouble.

> Yours in Jesus,
> M. Teresa M.C.[73]

Though determined to give God a free hand, she could not help questioning, "what pleasure He can draw from this darkness"? The meaning and the purpose of this interior trial, which she had accepted with complete surrender, had yet to be discovered.

TEN

"I Have Come to
Love the Darkness"

THE SPIRITUAL SIDE
OF THE WORK

For the first time in this 11 years—I have come to
love the darkness—for I believe now that it is a part a
very, very small part of Jesus' darkness & pain on earth.
You have taught me to accept it [as] a "spiritual side of
'your work,'" as you wrote.
—Mother Teresa

"If My Darkness Is
Light to Some Soul"

In 1957 Jesuit Father Joseph Neuner[1] wrote an
article about Mother Teresa and her work in
a German mission magazine, *Die Katholischen
Missionen*. Shortly thereafter she sought out his
help to respond to the letters directed to her from
readers. Their personal contact took a new turn
a few years later. Father Neuner, who taught the-

ology in Pune, India, came on occasion to Calcutta to teach at Morning Star College[2] and to direct retreats. In April 1961 he was invited to preach a retreat to the Missionaries of Charity in Calcutta. Mother Teresa attended the retreat and spoke to him privately. Father Neuner recalled the encounter:

In our meetings, Mother Teresa began to speak about the trials of her inner life and her inability to disclose them to anyone. So I asked her to write down her experiences which she did more explicitly than I expected. She gave me the papers with the explicit request to burn them as soon as I had read them. I was deeply impressed by the honesty and simplicity of her account, and the deep anxiety she was going through in utter darkness: Was she on the right path or had she become the victim of a network of illusions? Why had God abandoned her totally? Why this darkness whereas in her earlier life she had been so close to God? She had to lead her Sisters, initiate them into the love of God and into a life of prayer, which had been wiped out in her own life as she lived in total emptiness: Had she become a shameful hypocrite who spoke to others about the divine mysteries which had totally vanished from her own heart?—It is all contained in the document, I need not explain it.[3]

This document, most of which Father Neuner thought best to preserve,[4] concisely touches upon the highlights of her spiritual journey thus far:

In Loreto, Father I was very happy.—I think the happiest nun.— Then the call came.—Our Lord asked directly—the voice was clear & full of conviction.—Again & again He asked in 1946.— I knew it was He. Fear & terrible feelings—fear lest I was deceived.—But as I have always lived in obedience—I put the

whole thing before my spiritual father—hoping the whole time
that he will say—it was all devil's deception, but no—like the
voice—he said—it is Jesus who is asking you—& then you
know how it all worked out.—My Superiors sent me to Asansol
[in] 1947—and there as if Our Lord just gave Himself to me—to
the full. The sweetness & consolation & union of those 6
months—passed but too soon.

And then the work started—in Dec. 1948.—By 1950 as the
number of the Sisters grew—the work grew.—

Now Father—since 49 or 50 this terrible sense of loss—this
untold darkness—this loneliness—this continual longing for
God—which gives me that pain deep down in my heart.—
Darkness is such that I really do not see—neither with my mind
nor with my reason.—The place of God in my soul is blank.—
There is no God in me.—When the pain of longing is so great—
I just long & long for God—and then it is that I feel—He does
not want me—He is not there.—Heaven—souls—why these are
just words—which mean nothing to me.—My very life seems so
contradictory. I help souls—to go where?—Why all this? Where is
the soul in my very being? God does not want me.—Sometimes—
I just hear my own heart cry out—"My God" and nothing else
comes.—The torture and pain I can't explain.—From my
childhood I have had a most tender love for Jesus in the Blessed
Sacrament—but this too has gone.—I feel nothing before Jesus—
and yet I would not miss Holy Com. [Communion] for anything.

You see, Father, the contradiction in my life. I long for God—
I want to love Him—to love Him much—to live only for love of
Him—to love only—and yet there is but pain—longing and no
love.—Years back—about 17 years now[5]—I wanted to give God
something very beautiful.—I bound myself under pain of Mortal
Sin not to refuse Him anything.—Since then I have kept this

promise—and when sometimes the darkness is very dark—& I am on the verge of saying "No to God" the thought of that promise pulls me up.

I want only God in my life.—"The work" is really and solely His.—He asked—He told me what to do—He guided every step—directs every movement I take—puts the words in my mouth makes me teach the Sisters the way.—All that & everything in me is He.—This is why when the world praises me—it really does not touch—not even the surface—of my soul. About the work I am convinced it is all He.

Before I could spend hours before Our Lord—loving Him—talking to Him—and now—not even meditation goes properly—nothing but "My God"—even that sometimes does not come.—Yet deep down somewhere in my heart that longing for God keeps breaking through the darkness. When outside—in the work—or meeting people—there is a presence—of somebody living[6] very close—in very me.—I don't know what this is—but very often, even every day—that love in me for God grows more real.—I find myself telling Jesus unconsciously most strange tokens of love.—

Father, I have opened my heart to you.—Teach me to love God—teach me to love Him much. I am not learned—I don't know many things about the things of God.—I want to love God as and what He is to me—"My Father."

Very often I long to make use of the food I give my Sisters[7]—but I can never do it—the same for spiritual books.

All these things were so natural to me before—until Our Lord came fully in my life—I loved God with all the powers of a child's heart. He was the centre of everything I did & said.—Now Father—it [is] so dark, so different and yet my everything is His—in spite of Him not wanting me, not caring as if for me.

When the work started—I knew what it will all mean.—
But with my whole heart I accepted then everything.—Only
one prayer I made—to give me grace to give saints to the Church.

My Sisters, Father, are the gift of God to me, they are sacred
to me—each one of them. That is why I love them—more than I
love myself.—They are a very great part of my life.

My heart & soul & body belongs only to God—that He has
thrown away as unwanted the child of His Love.—And to this,
Father, I have made that resolution in this retreat—

To be at His disposal.

Let Him do with me whatever He wants, as He wants, for as
long as He wants. If my darkness is light to some soul—even if it
be nothing to nobody—I am perfectly happy—to be God's flower
of the field.[8]

This summary of her call is the only instance where Mother
Teresa revealed something of the inspiration of 1946 to someone
other than Archbishop Périer and Father Van Exem. Considering
the rich spiritual experiences she had during the months following
September 10, 1946, Mother Teresa could have disclosed much
more about herself, but with her habitual humility she shared just
enough for Father Neuner, who was assuming a role as her spiritual
director, to grasp her interior journey and be of help.

What she did reveal is significant and very personal: her moving
account of the "untold darkness" she had been enduring since the
work started, her private vow and the impact it had had on her life,
and her recollection of the time when she could spend hours with
Jesus, loving Him.

The reality of her relationship with Jesus was truly a paradox.
He was living in and through her without her being able to savor the
sweetness of His presence. At prayer she would turn to Jesus and
express her painful longing for Him. But it was only when she was

with the poor that she perceived His presence vividly. There she felt Him to be so alive and so real.

Having realized that Father Neuner was capturing the pattern of God's working in her soul, Mother Teresa revealed to him details about her childhood that she had not shared with her previous spiritual directors, such as her early love for the Eucharist. Though she no longer felt Jesus' presence, she "would not miss Holy Com. [Communion] for anything." A senior sister, daily witness of Mother Teresa's actions, testified to this great faith in the Eucharist:

> Mother received Holy Communion daily with tremendous devotion. If there happened to be a second Mass celebrated in Mother House on a given day, she would always try to assist at it, even if she were very busy. I would hear her say on such occasions, "How beautiful to have received Jesus twice today." Mother's deep, deep reverence for the Blessed Sacrament was a sign of her profound faith in the Real Presence of Jesus under the appearances of bread and wine. Her adoring attitude, gestures such as genuflections—even on both knees in the presence of the Blessed Sacrament exposed, and that well into old age—her postures such as kneeling and joining hands, her preference for receiving Holy Communion on the tongue all bespoke her faith in the Eucharist.

With a nostalgic tone Mother Teresa recalled the love and union she had known. At the same time, she knew that her perception of her spiritual state with all its darkness was not the whole picture. She could catch a glimmer of her love for God: it was becoming more real, and "most strange tokens of love" arose spontaneously into her consciousness. And while she felt "as if" God was not caring for her, she knew she was a "child of his Love."

Years later, Father Neuner summed up his reaction to Mother Teresa's self-revealing notes:

🌾 My answer to the confession of these pages was simple: there was no indication of any serious failure on her part which could explain the spiritual dryness. It was simply the dark night of which all masters of spiritual life know—though I never found it so deeply, and for so many years as in her. There is no human remedy against it. It can be borne only in the assurance of God's hidden presence and of the union with Jesus who in His passion had to bear the burden and darkness of the sinful world for our salvation. The sure sign of God's hidden presence in this darkness is the thirst for God, the craving for at least a ray of His light. No one can long for God unless God is present in his/her heart. Thus the only response to this trial is the total surrender to God and the acceptance of the darkness in union with Jesus."[9]

"I Have Come to Love the Darkness"

Father Neuner was able to impart to Mother Teresa invaluable insight into her trial, which she appreciated greatly.

🌾 Dear Father,
I can't express in words—the gratitude I owe you for your kindness to me.—For the first time in this 11 years—I have come to love the darkness.—For I believe now that it is a part, a very, very small part of Jesus' darkness & pain on earth. You have taught me to accept it [as] a "spiritual side of 'your work'" as you wrote.—Today really I felt a deep joy—that Jesus can't go anymore through the agony—but that He wants to go through it in me.—More than ever I surrender myself to Him.—Yes—more than ever I will be at His disposal.—

Your instructions & meditations have also been a great strength for me.—For though my instructions to the Sisters are not so beautiful & full as yours—but it is the same food—that of love and trust—that of personal love for Christ.—Now I feel that it is He & not I who helps those Sisters.—Yes, they are my treasure—my strength and God's gift to me.—They are His.

Thank you once more for your readiness to help.—I do not believe, Father, in that continual digging into one's spiritual life—by long & frequent visits & talks. The help you have given me—will carry me for a long time.—Our spiritual life must remain simple—so as to be able to understand the mind of our poor.

It must have been very difficult for you to bring yourself to our level—and make things so beautifully easy for us to understand—God reward you.

Dear Rev. Fr. Neuner—I don't know what the rules are regarding your expenses—but please accept this for your train journey.

My Sisters & I join to thank you for all the good you have done to us.

Pray for me.

Yours in Jesus,
M. Teresa, M.C.

I would like to go to confession—before I start seeing the Sisters.—There is still a big group waiting. Each one wants the blessing of obedience on her resolutions—& so I have to take a part in their joys & sorrows.[10]

Thanks to Father Neuner, Mother Teresa's understanding of her interior condition deepened considerably: she came to realize that her darkness was the spiritual side of her work, a sharing in Christ's redemptive suffering. Regardless of how she had understood it, this trial of faith, hope, and love was not a purification from the defects characteristic of beginners in the spiritual life or even from those

defects common to those advanced on the path of union with God.
At the time of the inspiration, she had frankly stated to Archbishop
Périer that she had "not been seeking self for sometime now."[11]
Moreover, in the months prior to the inspiration of September 10,
she was, in the estimation of her confessor, near the state of ecstasy.

Her darkness was an identification with those she served: she
was drawn mystically into the deep pain they experienced as a result
of feeling unwanted and rejected and, above all, by living without
faith in God. Years before, she had been willing to offer herself as a
victim for even one soul. She was now called to be united in the
pain, not only with one soul, but with a multitude of souls that suffered in this terrible darkness.

Father Neuner later shed light on the transformation that took
place in her soul:

It was the redeeming experience of her life when she realized
that the night of her heart was the special share she had in Jesus'
passion. . . . Thus we see that the darkness was actually the
mysterious link that united her to Jesus. It is the contact of intimate
longing for God. Nothing else can fill her mind. Such longing is
possible only through God's own hidden presence. We cannot long
for something that is not intimately close to us. Thirst is more than
absence of water. It is not experienced by stones, but only by living
beings that depend on water. Who knows more about living water,
the person who opens the water tap daily without much thinking,
or the thirst tortured traveler in the desert in search for a spring?[12]

Henceforth Mother Teresa began to love the darkness as an integral part of her call. She had been praying, "let me share with you
His pain," and she now recognized that this prayer had been answered. Jesus was letting her relive His agony and because it was
His, she was happy to take it upon herself.

Father Neuner had apparently suggested more frequent meetings to assist her better. Satisfied with what she had received, she refused. Not even for spiritual direction did she allow herself to drift from the poverty of the poor. The simple help that God made available would suffice to carry her along. This complete trust in divine providence for everything, even for her spiritual needs, was a hallmark of her life.

In her second letter (actually, a short note) to Father Neuner written during the same retreat, she mentioned a grace she had received. She also reaffirmed her total abandonment to God's good pleasure.

Dear Rev. Fr. Neuner,

Thank you for your prayer. I need not force myself to be happy or to keep up a smiling face to others.—I am very happy for the good God has given me one big grace—I have surrendered completely—I am at His disposal.

"A hearty 'Yes' to God and a big smile for all."[13]

Pray that I live up to His desire—I will come and talk to you—as soon as I finish with the Sisters.

Yours in Jesus,
M. Teresa[14]

A few weeks later she wrote a warm letter to two co-workers in England:

I got two or three parcels of Cat. [Catholic] Magazines—& today your book of St. John of the Cross arrived.—I am just reading his works. How wonderfully He writes about God. . . .

We had such a wonderful retreat—Rev. Fr. Neuner spoke only of God, His love—our love—and God's Poor. Everything was so beautifully joined—that now it does not really seem so hard—to love God with our whole Heart.—

You know—often I pray for you and each time I ask the same thing—make them holy. The rest I think He will give you if you have His holiness—His love.

... Keep smiling— ... —Pray together—and Jesus will always fill your hearts with His love—for each other.[15]

Although she had written to Father Neuner that she couldn't profit from spiritual books, she was able to profit from the works of St. John of the Cross. Significantly, it was not the masterly description of interior purification during the "dark night" that attracted her attention, but rather all that the Spanish mystic had written about God. Though familiar with the Carmelite saint's thought, she did not label her own suffering as a "dark night." She had the intuition and now a confirmation from her spiritual director, that, though the sufferings were similar, their purpose was different.[16] Her friends would not have known what she was referring to when she hinted at the change within her: "now it does not really seem so hard."

"A Hearty 'Yes' to God and a Big 'Smile' for All"

The darkness did not lessen, the pain did not diminish, but a greater peace and a more serene acceptance were evident in Mother Teresa's soul. Father Neuner had led her to a turning point in the understanding and living of the darkness. However helpful Archbishop Périer and Father Picachy had been, their advice had proved to be more of a support and an encouragement than a light on her interior state. She nonetheless missed that help, as she wrote to Father Picachy:

Each time you have been to Calcutta I have missed you—but the Lord must be wanting it like this.—He wants to make sure to drain out of me every drop of self.—Those weekly helps He has taken also, so the darkness is so dark and the pain so great, but in spite of it all—my retreat resolution was the same

A hearty "Yes" to God

A big "Smile" to all.

and it seems to me that these two words are the only thing that keep me going.—

     . . . Next time you come to Calcutta I hope I will be here. . . .

     Pray for me Father, that I may just keep the two words "Yes" & "Smile."

     You know I pray for you daily.[17]

For almost twenty years Mother Teresa had been living faithfully her private vow not to refuse God anything, aspiring to be completely at God's disposal. She was well aware of the implication of her "hearty 'yes' to God": it not only confirmed her pledge to Him, it also expressed her resolve to respond even more generously and wholeheartedly to His will in every detail of her life.

"A big smile to all" did not mean that Mother Teresa was approving of everyone. Though warm and loving, she could at times be strong and demanding with her sisters and friends. She did not want their energy or efforts to be "wasted" on lesser things than God Himself. He was all to her: His love, His interests, His plans, His will were of supreme importance for her and she wished it would be likewise for those she loved.

Part of the Redemption

With Father Neuner's assistance, Mother Teresa had reached the point where she could rejoice in her suffering and repeat the words of St. Paul: "Now I rejoice in my sufferings for your sake, and in my flesh I complete what is lacking in Christ's afflictions for the sake of his body, that is, the Church."[18] A clear expression of her new understanding of her hidden trial as a sharing in the redemptive mission of Jesus and a part of her mission for the poor emerges in the advice she gave to her sisters in the general letter she wrote in July 1961:

> Try . . . to increase your knowledge of this Mystery of Redemption.—This knowledge will lead you to love—and love will make you share through your sacrifices in the Passion of Christ.
>
> My dear children—without our suffering, our work would just be social work, very good and helpful, but it would not be the work of Jesus Christ, not part of the redemption.—Jesus wanted to help us by sharing our life, our loneliness, our agony and death. All that He has taken upon Himself, and has carried it in the darkest night. Only by being one with us He has redeemed us. We are allowed to do the same: all the desolation of the poor people, not only their material poverty, but their spiritual destitution must be redeemed, and we must have our share in it.—Pray thus when you find it hard—"I wish to live in this world which is so far from God, which has turned so much from the light of Jesus, to help them—to take upon me something of their suffering."—Yes, my dear children— let us share the sufferings—of our poor—for only by being one with them—we can redeem them, that is, bringing God into their lives and bringing them to God.[19]

Although she had some notion of it much earlier, it had taken her over a decade to grasp the meaning of her trial. The degree of abandonment and trust this new understanding helped her achieve is reflected also in her correspondence with Father Picachy:

As for me—thank God we have been told to follow Christ.—As I have not to go ahead of Him, even in darkness the path is sure.

When some days are above the average—I just stand like a very small child and wait patiently for the storm to subside. . . . Pray for me.[20]

Even in darkness the path was sure: there was no need to "find the way" but rather to "follow the way" that Jesus had already walked. This conviction she transmitted to her sisters:

Once I saw a Sister with a long face going out for apostolate, so I called her to my room and I asked her, "What did Jesus say, to carry the cross in front of Him or to follow Him?"[21] With a big smile she looked at me and said, "To follow Him." So I asked her, "Why are you trying to go ahead of Him?" She left my room smiling. She had understood the meaning of following Jesus.[22]

"The Darker the Darkness the Sweeter Will Be My Smile at God"

As Mother Teresa followed Jesus in darkness, He provided needed help and support. She was attentive to signs of His love along the way, as she related to Father Neuner:

Your letter was an answer to a desire I expressed—"I wish Father would write since I have no time"—and here was a little token of His thoughtfulness. . . .

The Internuncio[23] & our Archbishop want me to go to Bombay for the Superiors meeting. It is really an act of blind obedience for me, it is a very big sacrifice. . . . It would be wonderful if I could see you.

As for myself, Father—I have nothing to say—for the darkness is so dark, the pain is so painful. Sometimes the grip of pain is so great—that I can hear my own voice call out—My God, help me. When I help my Sisters draw very close to Jesus—when I teach them to love Him with a deep—devoted—personal love—I long to be able to do the same.—The Sisters in front of my very eyes I see them love God—come so close to Him—grow daily so much like Him—and I, Father—am just "alone"—empty—excluded— just not wanted. And yet in all the sincerity of my heart—I am happy to see Him loved—to see the Sisters grow like Him. I am happy to love Him through them.—Rev. Fr. Van Exem was here for 8 days giving the Superiors retreat—not a word came from me.—It hurt me—because I have never kept anything from him.— But now I really have nothing to say.—And yet it is so painful to be lonely for God. Faithfully I have kept my retreat resolution—The greater the pain and darker the darkness the sweeter will be my smile at God.—Pray for me that I may love Jesus.

Please ask your theologians[24] to pray for your Missionaries of Charity. The Sisters were very happy to get your letter.[25]

Loneliness continued tormenting her and she could do nothing to relieve it. It still hurt her deeply to be unable to communicate, even with Father Van Exem, to whom she had been "an open book." She had great sympathy toward others in similar situations: "It must be a terrible torture for him[26]—to want to speak & not to be able to,"[27] Mother Teresa wrote to her friend Eileen. She too was undergoing this "terrible torture." Estrangement from God and estrangement from people were her daily lot.

In deciding that "the greater the pain and darker the darkness the sweeter will be my smile at God,"[28] she was echoing her patroness, St. Thérèse of Lisieux.[29] Like her, Mother Teresa always seemed to find a way to give God even more.

"Thank God That He Still
Stoops Down to Take from Me"

At the first general chapter in October 1961, Mother Teresa was
elected superior general. This title only reaffirmed the deeply spiritual
bond that existed between her and her sisters. She was their leader and
their model, but above all she was their "mother." She, in turn, aspired
to no other role, as her letter to Father Neuner makes plain:

Dear Father J. Neuner.

Many thanks for your letter. I am glad you like our printed
news.—You congratulate me on being elected Mother General.—
You are the first one—and I hope you are the last. To the Sisters
& to me it is only a title for the official documents, but to us it
makes no difference.—I want to be to them what Mary was to
Jesus—their mother.—

I am looking forward to my visit to Bombay. Meetings have a
terrible sickening effect on me.—It is a real sacrifice and an act of
blind obedience to me.—I would gladly come to Poona to ask
those 400 theologians to pray for me and our Sisters, but your
proposal to speak to them makes me feel cold.—You have written
not to say NO before I think it over. My thinking it over—is to
ask His Grace what is his wish.—If he says Yes—I will do what
you want me to do—I will come and speak and tell them of God's
beautiful work.

No, Father, I am not alone.—I have His darkness—I have
His pain—I have the terrible longing for God—to love and not
to be loved. I know I have Jesus—in that unbroken union—for
my mind is fixed on Him and in Him alone, in my will.

In case I don't come to Poona—please don't take the trouble
to come to Bombay, as it is not worth your journey—if you come

and I have nothing to say.—Nowadays He has taken this also. So I give Him a big smile in return. Thank God that He still stoops down to take from me.—

I will send you a P.C. [post card] if His Grace says yes.

Pray for me.

Yours in Jesus,
M. Teresa, M.C.[30]

In response to a remark Father Neuner had made on her feeling of aloneness, Mother Teresa gave one of her most explicit statements of faith about the darkness. The darkness was not just "her" darkness: it was "*His* darkness"; she was sharing in "*His* pain." In pure faith she was certain she was in an "unbroken union" with Him because she found her thoughts "fixed on Him . . . alone." She was steadfastly united to Jesus in her will, although her feelings were telling her the opposite. The pain that never left her kept reminding her that Jesus was there, though all she could feel in "that unbroken union" was His agony, His Cross.

Following her resolution, she accepted with a big smile her incapacity to speak about her darkness. She was grateful to be considered worthy of God's attention, even if it only meant being deprived of something precious; in this instance the support of her spiritual director was a little gift she still could give Him.

I Accept Whatever You Give

After receiving this letter, Father Neuner offered to meet Mother Teresa in Bombay. But she objected:

I have absolutely no engagements, as I know nobody in Bombay.—I am only thinking of those 3 long days—sitting for

hours at the meetings.—Anyway this too can be for the G. G. G.
[Greater Glory of God]

Don't come—I have nothing to say. Only please pray for
me. I am happy. Today I made a new prayer—Jesus I accept
whatever you give—and I give whatever you take.—There is no
meaning in my words, but I am sure He will understand.—
If you write—that will be enough for me—but please do
not come.— . . .[31]

This prayer, one of Mother Teresa's favorites, was forged in the
depths of her darkness. It was the fruit of her lived experience, an act
of the will that went against her feelings. Later she transformed it
into her oft-repeated exhortation, "Take whatever He gives and give
whatever He takes with a big smile."[32] This prayer, expressing the
spirit of her congregation—total surrender, loving trust, and joy—
summed up her manner of living through the darkness. She articu-
lated the same resolution in another of her frequent counsels: "Give
Jesus a free hand and let Him use you without consulting you."[33]

Mother Teresa regretted refusing Father Neuner's visit. But
since she felt like an "ice block," she deemed it inappropriate to take
advantage of his availability and then waste his time. She was
nonetheless grateful for his letter:

I just received your letter—and it made me very happy.—

Thank God, Father, I don't have to speak. I pity the Nuns &
the Fathers who have to speak before so many.—But thank God
they have it all written—so it won't be so difficult.

I am sorry I told you not to come—but really it is not
worth [it] as my soul is just like [an] ice block—I have nothing
to say.—You say He is "so close that you can neither see nor
hear Him, not even taste His presence." I don't understand this,

Father—and yet I wish I could understand it. I don't know what is really happening to me—for even now when I am surrounded with so many nuns & people, with things that could preoccupy me completely—Father, my mind—my heart—my very thoughts & feelings seem so very far—so far that I don't know where they are, but on pulling myself [up] I find they are with God.

You say that you had "the feeling of a meeting in the midst of a desert." It must have been painful to you who are so much with Jesus in your personal love for Him.—The fact that you love God as you do helped me.—I was happy to find somebody loves God as I long to love Him—but can't do so. . . .

Rev. Fr. Miranda will tell you what I said.—I spoke as if my very heart was in love with God—tender, personal love.—If you were in place of Fr. Miranda—you would have said—what hypocrisy. Most of the nuns thanked me for speaking.—I really did it because you wrote to do so.—I can't tell you how very kind all these Sisters have been.—What love I received at St. Sophia College—all that because I belong to God.—

Excuse writing as I am writing in the moving train.[34]

Mother Teresa kept wondering at the paradox in her life: How could God be so close, as Father Neuner maintained, when her feelings indicated the opposite? Yet, while her feelings continued in this treacherous "game," she could not deny that her whole being was fixed on Him. Others were drawn to her precisely because they perceived this closeness to God. And though she still feared being a hypocrite, she was witnessing to resolute faith and genuine charity—the fruits of her intimate union with God that she could not sense. Judging herself unable to "reach" God, she still rejoiced in helping others to get closer to Him.

"The Joy of Having Nothing"

Only scant remarks on her inner agony were now found in Mother Teresa's correspondence with Father Neuner. Apart from being unable to say more, she knew that a few lines would suffice to remind him of her constant pain and need of prayers:

This will bring you the best wishes from everyone in the Society—and our poor.—We shall all pray for you.—Pray for us, Father—that our hearts may be the crib Our Lady chooses for her Baby. . . . For me—only pray—I now want it to be just like this—because Jesus wants it so.[35]

Rather than focusing on her own suffering, she shared her joy in the steady growth of her community, a constant reminder of God's work and of His care:

Dear Father Neuner,
We got 13 new postulants last Jan. and they all already seem full of the joy of suffering for God's poor.—We will have a nice group for May, please God.—And I just only look on and wonder. Nothing goes in. I have realised something these days. Since God wants me to abstain from the joy of the riches of spiritual life—I am giving my whole heart and soul to helping my Sisters to make full use of it. I see them grow day by day in holiness—see them grow in the love of God—and the seeing makes me happy. As for myself, I just have the joy of having nothing—not even the reality of the Presence of God.—No prayer, no love, no faith—nothing but continual pain of longing for God.—These days I know Jesus has been giving to the Sisters such wonderful points.—After the

Instructions I tried my best to recapture those very thoughts and words that passed through me—but I could not recall a single thought. I want to write—but I have nothing more to say—but ask you to pray for me.—With my whole heart I want it to be just like this—because He wants it. . . .

Yours in Jesus,
M. Teresa, M.C.[36]

At this point in life, Mother Teresa even drew spiritual joy from her interior trial: Hers was "the joy of having nothing," of "absolute poverty," of the "poverty of the Cross" to which she had been aspiring from the beginning.

Newcomers to the life of the Missionaries of Charity had ample opportunities for sacrifice: the hardship of living in a crowded building, the lack of privacy, simple food and hard manual labor in serving the poor were among the many challenges. Mother Teresa was pleased to see her followers share in her "joy of suffering for God's poor." As her prolonged spiritual aridity continued, she willingly accepted being deprived of consolations while helping her sisters to "feast" on them. God was using her as a channel to pour His love on His children.

"I Want Only to Be a Real Missionary of Charity"

A few days after writing to Father Neuner, she affirmed in a letter to her friend Eileen her attitude in accepting awards and other honors:

I am sure you will be very happy that the Government of India has given me and through me to the Society the title Padma

Shri[37] for the work we are doing. I believe this is very good for the Church—as for me personally it means nothing. I want only to be a real Missionary of Charity like Our Lady was.[38]

The Padma Shri was Mother Teresa's first important award. This honor did not inflate her with pride; she had grown above that danger, as Father Neuner explained:

[Her union with Jesus] gave her the freedom which made her independent of praise and blame. When great honours were poured on her all over the world it did not affect her in the least. She had abandoned everything to God, her whole being. This was the intimate lifespring of her spirituality, which, I felt, must be preserved for her Sisters.[39]

She accepted this recognition, as she would future ones, with gratitude, in the name of and for the sake of her poor. All she aimed at was to remain a real Missionary of Charity as was Mary, whom she called "the first Missionary of Charity." "Like [Our Lady,]" she exhorted her sisters, "let us be full of zeal to go in haste to give Jesus to others."[40]

"If I Ever Become a Saint—I Will Surely Be One of 'Darkness'"

After guiding her for almost a year, it was Father Neuner's turn to fall short of words in the face of her spiritual ordeal. This did not sadden her: they both had the same attitude in the face of God's mysterious working in her soul.

☀ This will bring you the best wishes of every one at 54 A[41]—for a very happy and holy Feast. Our prayers, sacrifices & work will be for you all that day.

I did expect you—not to console me—but to help me—and I am very glad to know that you really have [nothing] to say. The day I wrote—I felt as if I could not suffer it any more.—But St. Paul has given me the answer in his epistle of Sexagesima Sund. [Sunday][42] and your letter also—so I am happy to suffer it still more and also with a big smile.—If I ever become a saint—I will surely be one of "darkness." I will continually be absent from heaven—to light the light of those in darkness on earth.—Keep in your prayers Kanpur, Amravati, Raigarh, Bhagalpur.—These may be our future mission houses. Pray much for me, pray often—that I may do the things that are pleasing to Him, who has called me.[43]

On a particularly dark day Mother Teresa had found light in the reading from 2 Corinthians 11:19–23, 12:1–9. She would have liked her darkness—the thorn in her life—to be removed, but like Saint Paul she grasped that in accepting it she could rely on the Lord's assurance that "my grace is sufficient for you."[44]

Just when she felt she had reached the limit of her strength, she formulated what may be called her mission statement: "If I ever become a saint—I will surely be one of 'darkness.' I will continually be absent from heaven—to light the light of those in darkness on earth." Not longing for its joys, she envisioned heaven as a new opportunity to love, to reach every "dark hole" and to light in each the light of God's love. Her zeal had not lessened. Strengthened in the furnace of suffering, she was ready to continue her mission until the end of time.

"Do We Really See Only Jesus in Us?"

God's blessing on her endeavors continued to be a reassurance of His presence and guidance through her interior desert. To her friend Eileen, Mother Teresa wrote, "God is so very wonderful to bless His own works in so many ways. Now more than ever I not only feel but know for certain—that really the work is His."[45] It was from this knowledge and conviction that she could confidently encourage her co-workers to live in union with Him:

The Loved Ones of Christ

Eileen has asked me to write—that you have all voted to have a few words from me for your March meeting. There must have been something wrong with that voting.—All the same, it gives me pleasure to come again near you & I think I can see still that burning desire for holiness I saw on your faces when I was with you.[46] God keep it burning. Daily we pray "let them look up and see only Jesus," but how often we look in and see only Jesus in us? Do we see Him in using our eyes, mind, & heart, as His own? Are we so given to Him—that we find His eyes look through ours, his tongue speaking, His Hands working, His feet walking, His Heart loving? Do we really see only Jesus in us?

You have to be in the world and yet not of the world.[47] The light you give must be so pure, the love you love with must be so burning—the faith you believe with must be so convincing—that in seeing you they really see only Jesus. Your apostolate is so beautiful to give Jesus. You can give Him—only if you have surrendered yourself totally to Him.—Often, very often, I pray for you—that you may be the fruit of Christ's love in the world—that you may grow in holiness—so that in you Christ's joy may be fulfilled. In our Society we often tell Our Lady she is the Cause of our Joy—because she gave us Jesus.—Would that we become the cause of her joy—because we give Jesus to others.

Keep close to Jesus with a smiling face.[48]

"Unwanted, Unloved, Unclaimed"

As Mother Teresa continued her mission of spreading God's love to the poor, the daily vivid "picture" of their distress implanted in her mind seemed to her the only fitting way to describe the state of her soul. Several weeks after writing to the co-workers, she wrote to Father Neuner:

How very kind of you—to pray for me—and to write. . . .

I have been reading "The Nun" St. Margaret Mary & the Sacred Heart by Margaret Trouner.[49]—Her love for Jesus gave me such painful longing, to love as she loved Him. How cold—how empty—how painful is my heart.—Holy Communion—Holy Mass—all the holy things of spiritual life—of the life of Christ in me—are all so empty—so cold—so unwanted. The physical situation of my poor left in the streets unwanted, unloved, unclaimed—are the true picture of my own spiritual life, of my love for Jesus, and yet this terrible pain has never made me desire to have it different.—What's more, I want it to be like this for as long as He wants it.—

Maybe in June I will come to Bombay. If Nirmala still wants to see me—I will be most willing either to go to Poona or let her come to the convent in Bombay.—It would also give her a chance to see the work. Pray for me—that I may in kindness and joy go about doing good.[50]

Yours in Jesus,
M. Teresa, M.C.[51]

The condition of the poor on Calcutta's streets, rejected by all and abandoned to their pain, was, she claimed, "the true picture of my own spiritual life." She had reached the point of complete identification with "her people," with their misery, loneliness, and rejection.

She too felt unwanted—not by people who needed her, but by the One who meant more to her than life, her God. She too felt unloved—not by the multitude that flocked around her, but by God whom she loved with all the powers of her soul. She too felt unclaimed—not by the poor who found a mother in her, but by God, the child of whose love she claimed to be.

Her interior darkness gave Mother Teresa the capacity to comprehend the feelings of the poor. "The greatest evil is the lack of love and charity, the terrible indifference towards one's neighbour who lives at the roadside assaulted by exploitation, corruption, poverty and disease,"[52] she would later say.

And she did her part, spending herself totally to help change the horrifying conditions of the poor. Not only did she meet their material needs; she offered more, for she knew that "people today are hungry for love, for understanding love which is much greater and which is the only answer to loneliness and great poverty."[53] Those she served knew that she loved them, understood them, suffered with them. They felt that for her, they were the only person in the world at that moment. It was not just the material help, but especially her love that made the difference.

She insisted with her sisters that they would not understand the poor unless they experienced poverty themselves:

Jesus was sent by His Father to the poor[54] and to be able to understand the poor, Jesus had to know and experience that poverty in His own Body and Soul. We too must experience poverty if we want to be true carriers of God's love. To be able to proclaim the Good News to the poor we must know what is poverty.[55]

Without her interior darkness, without knowing such a longing for love and the pain of being unloved, and without this radical identification with the poor, Mother Teresa would not have won over their trust and their hearts to the extent she did.

Mother Teresa's suffering was at the deepest possible level: that of her relationship with God. And in her zeal for the salvation of others, she willingly embraced the full measure of this suffering so that the poor she loved might experience the full measure of God's love. As a consequence, her darkness became her greatest blessing; her "deepest secret" was indeed her greatest gift.

ELEVEN

"At His Disposal"

TO BE THE ONE

I am ready to accept whatever He gives and to give
whatever He takes with a big smile.
—Mother Teresa

"I Want With My Whole Heart
What He Wants"

Beginning in mid-1962, Mother Teresa entered a
period of her life during which a few letters from
her spiritual guides and rare meetings with them
would be all the help she received. She continued
to correspond with Father Neuner and with Father
Picachy. Her letters are not detailed, but rather reminders of what they already knew; these letters
express more her resignation than her pain.

Since she considered Father Picachy a friend,
when he confided to her the difficulties of his
mission in Basanti in May 1962, she took them on
as her own:

Your difficulties and mine—we will offer to Jesus for souls.—I am sure you wonder as I do—how long will it all last. I know that I want with my whole heart what He wants, as He wants and for as long as He wants. Yet, Father—this "aloneness" is hard. The only thing that remains is the deep and strong conviction that the work is His.—With all these things that have happened in Delhi[1]—I did not even get a single thought of self-satisfaction.—It was one more painful sacrifice to make. The things of Basanti must be very painful to you—and I often pray for you that all may soon be finished.

Though I would like to write—but there is so much to be done—so many letters to be written—that I must put all these before my own self.[2]

Even in intense suffering, Mother Teresa's sense of humor did not fail her, and she could be impish in expressing her manner of following Jesus through the darkness. "I can do only one thing, like a little dog follow closely the Master's footsteps. Pray that I be a cheerful dog,"[3] she wrote to Father Picachy sometime later.

In July 1962 she learned that Father Picachy was to become a bishop. Mother Teresa was happy about his appointment, but felt that the separation was getting deeper. "It will be difficult for me to call you 'Your Lordship,'"[4] she wrote to him, "—but I will have to do it. . . . In your new life don't forget to pray for me."[5]

"Why Does He Give All These but Himself?"

The work of the Missionaries of Charity was bringing Mother Teresa more and more into the public eye. She realized that this too was the will of God for her. The separation from her sisters and the poor occasioned by her need to travel more often sharpened her sense of isolation. When alone among strangers she felt it keenly, as she wrote to her friend Eileen:

Here I am alone—how I would love you to be here.—You can't have all the good things.—

This afternoon I am flying to Manila and will stay there with the Daughters of Charity.—Personally I would prefer to be with my people—but the Lord has His own plans.—And as I want Him to be at full liberty to use me as it pleaseth Him, I am just as happy here or there. The Padma Shri & now Magsaysay[6] has helped many especially [in the] Gov. [Government] to understand the love of the Church for India & that the missionaries are the best gift the Church can give to a country.[7]

The honors bestowed upon her and her work accentuated the absence of intimacy with Jesus, which she longed for. She confided to Father Neuner:

For me, please pray. Would that I could tell—but that too is empty—and it seems to me I have nothing to tell you.—I wonder what He gets from all this—when there is nothing in me.

I had to go to Manila for the Magsaysay award. It was one big sacrifice. Why does He give all these but Himself? I want Him, not His gifts or creatures.—

I must not write like this—for it takes from the joy of letting God [be] free with me.—I am not only willing but also happy to be at His disposal. Let Him take all, even Himself—if this increases His pleasure.—In return I ask to make my Sisters holy.

Pray for me.[8]

When the anguished "why" disquieting her heart escaped her pen, she would take it back as soon as she wrote it, for fear of lessening her determination to give her "yes" to God and "a big smile for all." Thus, she remained happily at His disposal, even when she was seemingly deprived of God.

"I Give Whatever He Takes"

In September 1962, writing to now Bishop Picachy, Mother Teresa emphasized how dark her interior state was. In the most critical moment, when she was on the verge of saying "No," Mary, whom she often referred to tenderly as her "mother," came to her aid.

> Your Lordship,
>
> My thoughts, prayers and sacrifices were all the time with you on the 9th. I would have loved to be there—but the Lord has His own plans. Thank you for the picture— . . .
>
> Often I wonder what does really God get from me in this state—no faith, no love—not even in feelings. The other day I can't tell you how bad I felt.—There was a moment when I nearly refused to accept.—Deliberately I took the Rosary and very slowly without even meditating or thinking—I said it slowly and calmly. The moment passed—but the darkness is so dark, and the pain is so painful.—But I accept whatever He gives and I give whatever He takes. People say they are drawn closer to God— seeing my strong faith.—Is this not deceiving people? Every time I have wanted to tell the truth—"that I have no faith"—the words just do not come—my mouth remains closed.—And yet I still keep on smiling at God and all.
>
> Now that you are a Bishop—I must keep away—for you have many other more important works to do.—I thank you dear Father—for all the help you have given me for all these years, and pray for me—even though I must keep away.[9]

Not having the sense of believing, Mother Teresa still struggled with the fear of deceiving others. Yet when she wanted to disclose her apparent lack of faith she was deprived of the power to do so. This too was God's work in her life: He would not permit her to say something that was not true. She did have faith, a biblical faith, a blind faith, a faith that had been tried and tested in the furnace of suffering, and that traced the path to Him through darkness. Undeterred by feelings, she continued living by the faith she felt as lost.

Mother Teresa lived her commitment to total obedience in every situation of her life, even when she was given the difficult task of speaking in public. While she was at ease in instructing her sisters, she felt intimidated and inadequate to the task of addressing others. Declining again Father Neuner's invitation to speak to the seminarians, she wrote in January 1963:

> The Lord is having His own game—I give what He takes. He does not seem to want me [to] have the human consolation I would derive from my talking to you.—I am happy with whatever pleases Him best. I accept whatever He gives.
>
> I have nothing to say—nor have I the ability or the learning you need to speak to future priests. My Sisters are me—so I need not look for big learned words.—I just open my heart—and He talks.
>
> If you wish you may ask Archbishop D'Souza[10] what he thinks. If he tells me to do it—I have nothing to say—I will do it.[11]

Bishop Picachy had reassured her that she could count on his continued help. She thanked him for this important support:

> How very kind of you to write and to remember to pray for me. I thought now that you are a Bishop with a big diocese—[you]

would forget.—Thank God you did not forget and that you pray for me.

I am sorry I missed you each time—for I would have loved to have the chance to go to Confession. Nearly every other week I have a different priest for Confession—and I never can speak—and also I have nothing to say.—How long the good God will act this way, I don't know—and I am happy that He knows. This is the only thing I do at present—to "Let His hand free." He can do what He likes and as He likes.—Pray for me.[12]

"The Fragrance of Christ's Joy"

The thought that her imperfections could be the cause of this long suffering never completely left her. "I must have been so very full of self all these years—since God is taking so long to empty me.—I hope one day when I am fully empty He comes,"[13] she wrote to Bishop Picachy in February 1963.

Since she was under the impression that God was emptying her, the image of John the Baptist[14] came vividly into her mind; his joy would be hers as well, she wrote after one of her meetings with Father Neuner:

I tried last night to remember all you told me and could remember but one thing—that I belong only to God.—I had taken so much of your time and make no profit from it. I am determined more than ever to spread joy wherever I go—the fragrance of Christ's joy. Since they [the Sisters] are not mine—I will be a St. John Baptist to Jesus.—I will rejoice because the Bridegroom has His bride.[15] Jesus has the love of my Sisters and soon, God willing will have the love of the Brothers too.—Father, if possible sometimes write, just as you spoke—I want to [be] only for God. . . .

Please keep on reminding your future priests to pray for me and the Society—and also the more holy they become the more holy they will make our Sisters when they become their spiritual guides. Ask them very specially to pray for the 25th March.

I am grateful for making it possible for me to come to Poona & see your great work—& being so patient with me.

God be with you—[16]

The Missionaries of Charity Brothers, the first male branch of the Missionaries of Charity family, began on March 25, 1963, the Solemnity of the Annunciation of the Lord. Mother Teresa had put her whole heart into this foundation and was happy to inform Bishop Picachy of this expansion of her service to the poor. As she had associated her interior struggles with the rapid growth and success of her sisters, she questioned what "the price" for her brothers would be. She was ready to give even more.

You will be very pleased to know that on the 25th March—to Our Lady—the first offering of the Missionary Brothers of Charity will be offered. So please pray that all be only for Jesus.

I wonder what Jesus will take from me for them since He has already taken all for the Sisters. I am ready to accept whatever He gives and to give whatever He takes with a big smile.[17]

Still lamenting the fact that she could not share with her "official" spiritual director, Mother Teresa turned to her old confidant and spiritual guide Bishop Picachy for help:

Dear Bishop Picachy,

Fr. Van Exem has been my spiritual father since 1944.—I think—he still is so—but I feel I need someone to talk sometimes. For some years now I have found this difficult to do it with him.—I don't know why.

May I ask you to help me—for as long as God wants it as sp. [spiritual] father? Since you know already nearly everything. If you need something else—I will try to tell.

Pray for me—

Yours in Jesus,
M. Teresa, M.C. [18]

"Make Me Share With Thee Thy Pain"

Letting Jesus "have a free hand"[19] with her continued to be the measure of her self-giving: "I was very happy to go to Confession—but as usual nothing to say. Pray for me—that I remain at His disposal,"[20] she wrote to Bishop Picachy. This constant surrender brought with it a steady share in Jesus' pain. In April 1963 she wrote to Father Neuner:

How very kind of you to write. Yes, Father, Lent is nearly over.—The Passion of Jesus has passed by—without even touching my soul. My meditations like everything else—are so meaningless.—Day after day—the same thing I repeat—maybe only with my lips—"Make me feel what Thou hast felt. Make me share with Thee Thy pain."[21] I want to be at His disposal.

The opening went off very beautifully.—We have one brother—the 2nd is coming on Easter Sunday. It is wonderful to see & hear the reactions of the priests here.—Strange—but they all seem pleased & at the same time they were expecting this to happen one day. I am praying for Nirmala—Jesus will take care of her because she loves Him in His distressing disguise [of] His

Poor. She may still go back to Poona one day as an M.C. & do great things for God—with her generous nature.

I am glad you are on holidays.—We began our spiritual holiday—retreat on the 15th for the novices & on the 16th for the professed & the Superiors. I will not make mine this time.—I wish I could go somewhere alone—to be alone with God even though He may not want to be alone with me. . . .

Thank God you keep well.—My throat has been & is still giving trouble.—The best is that it does not pain when I talk—only when I drink—so I keep on all the talking—sometimes 3 or 4 or 5 instructions a day.—The Sisters were delighted with the instructions I gave them on chastity. I don't know from where it all came—but it has made the vow of chastity—the most lovable and the most natural vow for a religious to make. I wish I could feel what they feel.—Never mind—I am very happy & keep a big smile for all.—

Pray for me—and ask the theologians to pray for me.[22]

Throughout Lent, and in fact throughout her life as a Missionary of Charity, Mother Teresa's prayer—"Make me feel what Thou hast felt. Make me share with Thee Thy pain"—was being answered. Was she not experiencing the agony of Jesus and also the agony of her poor?

While she was living this ordeal, made ever more strenuous by her ardent longing for God, she fulfilled all her duties with her habitual fidelity and cheerfulness, and she exhorted her friend Eileen to do the same: "Live your life of love for Jesus with great joy—for what you have is all His gift—use it all for the greater glory of His name. . . . Keep close to Jesus always with a smiling face—so—that you can accept what He gives and give what He takes."[23]

"He Still Plays His Game"

In September 1963 the petition for papal recognition of her congregation was sent to Rome. She could not conceal her satisfaction from Father Neuner:

Many thanks for your kind letter—

I am very happy you are going to Rome[24] and that you will pray for me & the Sisters & Brothers. You will be glad to know something else is going to Rome—our Archbishop's petition, the letters of all the Bishops where the Sisters are, my petition & the report on the life & work of the Society. The petition is to get the Pontifical rite for the Society. Father, don't you feel happy? The God's little seed is slowly growing—and yet it is all His.—The only thing that keeps me on—is the conviction that the work—the Sisters, the Society—all is His—only—I claim nothing. . . .

Everybody is well and doing their best. Pray that [He may] empty my emptiness.—He still plays His game—and I still keep smiling during His game.[25]

"My Feelings Are So Treacherous"

The opening of the Missionaries of Charity community in Jamshedpur, in the diocese of Bishop Picachy, was an opportunity for Mother Teresa to meet him face-to-face and disclose her persistent struggles. At a time when it was already difficult to speak, having to confide her trial to a new spiritual director would have been very challenging.

ON MY WAY HOME[26]
8/1/64

Your Lordship,

I can't thank you & your people enough for all your & their kindness and affection you & they have shown our young Sisters.—I hope they will be a real cause of joy to you—and bring many souls to Jesus.—Our Sisters are young—take care of them as they are His. Guide them to fervour & sanctity—& the holier they become the more they will be able to radiate God's love among His poor. I am very grateful to God—to have given me the chance to work with you in your young diocese.

You must have prayed very fervently for me—because it is now about a month that there is in my heart a very deep union with the will of God. I accept not in my feelings—but with my will, the Will of God.—I accept His will—not only for time but for eternity.—In my soul—I can't tell you—how dark it is, how painful, how terrible.—My feelings are so treacherous.—I feel like "refusing God" and yet, the biggest and the hardest to bear—is this terrible longing for God.—Pray for me, that I may not turn a Judas[27] to Jesus in this painful darkness. I was looking forward to speaking to you.—I just long to speak—and this too He seems to have taken the power from me.—I will not complain.—I accept His Holy Will just as it comes to me. If you have the time please write & do not mind my inability to speak to you—for I wanted to speak—but I could not. . . .

Please excuse paper & writing. Thank you for all your kindness to me & mine.[28]

It is hard to imagine how Mother Teresa could be more surrendered to God, but, according to her own words, her conformity with God's will had become more complete. She was ready to accept remaining in darkness even for all eternity, though fearing she may turn a "Judas to Jesus." Yet the darkness was not the most painful.

"The biggest and the hardest to bear," Mother Teresa insisted, was "this terrible longing for God." More painful than the darkness itself was this thirst for God. She was in fact experiencing something of Jesus' thirst on the Cross, the same thirst that she had encountered on September 10, 1946. As the darkness increased, so did her thirst for the One whom it hid and her thirst "to radiate God's love among His poor." Her "terrible" thirst for God was expressed in her burning thirst for souls, especially for the poorest of the poor. She was incarnating the charism she had received.

Mother Teresa's increasing zeal for souls was reflected in the rapid spread of her mission. To her friend Eileen she happily related the increasing number of foundations: "Counting Heaven where we have 4 Sisters—now we have 15 houses—and one of the Brothers with 9 Brothers."[29] This zeal helped her overlook her own needs and sufferings and unite them to the sufferings of the poor she served. "Don't worry about me," she added in the same letter to Eileen, "—my throat is better—& it is good to have something [to suffer]—so that I can share a little the pain of my poor in Nirmal Hriday. . . . I long to light the light of love in the heart of every creature of God."[30]

"What a Terrible World This Is— Without the Love of Christ"

Mother Teresa's desire to sow love was especially challenged in times of hostility. As the sufferings of the poor increased, her compassion increased as well. When fighting broke out in Calcutta in

1964, leaving over one hundred dead and four hundred wounded, all she could see was the terrible effect of sin:

☀️ It will break your heart to see thousands of people left homeless—just over night. There has been trouble between the Hindus & the Muslims. Pray for our people. . . . What harm sin can do. What a terrible world this is—without the love of Christ. I just can't understand why did they do it. Why cause so much pain to the poor? Pray for them.[31]

"Terrible is hatred when it starts touching human beings,"[32] she wrote to Bishop Picachy. As the violence of war harvested its victims, she saw hatred in action and kept looking for ways to replace it with love. Again she shared her sentiments with Eileen:

☀️ Pray for our people.—India is passing through most difficult time.—We need much prayers & sacrifices from you people in other lands. . . .

I know this will make you very sad—as your heart is filled with working for peace—but my dear Eileen—offer everything & pray much that we be able to extinguish this flame of hatred—which is spreading. . . .[33]

"Only God Can Ask Sacrifices Like This"

To be a channel of God's peace and spread His love through the expansion of her mission exacted numerous sacrifices from Mother Teresa. Returning from opening a house in Carambolin, she confided to Father Neuner a particularly demanding sacrifice:

The Sisters are in Carambolin & have already started work
among God's poor. Pray for them that they may do well & bring
many souls to God. They are beautifully brave. I am happy to
open all the houses the good God wants & light the fire of love in
as many cities—but every time I leave the Sisters—a part of me,
as if, is out from me & so causes great suffering.—Only God can
ask sacrifices like this. . . .

Pray for me—for the life within me is harder to live. To be in
love & yet not to love, to live by faith and yet not to believe. To
spend myself and yet be in total darkness.—Pray for me.[34]

If parting from her sisters was painful, occasional meetings with
them gave her much joy:

I had all the Superiors in Cal. [Calcutta] for the retreat.—It was
wonderful to have them with me—all together. I don't know
what other people feel—but I love my Sisters as I love Jesus—
with my whole heart, soul & mind & strength. . . . Keep praying
for me—as I do for you.—Let us love Jesus with our whole heart,
soul & mind.[35]

Mother Teresa recognized that her darkness was the price of
lighting "the fire of love." She willingly agreed to pay the price and
exhorted the superiors of her communities to do the same, though
she gave no indication that she was speaking from direct experience:

You are there for your Sisters—the Sisters are not there for you.
You must be ready for any sacrifice—so to say, to be eaten up by
your Sisters. You may sometimes feel great loneliness—but this
is one of the sacrifices you can make for your Sisters. It often
happens that those who spend their time giving light to others,
remain in darkness themselves.[36]

"The Good God Called & I Said 'Yes'"

As the Holy See was considering her request for pontifical recognition, a brief historical outline of the origin and development of the institute was required. Mother Teresa, who had been particular about keeping secret the beginning of her congregation was now faced with the question of what to reveal. She presented an extensive report on the development and present activities of her community, but concerning the call she just wrote: "as for the origin—it was very simple—the good God called & I said 'Yes.'"[37]

Keeping her "Yes" to God, she remained open to His will manifested in the smallest detail and surrendered each time anew, no matter what He asked of her. It often meant personal sacrifice. "I would have loved to come—as I wanted so much to speak to you," she wrote to her trusted spiritual guide, "but the Lord wants it His own way."[38]

"How Terrible It Is to Be Without God"

Although she had come to terms with the meaning of her ongoing interior darkness, that didn't mean it was any easier to live with. God was despoiling her of every natural and supernatural support: her isolation was so total that she could compare it only to hell. After over fifteen years of darkness, she presented Father Neuner with this description:

> As for me—what will I tell you? I have nothing—since I have not got Him—whom my heart & soul longs to possess. Aloneness is so great.—From within and from without I find no one to turn to.—He has taken not only spiritual—but even the human help.

I can speak to no one & even if I do—nothing enters my soul.—I was longing to speak to you in Bombay—yet I did not even try to make it possible.—If there is hell—this must be one. How terrible it is to be without God—no prayer—no faith—no love.—The only thing that still remains—is the conviction that the work is His—that the Sisters & the Brothers are His.—And I cling to this as the person having nothing clings to the straw—before drowning.—And yet, Father—in spite of all these—I want to be faithful to Him—to spend myself for Him, to love Him not for what He gives but for what He takes—to be at His disposal.—I do not ask Him to change His attitude towards me or His plans for me.—I only ask Him to use me—to teach & help my Sisters & Brothers & our Poor to love Him, since I could not love Him.—How beautifully the Sisters & the Brothers love God.—How much they try to live up to whatever He gives them through me.—[39]

"How terrible it is to be without God," Mother Teresa wrote. How even more terrible it was for her who had been so close to Him, to have, as it were, lost all sense of His presence. In God's design, she was allowed to experience some of the dreadful reality of a life without God, which she likened to hell, the consequence of the ultimate rejection of His love and mercy. This experience fueled her unquenchable thirst to save souls by helping each person to know God and His love, and to love Him in return. Along with her whole-hearted service to the poor, she was offering to God her hidden agony so that others could draw closer to Him. In imparting to the sisters her interpretations of the feelings of Jesus, she was also reflecting the depths of her acceptance of Jesus' Cross:

At the Incarnation Jesus became like us in all things except sin; but at the time of the Passion, He became sin.[40]—He took on

our sins and that was why He was rejected by the Father. I think
that this was the greatest of all the sufferings that He had to
endure and the thing He dreaded most in the agony in the
Garden.[41] Those words of His on the Cross[42] were the expression
of the depth of His loneliness and Passion—that even His own
Father didn't claim Him as His Son. That, despite all His
suffering and anguish, His Father did not claim Him as His
beloved Son, as He did at the Baptism by St. John the Baptist[43]
and at the Transfiguration.[44] You ask "Why?" Because God
cannot accept sin and Jesus had taken on sin—He had become sin.
Do you connect your vows with this Passion of Jesus? Do you realize
that when you accept the vows you accept the same fate as Jesus?[45]

By her life of consecrated service to the poor, Mother Teresa had
embraced the same lot as Jesus. Like other saints called to help those
they served draw closer to God, she was called to share the lot of the
poor. In a way, she had to fight and resist their temptations so that
they could emerge victorious.[46] And the battle was intense. Her
statement, "If there is hell—this must be one," was not a questioning of the existence of hell but rather the assertion of "how dark"
her darkness was. She believed firmly that the possibility of going to
hell was a dreadful reality. Back in 1946 she was longing to leave
Loreto "to make Our Lord better known to the poor who suffer
most terrible sufferings and then also eternity in darkness." She was
now one with the "great crowd . . . covered in darkness" that she
had seen in the visions she had at the beginning of her new vocation,
the crowd that called out to her, "Come, come, save us—bring us to
Jesus."[47] By embracing their darkness she was bringing them to the
light—Jesus.

Even the consolation of seeing her sisters and brothers grow
closer to God was mixed with disappointment. The hardships of
their life and work with the poor demanded much strength and ded-

ication and not everyone persevered. In April 1965, on the occasion
of two sisters' leaving the congregation, she wrote to Bishop Picachy: "I have never felt sorrow like this, but it has been a great lesson for us all. Pray for them."[48]

"He Takes Every Drop of Consolation From My Very Soul"

On February 1, 1965, the Missionaries of Charity received the
hoped for pontifical recognition (Decree of Praise) whereby the
congregation was placed directly under the authority of the pope instead of the diocesan bishop. This was a decisive step in the life of
the "young Society." This mark of God's favor moved Mother
Teresa to think of St. John the Baptist. His words "He must increase, but I must decrease"[49] were both her inspiration and her aspiration, for she wanted all the attention to be on Jesus and not on
His instrument. She expressed her joy over the pontifical recognition to Father Neuner:

Thank you for your kind letter.—God has His own way in all
things.—Slowly I learn to accept everything just as He gives it.
Your absence from Goa was one of those acts—but I am glad He
did like this—I have still many, many things to learn.—

We had a beautiful day on the 2nd May. Our thanksgiving
day for all the graces our little Society has received—especially the
Decree of Praise.—And now we are a Pontifical Congregation.—
See what Our Lord does.—He pours Himself on the little
Society—and yet He takes every drop of consolation from my
very soul.—I am glad it is [so]—for I only want that Jesus in the
Society be more and more and I be less & less.

The Internuncio came all the way from Delhi only for this—
and he spoke beautifully.—He summarized the Society in
3 words—Dependence, Detachment, Dedication. Pray that we
live up to this.[50]

Because the internuncio, Archbishop James Robert Knox, was
the official representative of the pope, Mother Teresa took the occasion of his visit to reveal to him her darkness—the pivot of her
union with Jesus:

In Ceylon you told me that you took the place of our Holy
Father.—I love Holy Father.—Maybe this is why I feel better
for having spoken to you.—And because I want to believe, I
accept the darkness of faith with greater joy and confidence.
Thank you for teaching me this. Pray for me.[51]

Since Archbishop Knox stood in the place of the pope himself
his advice meant more for her than that of her confessors or spiritual
directors.

With her customary sense of humor, she would play with words
in referring to her suffering. In the same letter to the Internuncio
she wrote, "The heat here is just burning.—One big consolation for
me—since I can't burn with the love of God—at least let me burn
with the heat of God—and so I enjoy the heat."[52]

With Archbishop Knox she also shared her joy of opening the
first foundation outside India, in Venezuela. This milestone was a
major step in the life of the new congregation. Though happy that
her long awaited desire was fulfilled, she kept asking for his support
in prayer: "Pray for me—please—I need Our Lord."[53] To Bishop
Picachy she wrote a note hinting again at her pain: "I am trying to
be very brave & cheerful—in spite of what is within me. Pray for
me much & often."[54]

"*Pray for Me—That I Too Be Brave*"

In her letters to Archbishop Knox, Mother Teresa kept informing him about the growth of her young institute, and often added a line alluding to her suffering. "I was longing to speak to you at the airport—but no words would come—the little note you gave me is with me—I read it often—I know you pray."[55] After a week, she wrote from the newly opened house in Venezuela, urging him again, "Pray for me—that I too be brave[56]—I will have many things to tell you when I return."[57]

She shared with Archbishop Knox her joy at being able to help her sisters to love God (while maintaining that she herself could not!), as well as touching incidents from her life with the poor:

> I was sorry not to be able to be at the Mater Dei [College] for the meeting. About 60 Sisters were in retreat—so they had [a] chance to talk to Mother.[58] It is so consoling to help others love God— since I can't do it myself.—What deep, humble gratitude I owe God for what treasures He has given me in my children. . . .
>
> Three days ago we picked up two people eaten alive with worms. The agony of the Cross was on their faces.—How terrible poverty is, if unloved.—After we made them comfortable—you should have seen the change. The old man asked for a cigarette and how beautiful of God—in my bag there were two packets of [the] best cigarettes. A rich man gave them to me that morning in the street. God thought of this old man's longing.
>
> Why do I write all these foolish things to you—when you have so many other great things to be busy with?—Because it is the first article of the creed of our poor.[59]

The "first article of the creed of our poor" was the evidence of God's tender love for each one of them, manifested in the smallest details. She witnessed it daily and could not help marveling at it.

"No Reason to Be Sad"

Mother Teresa's awareness of God's Providence in her ministry and in her own spiritual life helped her through the hard times. "Thank God we don't serve God with our feelings, otherwise I don't know where I would be.—Pray for me,"[60] she wrote to Bishop Picachy. Yet she resisted falling into self-pity. In a letter to Father Neuner, she exhibited this same equanimity:

> Dear Father Neuner,
>
> I was very glad to get your letter—and to see that in spite of your many great things you have to do for the Church of God—you still remember me. You are sad for me—but we really have no reason to be sad. He is the Master.—He can dispose of me as it pleaseth Him alone.—I no longer count.—And yet it hurts so much.—Today I read something in Abbot Marmion, "Suffering With Christ": "when this fire (God's love) comes into contact with imperfection, it produces suffering." There must be so much of nothingness in me and so this fire causes so much pain. . . .
>
> Pray for me.[61]

In humility Mother Teresa continued to think that she still needed purification from her imperfections. In reality, her agonizing and interminable darkness was reparatory rather than purgative. It was a participation in the mission of saving souls; she was following the example of Jesus her Master, and of His Blessed Mother, who suffered immensely, not to be purified from sin, but to save sinners.[62]

In her correspondence with Archbishop Knox, rather than describing the darkness, Mother Teresa expressed her determination in the unrelenting struggle: "Pray for me—that I may kiss 'the hand' that strikes with love and joy.—"[63] At the same time she was grateful for the archbishop's support: "Your letter to me was a great help. Would that in my heart [it] was as hot as it is outside. Pray for me."[64]

Writing to Bishop Picachy she went on alluding to her inner agony: "Pray for me—that I may be able to keep giving with joy."[65] She often just asked for his prayers or reaffirmed her "Yes" to God: "As for myself I have very little if anything to say. I want to do His Holy Will—that is all. Though I scarcely understand it."[66]

Along with the darkness, the cherished memory of the origin of her call also found a place in her confidential correspondence. From Archbishop Knox, for instance, she requested prayers on the twentieth anniversary of the inspiration: "Please pray for me on the 10th Sept. 'The Inspiration day' as the Sisters call it—20 years of Grace, toil and love."[67]

"*I Know This Is Only Feelings*"

As Mother Teresa became busier, her desire to see her spiritual directors often went unanswered. "I wish I was able to come even for a few hours to see you—but the Lord has His own plans & I must accept His will—as you said. Pray for me much."[68] As was now usual when she met either Archbishop Knox or Bishop Picachy or Father Neuner, she remained without words.

L.D.M.

TRAIN TO BOMBAY

24/7/67

Dear Father,

It was very kind of you to come & give me so much of your time—for you have many more souls more worthy of your care and love than mine, which is so small & so empty & so weak.

Forgive me for asking you to come & then telling you nothing.—This shows you how terribly empty my soul is—but I am not afraid.—He has done marvels for me—Holy is His name.[69]—Pray for me that in this darkness I do not light my own light—nor fill this emptiness with my self.—I want with my whole will only Jesus.—

Father, I wanted to tell you—how my soul longs for God— for Him alone, how painful it is to be without Him—how my thoughts are only the Sisters & the Poor.—Is this distraction [or] are these thoughts the cause of my praying?—They are my prayer they are my very life.—I love them as I love Jesus—& now as I do not love Jesus—I do not love them either. I know this is only feelings—for my will is steadfast bound to Jesus & so to the Sisters & the Poor.

You spoke of "the Father" in your instruction.—I could have sat there for a long, long time and just [listened].—Though very little registers within—yet if even for that time only.—

I am very happy the Sisters are in Poona—for they will get much spiritual help and also whenever I come I may be able to see you.—"Selfish motive." There is beautiful work in Poona—& I think much good will be done both to the rich & the poor.

I would be grateful if you let me know of some good books.— When I face our library—I just find it difficult to choose the book I need.

Father, can you explain to me—when you have time—how to grow in the "deep personal union of the human heart with the Heart of Christ." From childhood the Heart of Jesus has been my first love.—Every Friday is the feast of the Sacred Heart for me. I love the Mass of the S H [Sacred Heart]—for in the words of the offertory reecho the words of 10th Sept.—"will you do this for Me." This M.C. [Missionaries of Charity] is only His work.

I only accepted to do it for Him.—I have tried to follow His plan of the Work—to the last word. Every foundation is each time another 10th Sept. for it is His doing. This [is] why I think whatever is said[70] does not register in my soul—because of Him.—Please remember "His Work" on the 10th Sept.—I am sure that once more He will come—before I die—& I will hear His voice.—

Our Sisters in Poona have a holy confessor. I am not afraid for them. They will do great work if they are guided properly.

I will be going to Amravati on the 26th night & from there to Bhopal, Jhansi, Agra, Delhi, Ambala & back home.—Pray for me—that I give Jesus everywhere I go.—If you write please write to Cal. [Calcutta] as I hope to be there the latest about the 10th Aug. . . .

Please pray for me.

Yours in Jesus,
M. Teresa, M.C.[71]

In apologizing again for not being able to speak because of the "emptiness" within, she also revealed her awareness that God, because of the "marvels He had done for her," was somehow at work through it all. Like Mary in her Magnificat,[72] she praised God for His gifts. She did not fear the emptiness itself, but was concerned that it could lead her to turn in on herself and fill the void with something other than God.

Her thirst for Jesus impelled her to seek help in order to grow in "deep personal union of the human heart with the Heart of Christ."[73] Her request to learn more about this "union" takes on added significance in the light of her claim that "from childhood the Heart of Jesus has been my first love."[74] Jesus was Mother Teresa's first love and her only love, in a relationship that grew more intense at each stage of her life. Her heart would be drawn with singular intensity to the Heart of Christ to the very day of her death.[75] One of the best descriptions of Mother Teresa is that she was a woman "totally, passionately, madly in love with Jesus."

"I Have Never Had Doubt"

"Will you do this for Me?" were the words that Jesus had addressed to her in the train to Darjeeling on September 10, 1946. In this encounter with Christ, Mother Teresa received the call and the charism of the Missionaries of Charity. The certainty that this came directly from Jesus and that her work "was only His work" carried her along throughout the years of darkness. Even when she felt as though she had lost her faith in God, she could not question the authenticity of that experience.

A journalist persistently digging into the extraordinary experience of "someone to whom God had personally spoken" inquired: "Were you not for a second in doubt? After all, Christ himself had moments of doubt. In Gethsemane."[76] Mother Teresa responded with conviction:

No. There was no doubt. It was only for a moment that He felt unsure. That was as a human being. That was natural. The moment you accept, the moment you surrender yourself, that's the conviction. But it may mean death to you, eh? The conviction comes the moment you surrender yourself. Then there is no doubt. The moment Jesus said, "Father, I am at your disposal, Thy will be done," He had accepted. That was His agony. He felt all the things you and I would feel as human beings. That's why He was like unto us in all things, except sin.

[If uncertainty remains] that's the time to go on your knees, eh? . . . In that prayer, God cannot deceive you because that prayer comes from within you. That is the time you want Him most. Once you have got God within you, that's for life. There is no doubt. You can have other doubts, eh? But that particular one will never come again. No, I have never had doubt. . . . But I am convinced that it is He and not I. That it is His work, and not my work. I am only at His disposal. Without Him I can do nothing. But even God could do nothing for someone already full. You have to he completely empty to let Him in to do what He will. That's the most beautiful part of God, eh? Being almighty, and yet not forcing Himself on anyone.[77]

"Be the One Who Will Satiate His Thirst"

"My heart hath expected reproach and misery. And I looked for one that would grieve together with me, and there was none: and I sought one that would console me, and I found none," reads the Offertory verse (Ps: 68: 21)[78] used for the Mass of the Feast of the Sacred Heart and Votive Masses of the Sacred Heart outside Easter time. This verse triggered in Mother Teresa's memory her crucial encounter with Jesus on the train and was a permanent challenge for her to "be the one." Years later, on a holy card of *Ecce homo*[79] with the printed words, "I looked for one that would comfort me and I found none," she would write, "Be the one." She loved to look at this image, a reminder of her call, and to give copies to her followers as an incentive to carry on.

She used to exhort her sisters:

Tell Jesus, "I will be the one." I will comfort, encourage and love Him. . . . Be with Jesus. He prayed and prayed, and then He went to look for consolation, but there was none. . . . I always write that sentence, "I looked for one to comfort Me, but I found no one."

Then I write, "Be the one." So now you be that one. Try to be the
one to share with Him, to comfort Him, to console Him. So let
us ask Our Lady to help us understand.[80]

One of the sisters recalled another similar exhortation:

Be the one. . . . be the one who will satiate the Thirst. Instead of
saying "I Thirst" say *"be the one."* . . . do whatever you believe
God is asking you to do to *be the one* to satiate Him.

As every new foundation was for Mother Teresa another September 10, the question *"Will you do this for Me?"* kept resounding
in her heart. How could she refuse? The memory of Jesus' words
gave her the strength to overcome herself and console Him by striving to light the fire of God's love in the heart of every person, in
spite of the terrible darkness within. She longed for Jesus' return
and wanted Him to find her "being the one," comforting Him in the
poorest of His brothers and sisters, since it was in their lives that she
saw His Passion being relived, as she explained to her friend Eileen:

Thank you for your letter of 25/8 [August 25] received.—Your
letter is so beautiful.—Yes, if we only went back to the spirit of
Christ—if we only relived the Eucharistic life, if we only
realised what the Body of Christ is—there would not be so
much suffering—so much of what we have today.—The Passion
of Christ is being relived once more in all its reality.—We must
pray much for the Church—the Church in the world—and the
world in the Church.—Here in India we are still fighting the
famine & then the hard days of food shortage & then the floods
have spread in so many places.—There is so much suffering—so
much misunderstanding—which brings so much hatred & all that
hatred can bring & give.—Thank God our Holy Father made

this year a year of faith.—Really we have never needed so much faith as we need it now.

If all goes well I should be leaving for Africa on the 17th Sept., but as the things are here, I wonder if I will be able to be away from home at this time. You must not grieve for Jim.—He is with God.—We are here to go there—home to God—and there is no unhappiness there, but only shanti—a real "shanti nagar."[81] So why should you be sad—if shanti is his companion now? . . .

Thank God we are in God's hands. He will take care of us—we have now really to trust Him blindly.[82]

"A Deep Longing for God and Death"

Trusting that God's Providence could draw good from any circumstance, Mother Teresa recognized in every suffering an opportunity for spiritual growth. To some friends she wrote:

Your nephew like so many in this hard & sad time of fight for the faith—is going through his purification.—If he only clings to the living Christ—the Eucharist—he will come from his darkness radiant with new light—Christ. . . .

Now you must pray much—as our little Society keeps growing—and we must more & more be His light—His way—His life—His love in the slums.[83]

She appreciated the occasions when she could speak with Father Neuner, though she had no new insights to offer him, only an expression of her ever-stronger determination to go ahead, regardless of the cost.

※ I was grateful to God for giving me the chance of speaking to
you—as I really feel much better.—I know He will never break
His promise if I keep my word to Him. I want to love Him as He
has never been loved before—with a tender, personal, intimate
love. Pray for me.[84]

As her love for God was becoming more ardent, the pain of
being separated from Him was becoming sharper. In this constant
strain, she felt the need for God and for human support. She reminded Bishop Picachy:

※ It is so unlike you not to write for Christmas—also not to answer
letters.—Maybe you were not in Jamshedpur when my letters
came. . . . I do hope you will be coming to Calcutta and then I will
be able to have a good talk. I have such a deep longing for God
and death. . . . Pray for me that I may use the joy of the Lord as
my strength.—[85]

Deep longing for God and deep longing for death were two
sides of the same coin. For her, death was "going home to God."
And now that the yearning for Him was almost unbearable, and the
light at the end of the tunnel was not in sight, she longed for eternity, not to end her sufferings but to be reunited with Him.

"Be Happy for We Share the Passion of Christ"

More than twenty years had passed since Mother Teresa began her
mission among the poor. At this stage, she spoke very little about
her own interior darkness, but never missed the chance to connect
the reality of the human suffering she was facing with the sufferings

of Jesus. Her heart was "one" with His. His wounds were so im-
printed on her soul that they had become hers. She suffered intensely at seeing the sufferings of those she loved, but she kept
highlighting the value and the meaning of human suffering as a
means of sharing in the Passion of Jesus. She wrote in August 1969:

> Keep the light of faith ever burning—for Jesus alone is the way
> that leads to the Father. He alone is the life dwelling in our
> hearts. He alone is the light[86] that enlightens the darkness.[87]
> Be not afraid.—Christ will not deceive us. . . .
>
>   Don't worry about me.—My head[88] does not give trouble at
> all.—Only in the mornings I feel tired—but this is nothing if
> you saw what our poor suffer without any relief . . .
>
>   My heart is full of sorrow because of you all, so dear to me
> and to the Heart of Jesus, have to suffer so much, but be happy
> for we share the Passion of Christ and so through our sharing,
> give the world another proof that Christ is the same yesterday—
> today—tomorrow[89] in His Church.[90]

Jesus' words in St. Matthew's gospel, "whatever you did to the
least . . . you did it to me" were a rock on which her convictions
were built. Knowing that Jesus could not deceive her, she clung to
this word; His presence in the poor remained a beacon in her night.
She wrote to her friend Eileen:

> You write so little of yourself—& yet your heart must be full.—
> But you know—as much as I do—Christ cannot deceive.—
> Therefore whatever we do to the least—we do it to Him.[91] Let
> the joy of the Lord be your strength.[92]—For He alone is the
> way[93] worth following, the light[94] worth lighting,—the life worth
> living,[95]—and the love[96] worth loving. I am longing to see you—
> it seems ages to me since I saw you last. . . .

If we feel like this—I wonder what Jesus must have felt during His agony, when He went through all these unspoken & hidden wounds. . . .

If you only knew how I long to light the fire of love & peace throughout the world.—Pray for me—that He may use me to the full.[97]

She Had Found Her Way

A letter Mother Teresa wrote to Father Neuner in November 1969 indicates that there was not much new in her soul:

☀ Many thanks for your kind thought in remembering me.—Your letter with the words of St. John was beautiful.—And you will I am sure be surprised that the works of St. John of the Cross seem to be books I am able to understand a little & enjoy sometimes.— His writings make me hunger for God—and then faced by that terrible feeling of being "unwanted" by Him.[98]

As there was nothing more to share about her inner state, Mother Teresa could go on without the support of her spiritual guides. During this time, her correspondence with Father Neuner nearly came to a halt. When she did communicate, she wrote about her congregation but hardly a line about herself. Father Neuner himself realized what was going on, as he later remembered:

☀ So I accompanied M. Teresa for many years from a distance, meeting her occasionally in Calcutta. In her letters she often referred to the inner darkness which continued. But I felt she had found her way and did not need my support any longer. So the correspondence came to an end—but the letters I kept as they reflected something of her inner life during these years.[99]

To Bishop Picachy, now the archbishop of Calcutta,[100] she also stopped mentioning her darkness; her letters at this time dealt mostly with practical matters. But in a letter written on December 21, 1969, she did remind him about an important date in her life: "Today in 1948—I went for the first time to the slums—my first meeting with Christ in His distressing disguise. Pray for me."[101]

What a difference between that first day—when she was working as a lone nun in the slums—and the present—when she had a thriving religious community with two branches. In the beginning she had only God's promise to hold on to; twenty-one years later she had almost three hundred sisters in thirty-three communities around the world. She knew that this was God's work. Although Christ seemed to have rejected and forgotten her, she was faithfully and lovingly serving Him in the distressing disguise of the poorest of the poor. And it was through her sufferings that He was bringing them the light of His love.

TWELVE

"God Uses Nothingness to Show His Greatness"

AN INSTRUMENT IN HIS HANDS

*I wonder at His great humility and my smallness—
nothingness.—I believe—this is where Jesus & I
meet.—He is everything to me—and I—His own
little one—so helpless—so empty—so small.*
                                        —Mother Teresa

In 1975 the Missionaries of Charity, numbering
over a thousand sisters in eighty-five foundations
in fifteen countries, celebrated the silver jubilee
of their foundation. The succeeding years would
be marked by the rapid expansion of the congregation throughout the world and the increasing
attention of the world's media on Mother Teresa
and the work she had started in the obscurity of
Calcutta's slums. Though she had made no mention of it for the past six years, the darkness still
had its unrelenting grip on her soul.

It was during this time that Mother Teresa met
Father Michael van der Peet, a member of the

Priests of the Sacred Heart.[1] In October 1975, while walking down the street in Rome, he saw Mother Teresa waiting for a bus with another sister. "My first impulse was to go to her, but I said to myself, 'Leave the woman alone. Everybody is always staring at her.' I walked on, my heart pounding, but suddenly I thought, 'She's a saint and I'm a sinner. Let the sinner go to the saint and ask her to pray for me.'"[2] So he returned. After a short greeting, Mother Teresa, in her usual fashion, asked him to give a conference on prayer to her novices two days later. Following the conference in the convent on the outskirts of Rome, Father van der Peet accepted Mother Teresa's invitation to preach a retreat for her community in November.

"Remember My Face Before Jesus"

Mother Teresa's first letter to Father van der Peet was in fact a note she wrote during that retreat. She professed her emptiness and smallness and questioned the usefulness of seeking spiritual help in this state. Asking for his prayers, she alluded to the private vow that had been carrying her through the agonizing struggle.

> Dear Father Michael,
> God love you for all the love you have given to each one of us.—
>   Keep the joy of giving only Jesus to all who come in touch with you.—
>   I would be grateful if I could turn to you for spiritual help, but I am absolutely too small and empty.—Only Jesus can stoop so low as to be in love with one such as me.
>   Pray for me that "No" does not pass through my heart & lips—when Jesus asks.
>
> *Yours in Jesus,*
> *M. Teresa, M.C.*[3]

Father van der Peet's impressions from this and subsequent meetings with Mother Teresa leave no doubt as to the holiness and union with God that she radiated:

Whenever I met Mother, all self-consciousness left me. I felt right away at ease: she radiated peace and joy, even when she shared with me the darkness in her spiritual life. I was often amazed that someone who lived so much face to face with suffering people and went through a dark night herself, still could smile and make you feel happy.... I believe that I can say that I felt in God's presence, in the presence of truth and love.

I could not help but think: Here is a person God dreamed of in Paradise, truly a touch of God. Yet I have to say at the same time that she was one of the most down-to-earth persons I have ever met.

This practical spirit came to the fore especially in the way she directed her congregation and managed to stay on top of the myriad demands on her time by so many people within and outside her religious family. Yet despite the numerous activities, the frequent travels to visit the increasing number of houses, the growing needs of the poor she witnessed daily, and the persistent interior darkness that troubled her, her fidelity to prayer was categorical:

Dear Father Michael,

Your letter of Christmas and this one of 26/2 [February 26] brought me much joy—for the gift you keep on giving—praying for me. I think I do the same for you.

Forgive me for the delay, I just could not make it.—The whole of Jan. I spent it travelling in the South [of India].—The whole Feb. in Calcutta & round & now again I am going to the South for another 2 weeks to finish the remaining houses.

I make my holy hour with Jesus straight after Mass—so that I get the 2 hours with Jesus before people & Sisters start using me.—I let Him use me first.—

You write so beautifully of nothingness, we—and fullness—God.—And to think that those two are so apart—and yet the humility of God has made it one—Jesus. . . .

Keep the joy of loving only Jesus for you & for me.

Yours in Jesus,
M. Teresa, M.C.[4]

Mother Teresa's uncompromising fidelity to prayer was one virtue that her sisters had observed back when she was in Loreto. Her first followers were struck by it as well. It continued to impress generations of Missionaries of Charity, and in later years the numerous visitors to the chapel of the motherhouse. "People were fascinated just watching Mother pray. They would sit there and watching her be really drawn into this mystery," one of her followers observed. Hearing her loud and clear voice in prayer or seeing her penetrating gaze fix on the tabernacle left an impression of great intimacy with God. Little did they know that she had not enjoyed the fruits of that intimacy for decades.

Indeed, one of the great challenges of the darkness was this absence of a vivid sense of God's presence in prayer; it was something she still longed for. In September 1959 she had written to Jesus at the request of Father Picachy:

I don't pray any longer.—I utter words of community prayers—and try my utmost to get out of every word the sweetness it has to give.—But my prayer of union is not there any longer—I no longer pray.—My soul is not one with You.—[5]

At that time her prayer, which she labeled as "miserably dry & frozen,"[6] proved effective and obtained many graces for others.

A letter reveals one of her ways of praying during these years of impenetrable darkness: "often during Adoration—faces of the people I have met come before me and I remember them to Jesus.—Do this for me as I do for you—remember my face before Jesus."[7]

"So Helpless—So Empty—So Small"

Mother Teresa's letters to Father van der Peet did not depict the details of her interior trial as her writings to her previous spiritual directors had. There were brief allusions, however, in letters that focused more on the work of her community, and these were revealing, as he later recalled:

> [Her letters] reflect many beautiful things, but she also mentioned this emptiness, this darkness. It was not in every letter, but it was definitely a theme that would occur.[8]

The mystery of God's greatness and her nothingness had become a recurrent theme in her speaking and writing. Her smallness, an essential element of the way she related to God and to others, had shaped her way of praying and acting, her very life. She even welcomed the growing publicity from His hand, since in her smallness she neither made any claims nor wished to place any obstacles in the way of His action.

> Dear Father Michael,
> Thank you for your letter of 23/5 [May 23]. It was so good of you to write. I want to write—but I have nothing to say, but that I wonder at His great humility and my smallness—nothingness—I believe this is where Jesus & I meet.—He is everything to me—

and I—His own little one—so helpless—so empty—so small. I am so small that all these things that the people keep pouring at and round me—cannot enter within me. Maybe because of the darkness I do not see.—Maybe He just wants it to be so. I let Him have His way.—I smile at the cardboard box[9] getting filled with all kinds of things—big things most of which I do not understand. But I know that I am being used—only—for & by them so that they proclaim the presence of the poor—& their concern for the poor, & so I accept everything with a smile in their name.—

I am leaving for Rome on the 3rd & will be able to make my retreat with the Nov. [Novices]—& have the profession on the 14th.—I will return to N.Y. [New York] by the 17th as to be able to join the triduum[10] as preparation for the Sacred Heart feast when we hope to begin the new branch "The Sisters of the Word."[11] Pray much for this. It will be lovely if you could make it to be present. . . . I am longing to be back in India—but I know this is where He wants me to be now—& so I accept with a big smile.

I wanted to write a real spiritual letter—but more than this does not come.—

I pray for you that you let Jesus use you without consulting you. Do the same for me.—

> *Yours in Jesus,*
> *M. Teresa, M.C.*[12]

Mother Teresa had reached the point in her life when she no longer ventured to penetrate or question the mystery of her unremitting darkness. She accepted it, as she did everything else that God willed or at least permitted, "with a big smile." Though the pain was deepening as the years went by, she had made friends with it, and had even come to love it.[13]

Aspiring to be completely at God's disposal, she marveled at His humility in using her "nothingness." Her very poverty was her meeting place with God. She was convinced that He used it in order to reach others:

> His ways are so beautiful.—To think that we have God almighty to stoop so low as to love you & me & make use of us—& make us feel that He really needs us.—As I grow older my wonder at His humility grows more and more & I love Him not for what He gives but for what He is—[the] Bread of Life—the hungry One.[14]

"I Want Him . . . Not to Mind Even the Darkness That Surrounds Him in Me"

So empty of self had Mother Teresa become that she spontaneously kept shifting the focus of her letters from herself to Jesus, to His work among the poor or to her community. This attitude was evident not only in her correspondence, but also in her conversation. Her sisters were the first ones to notice it:

> She did everything as she says, "We must keep Him continually in our hearts and minds." I think, wherever she went and whatever she did, she did very consciously, maybe not very ostentatiously but very consciously, to become a bridge between people and God, and to bring them God's salvation and bring them to God. So even in small things that she did, she wanted to talk about [Jesus]; people would say, "After two minutes, she will be on Jesus." So, that was her constant, I would say, red thread through her life.

To be absorbed with Jesus required being forgetful of self, as she explained to her sisters:

> It is only when we realise our nothingness, our emptiness, that God can fill us with Himself. When we become full of God then

we can give God to others, for from the fullness of the heart the mouth speaks.[15]

Mother Teresa's correspondence with Father van der Peet reflected her heart's desire: to love Jesus more deeply in spite of the poverty and littleness she felt.

Dear Father Michael,

I hope all is well with you and that your love for Jesus keeps growing and bringing much fruit. . . .

You must pray much for this that the Society be fully at the disposal of the Church. I enclose the Jesus prayer I wrote for our Sisters.—They are trying to put the music to it.—Maybe you could help them when you go in Aug.

My love for Jesus keeps growing more simple and more, I think, personal.—Like our Poor, I try to accept my poverty of being small, helpless, incapable of great love. But I want to love Jesus with Mary's love, and His Father with Jesus' love.—I know you are praying for me.—I want Him to be at ease with me—not to mind my feelings—as long as He feels alright—not to mind even the darkness that surrounds Him in me—but that in spite of everything Jesus is all to me and that I love no one but only Jesus.—Pray on the 25th.

Yours in Jesus,
M. Teresa, M.C.[16]

By the latter part of the 1970s the distressing thoughts that had been puzzling her in the early 1950s and tormenting her in the 1960s had given way to serenity and peace. In her relationship with Jesus she wanted Him to be at ease with her, not even to mind her feelings. While the painful darkness persisted, a deep joy permeated her words and deeds. She was able to communicate her understanding to others and encourage them to surrender completely, as can be seen in this letter she had written to a priest nearly two years earlier:

Dear Co-worker of Christ,

You had said "Yes" to Jesus—and He has taken you at your word.—The Word of God became Man[17]—Poor.—Your word to God—became Jesus—poor and so this terrible emptiness you experience. God cannot fill what is full.—He can fill only emptiness—deep poverty—and your "Yes" is the beginning of being or becoming empty. It is not how much we really "have" to give—but how empty we are—so that we can receive fully in our life and let Him live His life in us.

In you today—He wants to relive His complete submission to His Father—allow Him to do so. Does not matter what you feel—as long as He feels alright in you. Take away your eyes from your self and rejoice that you have nothing—that you are nothing—that you can do nothing. Give Jesus a big smile—each time your nothingness frightens you.

This is the poverty of Jesus. You and I must let Him live in us & through us in the world.

Cling to Our Lady—for she too—before she could become full of grace—full of Jesus—had to go through that darkness "How could this be done?—" But the moment she said "Yes," she had need to go in haste and give Jesus to John & his family.[18]

Keep giving Jesus to your people not by words but by your example—by your being in love with Jesus—by radiating His holiness and spreading His fragrance of love everywhere you go.

Just keep the joy of Jesus as your strength.—Be happy and at peace.—Accept whatever He gives—and give whatever He takes with a big smile.—You belong to Him—tell Him I am Yours & if you cut me to pieces every single piece will be only all Yours.

Let Jesus be the victim & the priest in you.

I have started going round our houses in India—so I have beautiful time alone with Jesus in the train.

Pray for me as I do for you.

Yours in Jesus,
M. Teresa, M.C.[19]

These words provide a glimpse of the way Mother Teresa lived through these long years of darkness: the unconditional surrender to this painful emptying of self, the effort of letting God live His life in her, the self-forgetfulness in spreading His love to others.

"Keep the Light Jesus Burning"

"Pray for me—that I keep my hand in His hand and walk all the way with Him alone,"[20] Mother Teresa wrote to Cardinal Picachy in June 1976. After almost fifty years, her mother's parting words to her were still stirring her to a loving fidelity to Jesus. Through the thick darkness, she had steadfastly held Jesus' hand and walked alone with Him, resisting the temptation to light her own light. Bravely refusing to give in to her feelings, she followed the path God had traced for her and encouraged others to do the same:

Keep the light, Jesus, burning in you with the oil of your life. The pain of your back—the poverty you feel are drops of oil that keep the light, Jesus, burning & dispelling the darkness of sin everywhere you go. Do not do anything that will increase the pain—just accept with a big smile the little He gives you with great love.[21]

Her long experience of darkness, her sense of rejection, her lone-liness, the terrible and unsatisfied longing for God, each sacrifice and pain had become for her as one more "drop of oil" that she readily offered to God, to keep the lamp—the life of Jesus within her—burning, radiating His love to others and so dispelling the darkness.

"His Tender Concern for Me and My Nothingness"

As the correspondence continued, Father van der Peet rejoiced in the privilege of this exchange with Mother Teresa. "It was a gift from God for which I am most grateful," he later admitted:

> The impression that I got was that I was dealing with a woman who somehow saw God and felt God in the distress of the poor, and a woman who had an incredible faith in light and darkness. She saw the suffering of Christ, but it was not that she was taken up in ecstasy or things like that — that was not part of her life, although people might be tempted to think that. . . . I really believe that the reason Mother Teresa had to undergo so much darkness in her life is that it would bring about a greater identification with the poor."[22]

The darkness as being a means of "greater identification with the poor" was an insight that Mother Teresa had obtained earlier with Father Neuner's guidance. Father van der Peet pointed in the same direction, thereby helping Mother Teresa to have confidence in him. Her contact with him was also God's gift to her, offering her one more proof of His tender love, a confirmation of His care in the midst of her abiding interior trial.

L.D.M.

Dear Father Michael,

By now you must have received the note I sent you & the book.—
Since then I have had to come to Rome on some urgent work . . .

You ask the question why Jesus wanted you to meet me that
day in Rome.—We have received much from accepting to meet—
without being consulted or prepared. I do not know how He does
with you—but with me He always does so—just to make me
realize His tender concern for me and my nothingness—His
fullness and my emptiness—His infinite love and my childlike
love. Let not your infidelity [to spiritual exercises and daily
religious duties] & hesitancy, as you say, preoccupy you—but
accept all that He gives, and give whatever He takes with a big
smile. For this is holiness—to do His will with a big smile.

I am very happy you visited the Sisters at Union Ave[23]—I
feel Jesus will use them for [the] greater glory of His Father.—It
is good that the cross takes us to Calvary and not to a sitting
room.—The Cross—the Calvary has been very real for some
time. It no longer hurts me the hurt, but the hurt the person
hurts herself with in doing so. I understand better what Jesus said
to St. Margaret Mary of the pain He felt from those who were
His own— . . .

The days in U.S., especially in Philadelphia,[24] were so full
of sacrifice. I was really living "The Mass."—It was all one act of
blind obedience.—I began to understand the Stations of the
Cross with a deeper meaning. The police, the crowds, it all seemed
as if Calvary [was] today being re-enacted all over again.—Jesus
gave one very big grace—to accept everything with a big smile.

The other day a young priest spoke of how the MC are the
witness of God's existence—and if He did not exist, our work

would have no meaning at all, & how the MC have made his faith alive & fruitful.

Next time you write, please send the Jesus prayer & the music as in Mother House we don't have it.—More & more I begin to learn why Jesus wants us to learn from Him to be meek and humble of heart. For because without meekness we can never be able to accept others nor love the other as He loves us.—And so before we learn humility, without which we cannot love God— we have to learn to love each other.—We need meekness & humility to be able to eat the Bread of life.—We need meekness & humility if we want to feed Him in the hungry One. I would be happy if you wrote about the hunger of man and the Bread of life, the hunger of God and the Hungry One in the distressing disguise of the Poor.

At the Mother House since we have 10 groups of Sisters, 8 novices & 2 professed we have 10 hours of Adoration in two chapels. Here lies our strength and our joy. . . .

I will not ask you to pray for me for I know you pray for me.—But I ask you to tell Jesus—when at your word the Bread becomes His Body and the wine becomes His Blood[25]—to change my heart—[to] give me His own Heart—so that I can love Him as He loves me. Happy & holy Christmas—in case I am not able to write.

Yours in Jesus,
M. Teresa, M.C.[26]

Mother Teresa did not mention her darkness in this letter, but the fruits of this experience were evident. The "meekness & humility of the Heart of Jesus"[27] that she had been trying to imitate for years could be seen in the way she lived. God's tender love and concern that touched her each time anew, had mellowed her iron will, not lessening her determination but enriching it with tenderness. She was childlike in her love and in her life. A few years earlier she had written to Malcolm Muggeridge, encouraging him in his spiritual struggle:

I think I understand you better now.—I am afraid I could not answer to your deep suffering— . . . I don't know why but you to me are like Nicodemus[28] & I am sure the answer is the same— "Unless you become a little child."[29] I am sure you will understand beautifully everything—if you would only "become" a little child in God's hands.

Your longing for God is so deep and yet He keeps Himself away from you.—He must be forcing Himself to do so—because He loves you so much—as to give Jesus to die for you & for me.— Christ is longing to be your Food.[30] Surrounded with fullness of living food, you allow yourself to starve.—The personal love Christ has for you is infinite.—The small difficulty you have re His Church is finite.—Overcome the finite with the infinite.— Christ has created you because He wanted you. I know what you feel—terrible longing—with dark emptiness—& yet He is the one in Love with you.[31]

Mother Teresa indeed knew that "terrible longing—with dark emptiness." While wanting to be aflame with love, all she felt was icy cold darkness. Nonetheless, she had embraced her state with childlike simplicity and confidence. It was this same childlikeness that helped her encourage Father van der Peet not to be troubled with his infidelities and hesitancy.

Being a public figure was a real suffering—a "Calvary"—for Mother Teresa and she struggled mightily to overcome her natural feelings. Yet her smile, a "cloak" that covered this pain, too, prevented others from sensing what living in the spotlight cost her. To smile required an effort, as she explained during a speech in 1977 with her characteristic humor:

I remember some time ago a very big group of professors came from the United States and they asked, "Tell us something that will help us." And I said, "Smile at each other." I must have said it in a very serious way, I suppose, and so one of them asked me, "Are you married?" And I said, "Yes, and I sometimes find it very difficult to smile at Jesus because He can be very demanding."[32]

People flocked to her, attracted by her kindness and simplicity; for everyone she had time, a word, a smile. She was able to provide solace, because it was Jesus she wanted to give to all:

Pray—I must be able to give only Jesus to the world. People are hungry for God. What [a] terrible meeting [it] would be with our neighbour if we give them only ourselves.[33]

Sorrow, Suffering, Loneliness Are "a Kiss of Jesus"

An important way Mother Teresa helped people encounter God was by helping them discover His presence in the midst of their suffering. She shared with her friend Eileen Egan one of the insights on suffering she had obtained from her reading:[34]

Sorrow, suffering, Eileen, is but a kiss of Jesus—a sign that you have come so close to Jesus that He can kiss you.—I think this is the most beautiful definition of suffering.—So let us be happy when Jesus stoops down to kiss us.—I hope we are close enough that He can do it.[35]

With similar words she encouraged one of her sisters as well:

Suffering, pain—failure—is but a kiss of Jesus, a sign that you
have come so close to Jesus on the Cross that He can kiss you.—
So my child be happy. . . . Do not be discouraged . . . so smile
back . . . For you it is a most beautiful chance of becoming fully &
totally all for Jesus.[36]

To her followers she further explained, "Your parents must have
kissed you as a real sign of love. If I am the spouse of Jesus crucified,
He has to kiss me. Naturally, the nails will hurt me. If I come close
to the crown of thorns it will hurt me."[37]

Seeking to use every means to bring Jesus' love to all and thus
build a happier world, she counseled even the sick to take part in this
effort: "I know you are no longer able to travel, but keep it up wherever you are—& use the pen whenever you can.—We must fill the
world with [the] love & compassion of Jesus and overcome all hatred & darkness."[38]

"Let the People Eat You Up"

While encouraging others in their struggle, Mother Teresa also felt
the need to seek help and prayers. In June 1977 she wrote to Father
van der Peet, "My prayer is very close to you.—I do hope you will
keep me close to you in your prayer—and love Jesus for me—for all
the times when my heart is cold and empty."[39] Some months later,
after Father Michael had informed her about his upcoming retreat,
she took the opportunity to write again:

Dear Father Michael,
By the time this letter comes to you—maybe you will be "alone
with Jesus" [in retreat]. It is just like you to ask to spend the 3
months with Jesus alone.—But if during this time the hunger for

Jesus in the hearts of His people is greater than yours for Jesus, you should not remain alone with Jesus for all the time. You must allow Jesus to make you bread to be eaten by all those you come in touch with. Let the people eat you up.—By the Word & presence you proclaim Jesus.

I will be in St. Louis on the 21st April for the "Religious Life" meetings.—I wish you would be there. We could maybe have adoration everyday and so bring and weave our lives with the Bread of Life.—No greater love not even God could give than in giving Himself as Bread of life—to be broken, to be eaten so that you & I may eat & live—may eat and so satisfy our hunger for love.—And He seemed yet not satisfied for He too was hungry for love.—So He made Himself the Hungry One, the Thirsty One, the Naked One, the Homeless [One] and kept on calling—I was hungry, naked, homeless. You did it to Me.[40]—The Bread of life and the Hungry One—but one love—only Jesus. His humility is so wonderful. I can understand His majesty, His greatness because He is God—but His humility is beyond my understanding, because He makes Himself Bread of Life so that even a child as small as I can eat Him and live.—Some days back—when giving Holy Communion to our Sisters in the Mother house, suddenly I realized I was holding God between my 2 fingers. The greatness of [the] humility of God. Really no greater love—no greater love than the love of Christ.[41]—You, I am sure, must feel often like that when at your word in your hands—the bread becomes the Body of Christ, the wine becomes the Blood of Christ.—How great must be your love for Christ.—No greater love—than the love of the priest for Christ his Lord & God.

I am on my way back from Manila where I have opened a novitiate. . . . Then on the night of the 2nd Feb. we had a five days retreat.—The priest cleaned our souls from all sin—and then gave only Jesus.—The day of the confession I told all my sins—and Jesus took all my sins.—After confession I heard my heart singing—Thank you, Jesus, for taking my sins. He really just took them all away. There is such a wonderful spirit in the new novitiate.—Maybe someday you could give them a retreat & I hope I will be there to make it with them. . . .

I am on my way back to Calcutta for the 8 days retreat we begin on the 19th evening . . . so I will have a number of days alone with Jesus & so will share your joy.—I am at His disposal— He can do with me just as it pleaseth Him, without even a thought of consulting me. I just want to be His own little one—if He so wants, otherwise I will be happy to be just nothing & He everything.

Pray for me.

> *Yours in Jesus,*
> *M. Teresa, M.C.*[42]

With these words, Mother Teresa was witnessing to the reality of God's presence within her. From her darkness she was giving light. She could not stop marveling at God's actions and being captivated by His love. Whether she was considered or seemingly overlooked by God did not matter any longer.

Though she could sense Jesus' presence neither in her heart nor in the Eucharist, she clung to Him in faith with all her might. She wondered at "the greatness of [the] humility of God" not only in making Himself the "Bread of life" to meet her hunger for His love, but also in making Himself present in the distressing disguise of the poorest of the poor. In serving them, in feeding them, she could in turn serve Him, feed Him, and so express her love.

Her profoundly Eucharistic spirituality was as mystical as it was practical. She believed that "our life must be woven with the Eucharist." From her realization that God gives Himself totally to man in the Eucharist sprang her desire to give herself totally to Him in serving others. She placed a radical demand on herself and her sisters: "we have no right to refuse our lives to others in whom we contact Christ."[43] And she insisted:

> Let the poor and the people eat you up. . . . Let the people "bite" your smile, your time. You sometimes might prefer not to even look at somebody when you had some misunderstanding. Then, not only you look, but give a smile. . . . Learn by heart you must let the people eat you up.[44]

Her sisters noticed how deeply she lived her own teaching. One of them remembered: "She never thought of herself but always thought of others. Her ill health did not stop her from being available to the poor. 'Let the people eat you up.' Mother lived this sentence to the full till the end of her life."

"Not I Live, but Christ Lives in Me"

Mother Teresa's correspondence with her spiritual guides during these years reflects the genuine simplicity and selflessness she had arrived at. Her focus remained Jesus and His work:

> Thank you for your understanding love.—I think your coming gave this gift. Thank you for explaining in life the poverty of Jesus—the mystery of God's love. Yes, I want to be poor like Jesus—who being rich became poor for love of us.[45] Thank you for explaining so simply—Not I live but Christ lives in me.[46]
>
> Thank you for praying for me.—I need to pray—I want to pray—I try to pray. God's love for the Society has been so wonderful.—This year we have made 11 new foundations.—How

great is His humility to allow Himself to be used in such a way. So many new tabernacles—so many daily Adoration hours.[47]

"I have been crucified with Christ; it is no longer I who live, but Christ who lives in me; and the life I now live in the flesh I live by faith in the Son of God, who loved me and gave himself for me,"[48] St. Paul wrote. These words describe well the reality of Mother Teresa's union with God: Christ was indeed living and acting in her, spreading His love in the world. She often stated, "God still loves the world through you and through me today,"[49] and she was letting Him do it.

In every new "tabernacle," as she called a new foundation, she saw "a great gift of God to the world which is dying for God & His love—& yet does not want God."[50] Each convent was another shrine where the sisters, nourished with the "Bread of life," were spurred on to go in search of the "hungry Christ" hidden in the poorest of the poor and offer Him humble service. Prayer and service flowed from the same contemplation of Jesus' presence under these two "disguises." For this reason, Mother Teresa never tired of repeating, "We are not social workers. We are contemplatives in the heart of the world. We are 24 hours a day with Jesus."[51]

Mary was Mother Teresa's model not only in her prayer and service, but also in every aspect of her life. A note of thanks to Cardinal Picachy gives a glimpse of her relationship with Our Lady:

The fidelity to the Rosary will bring many souls to God. [The statue of] Our Lady of Fatima is for your table.—I know how much you love Our Lady. Often I pray to her for you—and the little bird[52]—will remind you to pray for me.—This is where I want to be—at her feet.

Thank you for all the love and care you have always shown for our young Society—for the spiritual guidance you have given me for so many years.—Pray for me and with me—that I may become only all for Jesus.[53]

"Helpless Yet Daring"

With her characteristic modesty, Mother Teresa considered herself still far from the union with Jesus that she wished to reach. Her letters to Father van der Peet revealed more her humility than her suffering:

Dear Fr. Michael,

Forgive the long silence. I have received all your 3 letters. Your love for Jesus is so wonderful, so full of Mary's pure love. I thank God and especially Our Lady for loving Jesus in you and, through you, all the people you come in touch with through your retreats. Last year we celebrated the silver jubilee of Jesus[54] by giving Him 25 tabernacles. Beirut was the 25th foundation. I just understand less and less the humility of God made man for love of us. . . .

I know you pray much for me—I need Jesus' love.

Let us pray—

God bless you,
M. Teresa, M.C.[55]

Several months later, she wrote again:

Dear Fr. Michael,

Your letter of May 28 was waiting for me and I believe somebody has already written to you. . . .

Please pray to Fr. Leo Dehon[56] for our Society—especially during these coming days when we are preparing for our Chapter.

We shall have the Ch. Gen. [Chapter General] on the 21st Nov. Ask Our Lady to take care of our Society—which was born at her pleading and grew under her care.—I would love to be just a simple Sister.—I will not ask.—Let Jesus do whatever He wills without consulting me, for I belong to Him.—

I felt so bad on the day of the profession to have left you & the others.—It was really an act of perfect obedience to have to go with the Cardinal to the meeting re the boat people. The sea has become an open Calvary where the Passion of Christ is being relived. We have not been able to take any of them in India. In Manila our home for the sick and dying had a few suffering people.—You only wonder how people can suffer so much and never break. Looking at them I feel physical pain right in my heart.— The profession was really something beautiful for God—and now we have a Contemplative MC Community—a gift of God.

How happy you must be to have this wonderful gift of giving Jesus to souls through your retreats. How good your Sup. [Superiors] have been to have given you the permission to do so.

Jesus has a very special love for you—for you are so totally His that you live—not you—but Jesus lives in you and through you He proves His love for the world. As for me—the silence and the emptiness is so great that I look and do not see, listen and do not hear.—The tongue moves but does not speak.—Helpless yet daring.—I want you to pray for me—that I let Him have [a] free hand—and even if He chooses to cut me to pieces, that every single piece, however small, be only His.—

At the M.H. [Motherhouse] we have over 300 novices so beautiful so full of joy.—It does one good to just look at them and enjoy the gift of God, their love.—I know you pray for me.— Ask Our Lady to take care of me as she took [care] of Jesus.

God bless you,
M. Teresa, M.C.[57]

Seeing people suffer horribly daily, Mother Teresa pondered, "how people can suffer so much and never break?"

The same question could be put to her: How could she suffer so much and not break? She looked and listened but neither saw nor heard the One she sought. Only darkness and silence were there to make her loneliness painful and frightening. Yet in her "helplessness" she was truly "daring," for she was as determined as ever to "let Him have [a] free hand" with her.

She did not break, but, even more, she was joyful in her suffering. Given what is now known of her interior state her habitual cheerfulness proves all the more extraordinary, as a senior sister observed:

Mother always told us: "God loves a cheerful giver.[58] If you don't go to the people with a cheerful face, you only increase their darkness and their miseries and their sorrows." So Mother had the spiritual joy. . . . It is overwhelming for us to think how Mother could continue with a pleasant countenance and with such single-mindedness to cling to Jesus her one and only love, without her letting us ever know what she was going through.

Because she bore her own suffering and pain in silence and peace, she could effectively encourage others to walk the same path. Whatever failure or disappointment she or others faced, she always found a way to look at it from God's perspective and to draw good out of it.

I know what you feel—this [is] really the full meaning of the poverty of Jesus. He being rich became poor.[59] The riches of the company of His Father He gave up by becoming man like us in all things except sin.[60]—You too are experiencing that "giving up" for love of Him. Do not be afraid.—All will be well.—The seed has to die—if it has to produce fruit.[61]—I am more than sure that Jesus wants the M.W. [Missionary Brothers of the Word] by all means to exist—& this aloneness is the beginning of great love. You are not alone—"Jesus and you." [The] Tabernacle is the most beautiful sign for you to look at when you feel lonely. Don't be afraid.—He is there—in spite of the darkness & failure.—It was like that for Jesus in the garden—"Could you not watch one hour?"[62] He felt so lonely that night. Don't be afraid. Put your hand in Our Lady's hand and walk with her.—[63]

Mother Teresa willingly accepted being deprived of "the riches of the company" of Jesus so that others would know the delight of it. From her own experience of loneliness, disappointment, darkness, and poverty, she could reassure her sisters of Christ's presence in the midst of sufferings:

The Will of the Father was that terrible loneliness in the Garden [of Gethsemane], on the Cross.—He was completely alone. If we are true followers of Jesus, we too must experience the loneliness of Christ.—He perspired blood.[64]—It was so difficult for Him to go through the humiliation of His Passion.[65]

"You Did It to Me"

In November 1979, at the fourth general chapter of the Missionaries of Charity, Mother Teresa was again elected superior general. Though she had been longing to be "a simple sister in the community," she accepted this decision as the will of God.

Shortly after, on December 11, 1979, Mother Teresa received the Nobel Peace Prize. By now, she had learned that "Calcutta is everywhere." Just as in the three visions she had had in 1947, she had been led to understand progressively deeper levels of poverty—material, social, and spiritual—so in her mission among the poor she was led progressively to identify and address not only material poverty but also the forms of poverty, that exist as well among the rich in affluent countries.

It was about her poor that she spoke to her attentive audience when accepting the Nobel Peace Prize, challenging all present to look for those who lived the agonizing poverty of being unwanted, unloved, or uncared for by their own. Beginning at home, loving and caring for each one, everyone could be a "missionary of charity," she said. Through humble love and service, they could discover the face of Jesus under the distressing disguise of the needy.

[Jesus] makes Himself the hungry one, the naked one, the homeless one, the sick one, the one in prison, the lonely one, the unwanted one, and he says: "You did it to me."[66] He is hungry for our love, and this is the hunger of our poor people. This is the hunger that you and I must find, it may be in our own home. . . .

    I . . . [visited] a home where they had all these old parents. . . . I saw in that home they had everything . . . but everybody was looking towards the door. . . . And I turned to the sister and I asked: . . . "How is it that these people who have everything here, why are they all looking towards the door, why are they not smiling?" I am so used to the smiles on our people, even the dying ones smile. And she said: "This is nearly every day. . . . They are hoping that a son or daughter will come to visit them. They are hurt because they are forgotten." . . . This is where love comes. . . . Maybe in our own family we have somebody who is feeling lonely, who is feeling sick, who is feeling worried. . . . Are we there to receive them? . . .

    I was surprised in the West to see so many young boys and girls given into drugs, and I tried to find out why. . . . "Because there is no one in the family to receive them." Father and mother are so busy they have no time. . . . The child goes back to the street and gets involved in something. . . . These are things that break peace.

But I feel the greatest destroyer of peace today is abortion, because it is a direct war, a direct killing, direct murder by the mother herself. And we read in the Scripture, for God says very clearly: "Even if a mother could forget her child, I will not forget you. I have carved you in the palm of my hand."[67] . . . That unborn child has been carved in the hand of God. . . .

Many people are very, very concerned with children in India, with the children of Africa where quite a number die, maybe of malnutrition, of hunger and so on, but millions are dying deliberately by the will of the mother. And this is what is the greatest destroyer of peace today. Because if a mother can kill her own child, what is left for me to kill you and you to kill me? There is nothing between. . . . Let us ensure this year that we make every single child born, and unborn, wanted. . . . Have we really made the children wanted? . . .

We picked up [a man] from the drain, half eaten with worms, and we brought him to the home: "I have lived like an animal in the street, but I am going to die like an angel, loved and cared for." And it was so wonderful to see the greatness of that man who could speak like that, who could die like that without blaming anybody, without cursing anybody, without comparing anything. Like an angel—this is the greatness of our people.

And that is why we believe what Jesus has said: "I was hungry, I was naked, I was homeless, I was unwanted, unloved, uncared for—and you did it to me."[68]

Mother Teresa had great sympathy for those who felt rejected and unwanted: the forgotten parents left in an old people home, the lonely youth whose family did not care for him or her, and very especially, the unborn child. "I find the unborn child to be the poorest of the poor today—the most unloved—the most unwanted, the throw away of the society."[69] She fought to defend the precious gift of life and it became one of the recurrent themes of her speeches.

> But what does God say to us? He says, "Even if a mother could forget her child, I will not forget you. I have carved you in the palm of my hand." We are carved in the palm of His hand; that unborn child has been carved in the hand of God from conception and is called by God to love and to be loved, not only now in this life, but forever. God can never forget us.[70]

Mother Teresa realized that the Nobel Peace Prize had "helped many people to find the way to the poor,"[71] and it prompted her to ask for prayer for greater love and zeal in serving the poor. "Keep praying that we do not spoil God's work—but that through us and in us—and with us and our poor, God's love and compassion be proclaimed,"[72] she wrote to Father Neuner. Speaking to her own sisters, she explained, "The work is God's work and not our work, that is why we must do it well. How often we spoil God's work and try to get the glory for ourselves."[73] This possibility frightened her, and she prayed constantly to be protected from this presumption. In this challenge, the awareness of her nothingness was her protection, as Father van der Peet later testified:

> I felt enough at home with Mother Teresa as to ask her some personal questions like: "Wherever you go, people follow you like a movie star. You have received all those prestigious awards. The Holy Father treasures you, You met with Indira Gandhi, Queen Elizabeth, President and Nancy Reagan. . . . How do you handle that kind of admiration?" In our different conversations she had various answers to that. The most beautiful one I remember was:

"Father, Jesus has given me a very great grace and that is: the deepest conviction of my total nothingness. If He could find a poorer woman through whom to do his work, He would not choose me, but He would choose that woman." Another answer was (and she often smiled when she said those things): "I am too small to understand it all" or "Father, it goes in here (pointing to her ears) and it comes out there; it goes right through me." Another reaction . . . to all the admiration of people: "It is true crucifixion."

A Much Greater Disease Is to Be Unwanted, Unloved

In October 1980, Mother Teresa was invited to attend the Synod of Bishops. From Rome she wrote to Father van der Peet:

Dear Fr. Michael,

Your letter has come with me right up to the Synod.—Thank you.—God love you.—Forgive the long delay in writing. A bishop told me that I will spend my purgatory in writing letters—because I am so bad in answering.—However long purgatory may be—there is the beautiful hope of seeing Jesus one day.

You must be alone with Jesus [in retreat] in Canada by now—and I am sure you must be praying for me—for can you imagine me in the Synod with all the big people of the Church. I had to speak—and I asked the Holy Father to give us holy priests if he wants families to be holy. Many of the Bishops said "Thank you." Jesus once more He did it—in His own way.

Your beautiful letter so full of Jesus has been a gift of Jesus to me. Christ's love is stronger than all that we have or are. Let us grow more and more in the likeness of Christ—so that all we meet—when they look up see only Jesus in us and through us.

I find this little prayer a great help, "Jesus in my heart, I believe in your faithful love for me. I love you." or "In union with all the Masses being offered throughout the world I offer Thee my heart. Make it meek & humble like yours." Pray this prayer for me sometimes—for I ask for this only—that my heart be like His meek & humble. . . .

Pray much for me—as I do for you.

Let us keep the joy of loving Jesus in our hearts and share this joy with all we meet.

> *Yours in Jesus,*
> *M. Teresa, M.C.*[74]

The assurance that "Christ's love is stronger than all that we have or are" had helped her not to succumb to the interior darkness and the pain of nothingness. It was in this state, when she felt that in her heart there was "no faith—no love—no trust"[75] that she had formulated the prayer "Jesus in my heart, I believe in your faithful love for me. I love you." Later she would alter the prayer by replacing "faithful" with "tender."

Though Mother Teresa felt uneasy about addressing "big people" at the Synod, she was convinced that Jesus was using her to proclaim God's great love for His poor. Her simple but eloquent message was a summary of what she had been living for thirty years. Through her interior darkness, she was well acquainted with the feelings of being unwanted, unloved, uncared for; and she knew that this deep pain was far worse than any physical disease. In her address, she pointed especially to loneliness as a new kind of poverty:

Recently, a man met me on the street. He said: "Are you Mother Teresa?" I said, "yes." He said: "Please send somebody to my house. My wife is half mental and I am half blind. But we are longing to hear the loving sound of a human voice." They were well-to-do people. They had everything in their home. Yet they were dying of loneliness, dying to hear a loving voice.

How do we know some one like that is not next to our house? Do we know who they are, where they are? Let us find them and, when we find them, love them. Then when we love them we will serve them.

Today God loves the world so much that He gives you, He gives me, to love the world, to be His love, His compassion. It is such a beautiful thought for us—and a conviction—that you and I can be that love and compassion.

Do we know who our own poor are? Do we know our neighbor, the poor of our own area? It is so easy for us to talk and talk about the poor of other places. Very often we have the suffering, we have the lonely, we have the people—old, unwanted, feeling miserable—and they are near us and we don't even know them. We have no time even to smile at them.

Tuberculosis and cancer [are] not the great diseases. I think a much greater disease is to be unwanted, unloved. The pain that these people suffer is very difficult to understand, to penetrate. I think this is what our people all over the world are going through, in every family, in every home.

This suffering is being repeated in every man, woman and child. I think Christ is undergoing his Passion again. And it is for you and for me to help them—to be Veronica,[76] to be Simon[77] to them.

Our poor people are great people, a very lovable people. They don't need our pity and sympathy. They need our understanding love and they need our respect. We need to tell the poor that they are somebody to us, that they, too, have been created, by the same loving hand of God, to love and be loved.[78]

In this very suffering, her own and that of her poor, Mother Teresa recognized Christ once again reliving His Passion in His distressing disguise. At the beginning of her work among the poorest of the poor, she had exhorted her little band of followers to "find Jesus in the dark holes of the slums, in the most pitiful miseries of the poor."[79] Now she found Him as well in the loneliness of the well-to-do.

"Whose Thirst Is Greater, His or Mine for Him"

With a faith penetrating through the darkness of pain, Mother Teresa could move beyond appearances and perceive the face of God. This contemplation of Jesus' Passion, relived in the poor and in her own heart, had led her to a keener understanding and experience of His thirst. In December of 1980 she wrote to Father Neuner:

> I am really very happy to know that you are close to me in your prayer. I think this is the strength I continually need.—During this year I have had many opportunities to satiate the Thirst of Jesus for love—for souls. It has been a year filled with [the] Passion of Christ.—I do not know whose Thirst is greater, His or mine for Him.[80]

In 1980, because of the large number of Missionaries of Charity communities spread throughout the world, the decision was made to divide the houses into twelve regions. A corresponding regional superior was appointed to assist Mother Teresa in the governance of the congregation. The work for the poor was flourishing and twelve more foundations were opened that year. Yet she wrote to Father Neuner: "It has been a year filled with [the] Passion of Christ."[81]

Father Neuner would probably have taken her statement as referring primarily to her darkness. Besides her interior plight, however, she was also pointing to the painful realization that not all her followers were fully living up to their lofty vocation. Jesus was not being loved and served in the poor as ardently as she longed for Him to be. In addition, there were failures in the sisters' love for each other. All these deficiencies hurt her deeply, yet she gave no inkling of this pain in her letter to Father Neuner. But to her sisters, letter after letter carried the same message:

> My dearest children,
> This brings you Mother's love and blessing—but especially the joy of the assurance that Jesus loves you, and I only ask you to love one another as Jesus loves each one of you—for in loving one another you only love Jesus. . . .[82]

Or again:

> This brings you Mother's love, blessing and prayer for each one of you, that you may more and more grow in the likeness of Christ through meekness and humility, so that your Sisters in the community and the poor you serve feel His presence and His love in you and through you, and learn from you how to love Jesus in each other.[83]

Since her journeys were more frequent and demanding, Mother Teresa felt that she was not giving enough time to her sisters when they needed her most. For that reason, she asked the pope for permission to be released from public engagements. She conveyed his reply to her sisters:

> After Holy Father gave a big speech to the people, I said, "Holy Father, I want to see you five minutes." He sat there; I sat there at his feet. He had his arms crossed with his head in his

arms like this looking down at me. He said, "You got problems."
I said, "Holy Father, I am finding it very difficult. I have so many
Sisters, 342 at the Mother House now in India, they need me
and I need them, and now this continual calling.[84] It is your will,
I know, whatever you say I will do, but what do you want me to
do?" He said, "Continue doing what you are doing. Do not refuse
Jesus. You have never refused Him before, do not refuse Him
now. I will pray for you and give you the answer the next time I
see you." Just like that, simply like a child. Holy Father's words to
me, "Do not refuse Jesus."[85]

The Holy Father eventually sent the word: "Give necessary
care to the sisters and loving care to the poor and people." Mother
Teresa remarked, "See Sisters, for Mother it is not easy." And it was
truly not easy to give less time to her sisters and go out to the world.
Yet she chose "not to refuse Jesus," who had challenged her, this
time through His representative on earth. It was "real blind obedience," she affirmed. She wrote to Cardinal Picachy a special request:
"When you see Holy Father—ask him to pray for me—as this time
obedience is a Sacrifice."[86]

With the blessing of obedience, Mother Teresa continued her
mission of service to the world's poor. She, a docile instrument in
God's hand, was letting Him use her nothingness to show His greatness. She was embodying the prayer[87] that for her expressed the goal
of a Missionary of Charity: to spread His fragrance everywhere she
went, to be His radiance, His light, and to be "only Jesus" to each
person she met. In all this, she was satiating His thirst for love and
souls.

THIRTEEN

Radiating Christ

NO LONGER ME, BUT ONLY JESUS

The joy of loving Jesus comes from the joy of sharing in His sufferings. So do not allow yourself to be troubled or distressed, but believe in the joy of the Resurrection. In all of our lives, as in the life of Jesus, the Resurrection has to come, the joy of Easter has to dawn.
—Mother Teresa

The last two decades of Mother Teresa's life were a period of intense activity, even as her health deteriorated. Endowed with an extraordinary energy, she traversed the world proclaiming the good news of God's love and of His presence in the poorest of the poor. Her love and zeal for God and souls was boundless and inspired her to make numerous foundations all over the world. Her presence and words had such influence that in 1985 she was called the most powerful woman in the world by the Secretary General of the United Nations, Javier Perez de Cuellar. Yet the terrible darkness remained.

Jesus Is . . . the Light I Light

Nothing could impede her from spreading the light of God's love in the most troubled places of the world. In August 1982 she ventured to war torn Lebanon and from there wrote to her sisters:

> We have just left Beirut.—It has been one continual action of God loving us and His people—by continual love actions in tenderness and love.—I brought a big Easter candle with the image of Our Lady with the child on it.—On Thursday the bombing was terrible.—I lit the candle that evening about 4 p.m.—At 5 p.m. all stopped [all] of a sudden.—Since then there is perfect quiet.— We went over and brought 38 crippled and mental little children.—The candle finished last night.—If you have the Easter candle, please light it before Our Lady in thanksgiving— the rest I will tell you when I return.[1]

While on visitation in Rome in 1983 she fell out of bed and was hospitalized. A serious heart condition was providentially discovered. While in the hospital, Mother Teresa wrote her intimate response to Jesus' query in Matthew 16:15: "Who do you say that I am?"

> *You are God.*
> *You are God from God.*
> *You are Begotten, not made.*
> *You are One in Substance with the Father.*
> *You are the Son of the Living God.*

You are the Second Person of the Blessed Trinity.

You are One with the Father.
You are in the Father from the beginning:
All things were made by You and the Father.
You are the Beloved Son in Whom the
Father is well pleased.
You are the Son of Mary,
conceived by the Holy Spirit in the womb of Mary.

You were born in Bethlehem.
You were wrapped in swaddling clothes by Mary
and put in the manger full of straw.
You were kept warm by the breath of the donkey
that carried Your mother with You in her womb.
You are the Son of Joseph,
the Carpenter, as known by the people of Nazareth.
You are an ordinary man without much learning,
as judged by the learned people of Israel.

WHO IS JESUS TO ME?
Jesus is the Word made Flesh.
Jesus is the Bread of Life.
Jesus is the Victim offered for our sins on the Cross.
Jesus is the Sacrifice offered at the Holy Mass
for the sins of the world and mine.
Jesus is the Word—to be spoken.
Jesus is the Truth—to be told.
Jesus is the Way—to be walked.
Jesus is the Light—to be lit.
Jesus is the Life—to be lived.
Jesus is the Love—to be loved.

Jesus is the Joy—to be shared.
Jesus is the Sacrifice—to be offered.
Jesus is the Peace—to be given.
Jesus is the Bread of Life—to be eaten.
Jesus is the Hungry—to be fed.
Jesus is the Thirsty—to be satiated.
Jesus is the Naked—to be clothed.
Jesus is the Homeless—to be taken in.
Jesus is the Sick—to be healed.
Jesus is the Lonely—to be loved.
Jesus is the Unwanted—to be wanted.
Jesus is the Leper—to wash his wounds.
Jesus is the Beggar—to give him a smile.
Jesus is the Drunkard—to listen to him.
Jesus is the Retarded—to protect him.
Jesus is the Little One—to embrace him.
Jesus is the Blind—to lead him.
Jesus is the Dumb—to speak for him.
Jesus is the Crippled—to walk with him.
Jesus is the Drug Addict—to befriend him.
Jesus is the Prostitute—to remove from danger and befriend.
Jesus is the Prisoner—to be visited.
Jesus is the Old—to be served.

TO ME—
Jesus is my God.
Jesus is my Spouse.
Jesus is my Life.
Jesus is my only Love.
Jesus is my All in All.
Jesus is my Everything.

Jesus, I love with my whole heart, with my whole being.
I have given Him all, even my sins, and He has espoused me to
Himself in tenderness and love.
Now and for life I am the spouse of my Crucified Spouse. Amen.[2]

Although she recovered, her strength began to fail and she was never long without sickness and physical pain. Yet she was continually active and even more determined, no matter the cost, to give her "Yes" to God and "a big smile for all." She maintained the same busy schedule[3] almost to the end, living to the full her fourth vow of wholehearted and free service to the poorest of the poor. Her body was getting weaker, but her spirit was indefatigable. She wanted to conquer the world with love, as a sister recalled:

Mother one day brought a map of Europe and spread it before me. At that time, the Soviet Union had not yet broken up and half of Europe was under Communist rule with no permission for missionaries to enter *as missionaries*. But Mother just went with her finger from country to country, like: "France, we are here. Germany, we are here. Austria, we are here. Hungary, not yet. Bulgaria, not yet." And so she went on. Then she started to count the countries where we were "not yet" on her fingers. . . . she was in dead earnest that "a tabernacle" (meaning a house) should be opened in each country of the world. Mother had a big vision of what she wanted to give her Lord and God.

"Conviction of My Nothingness"

Mother Teresa dedicated much of her time and energy in the last years of her life to the development and growth of the male branches of her religious family. The Missionaries of Charity—Contemplative, made up of priests and brothers, was founded on March 19, 1979, the feast of St. Joseph. An international movement to foster priestly holiness called the Corpus Christi Movement was officially recognized by the Sacred Congregation for the Clergy on the feast of the Sacred Heart, June 26, 1981. And the Missionaries of Charity Fathers began on October 13, 1984, in New York.

In 1985, with the fifth general chapter approaching, Mother Teresa again expressed her desire to be freed from her responsibility as superior general and her longing to be "just a simple sister in the community." She shared her thoughts with Cardinal Picachy:

> I have already written to our Sisters to pray and to vote for somebody else in my place. There are many Sisters who can do even better. I have done with God's grace—much—because I gave Jesus a free hand—knowing that I can't do anything by myself.—The conviction of my nothingness has made the work & the whole Society completely His. He will do still greater things if He finds somebody more nothing than I. (I don't think there is one.) I will be happy, very happy to be free—and to be just a simple Sister in the Com. [community]—after nearly 35 years.—I am longing for this.—I will always do what the Church—through the Holy Father & you—want me to do but I am longing to be only all for Jesus—through Mary, a simple MC.[4]

But this was not God's plan for her. She was reelected as superior general, a decision she accepted as coming from God's hand. As before, she kept asking for prayers for her religious family: "Please pray for us especially during Holy Mass—that we do not spoil God's work—that it remains His."[5]

It was at this time that Mother Teresa decided to share her interior struggle with another priest, Jesuit Father Albert Huart[6] of the Calcutta province. He remembered:

It was very probably at the retreat previous to the General Chapter in 1985. Mother came . . . to speak about the excruciating night in her soul. It was not a passing phase but had gone on for years. What immediately struck me is what she added to the description of this painful and enduring night . . . : "Father, I do realize that when I open my mouth to speak to the sisters and to people about God and God's work, it brings them light, joy and courage. But I get nothing of it. Inside it is all dark and feeling that I am totally cut off from God." This sounded to me like pure John of the Cross.

The contrast between her inner night and her ability to communicate God in word and deed to others enabled me to do my best to reassure her that God was powerfully at work in her, and encourage her to accept the darkness as part of His work. But, in this kind of night, a few words well meant will not relieve the pain, or not much.[7]

The "night" continued as dark as ever. Father Huart offers this particularly apt metaphor for Mother Teresa's experience:

As I listened to her, the image that emerged in my mind was that of a chalet basking in warm bright sunshine, surrounded by lush vegetation and flowers, yet, within, all dark and cold.[8]

She had stopped writing about her darkness and rarely spoke about it, but suffered from it as intensely as she had for the past thirty-five years. Yet, in spite of it or rather because of it, Mother Teresa continued to be a source of light and inspiration to others.

"Where Is Jesus?"

Another priest was introduced into the depth of her interior trial in the course of the last years of her life. Father William G. Curlin,[9] then pastor of a parish in Washington, D.C., recalled:

I have been privileged to direct several spiritual retreats for Mother Teresa in Calcutta and again in the United States. I recall how intense was her hunger to deepen her relationship to Jesus Christ. I note in particular one evening when Mother Teresa and I were discussing spiritual aridity. One of her Sisters overheard our discussion and remarked, "Mother must have great consolation from God to support her mission to the poorest of the poor." Later that evening during a Holy Hour one of the members of her religious family handed me a written note from Mother Teresa. I read her words and then looked to where she was seated in the Chapel. She returned my look and then knelt up and faced the Blessed Sacrament enthroned in the Monstrance. That gesture confirmed her words: "Dear Father, pray for me. Where is Jesus?" Throughout [the] years of my friendship with Mother Teresa, she frequently shared with me the spiritual dryness that accompanied her labors as a Missionary of Charity.[10]

A Witness to the Primacy of Love

Mother Teresa was in constant contact with human distress, yet she never got accustomed to it. Each time she encountered the suffering poor, it made a real impact on her. She would repeat: "I have never seen so much suffering." She saw God's greatness in the ability of the poor to bear so much suffering without complaining, and their witness was a source of strength for her, as she shared with Father van der Peet:

So kind of you to write in spite of my not writing—but I know your prayer is always with me and also mine for you, that you may more and more be humble like Mary and holy like Jesus. On Christmas day I went to Addis [Ababa]—Ethiopia to be with our Sisters and their Poor. I did not realize that their Christmas is actually today. I have never seen so much suffering—so much pain and without complaint.—I only saw an open Calvary— where the Passion of Christ was being relived in the bodies of crowds & crowds of people.

We already have 4 houses and the 5th is a camp with 8,000 feeding[11] and 600 sick crippled, mental [mentally ill] men, women, children. Our Sisters are really Jesus' presence to them, their touch so gentle, so full of love.—Pray that I be able to send some more Sisters.—There are 7 million people facing this suffering.[12]

Many more honors continued to be bestowed upon Mother Teresa, but the highest and dearest, in her estimation, was the visit of Pope John Paul II to Nirmal Hriday in Kalighat (the Home for the Dying in Calcutta) on February 3, 1986. After greeting each patient, the Holy Father shared a brief reflection summarizing Mother Teresa's whole endeavor:

I am grateful to God that my first stop in Calcutta has been at Nirmal Hriday Ashram, a place that bears witness to the primacy of love. Through Mother Teresa and the Missionaries of Charity, and through the many others who have served here, Jesus has been deeply loved in people whom society often considers "the least of our brethren." Nirmal Hriday is a place of suffering, a house familiar with anguish and pain, a home for the destitute and dying. But, at the same time, Nirmal Hriday is a place of hope, a house built on courage and faith, a home where love reigns, a home filled with love. . . . In Nirmal Hriday, the mystery of human suffering meets the mystery of faith and love.[13]

Desiring to be close to all the different "Calvaries" in which Jesus in many disguises relived His Passion, Mother Teresa was very alert to new forms of suffering and poverty in the world. In the late 1980s AIDS sufferers were the object of her particular concern and sympathy. Counting on his prayers, she wrote to Father van der Peet:

I know you are praying for me, for it is this only that keeps me up.

The work for the "Aids" keeps growing fruitfully. No one has died without Jesus. There is so much suffering among our poor all round the world.—We are now in 77 countries over 350 houses. Can you imagine—poor people entering heaven from all sides— . . . in New York—already over 50 have died a beautiful death— . . .

At the beginning St. Peter would not let me enter heaven because there were no slums in heaven.—Now heaven is full of slum people. Jesus must be very happy to have those thousands coming to Him, with love from Calcutta—

I know you will enjoy this gospel story in full reality.

Please pray for me that I be only all for Jesus through Mary.[14]

"Tell Mother Teresa, 'I Thirst'"

The mission Mother Teresa had begun was developing to an extent and in ways that far surpassed what she could have envisioned at the beginning. She saw the good news of God's love coming alive in the works of her community. At the same time, she was very much distressed at the thought that she and her sisters were not fully answering Jesus' plea:

My children, you do not know the terrible pain there is in my heart for not being able fully to answer to the terrible thirst Jesus asked me to satiate through the Society, through each one of you.

If I am feeling like this, I wonder what the Heart of Jesus must feel. Is it not at this time again, as He did 10th Sept., is He not looking at each one of us: "I chose you and called you to be a Missionary of Charity to satiate My painful thirst, and where are you?" Jesus told a priest in Rome, "Tell Mother Teresa, 'I thirst.'" My children, hear your own name. He is saying it to you.[15]

This priest, a confessor in the novitiate in Rome, later shared the circumstances of the message he gave to Mother Teresa:

On Palm Sunday of 1987, I was sitting in our prayer chapel in our general house. . . . It was a small room designated specifically for prayer, but did not have the Blessed Sacrament present. While I was praying Morning Prayer silently with my office book, I suddenly had a thought insinuated in my head—as if someone had spoken, but I didn't hear it with my ears. But, it seemed quite clear: "Tell Mother Teresa, 'I thirst.'" I thought to myself, "What an odd interruption in my prayer." Thinking no more of it, I returned to praying the office. A couple minutes later, I "heard" again (in my thoughts): "Tell Mother Teresa, 'I thirst.'" I thought once again, "How strange!" Then I looked up at the large crucifix hanging on the wall and said (not out loud), "Are you talking to me?" And I "heard" once again (as a strong thought coming into my mind), "Tell Mother Teresa, 'I thirst.'"

At that point, I felt like the inspiration was coming from Jesus and heard not as a request, but more as a command. At this point, I must clarify that I had never had an experience like that before—I have never had one since. I am not prone to suggestion. I have not had, and do not expect to have visions or locutions. If anything, I am by nature wary of "supernatural" manifestations. However, I felt strongly moved to answer this particular inspiration. So I went to my room and wrote a letter in handwriting to Mother Teresa, telling her that perhaps she would think me crazy, but that I had felt moved to communicate my experience. . . .

When I met Mother Teresa, her first question was, "Are you the one who heard Jesus say: 'Tell Mother Teresa: I thirst'?" I said yes, that I had written the letter to her about my experience. She looked at me for a moment and asked, "What else did He say?" I was surprised by the question, but answered immediately, "Nothing. That was all I 'heard'." Then she asked, "What did he mean?" I said, "I don't know. I know only what I felt compelled to communicate to you. I am only the messenger."

The "Voice" that she had first heard on the train journey to Darjeeling had been silent for a very long time. She had been longing to hear it again, and now, though the cherished "Voice" was not speaking to her directly, His message was clear: He was still thirsting and looking for one to console Him. And she was ever aflame "to be the one."

"People Are so Hungry for God"

By the end of 1989, a new phase began in Mother Teresa's life. Her heart condition was worsening, and several times she was at death's door. In December 1989, after she had a permanent pacemaker inserted, she wrote to Brother Roger of Taizé, "One very good thing was the fruit of my sickness—that the whole world prayed to the same God to make me well."[16] It was important to Mother Teresa that people be drawn to God, and if her sickness helped bring this about, she was grateful. As soon as she regained a little strength, she was on her feet again spreading God's love in every possible way.

In the 1990s, with the collapse of the communist system in Eastern Europe, she was on the move, in spite of her heart condition and contrary to the doctors' advice. She had been longing to bring the light of God's love to the Central and Eastern European countries that had suffered restrictions on religious freedom. She opened foundations in most of the countries of the former Soviet Union, including several in Russia, and in Czechoslovakia, Hungary, and finally Albania. "People are so hungry for God," she repeated after witnessing the deep desire for God that had been suppressed for too many years in these countries. After her visit to Albania, she wrote to her sisters, "I feel Jesus and Mary want me here at this time of opening of churches in the country of Albania where God's love has been so rejected for many years and people were starving spiritually."[17]

Be Only All for Jesus Through Mary

Though Mother Teresa was traveling extensively, her congregation had spread to such an extent that she could not possibly reach all of her sisters, as she wished to. She was eager to be present to them through her monthly general letters. Her letters were full of gratitude, encouragement, advice, and recommendations. She had much to tell her sisters and brothers and time was running short. She was a guide, a teacher, an example, but in all she was always a mother.

LDM

My dearest children, Sisters, Brothers, Fathers, Lay Missionaries, Co-workers,

This brings you my prayer and blessing for each one of you—my love and gratitude to each one of you for all you have been and have done all these 40 years—to share the joy of loving each other and the Poorest of the Poor.

Your presence and the work you have done throughout the world for the glory of God and the good of the Poor has been a living miracle of love of God and yours in action. God has shown His greatness by using nothingness—so let us always remain in our nothingness—so as to give God [a] free hand to use us without consulting us. Let [us] accept whatever He gives and give whatever He takes with a big smile.

As the days of the General Chapter draw near my heart is filled with joy and expectation—of the beautiful things God will do through each one of you by accepting with joy the one God has chosen to be our Superior General. Beautiful are the ways of God if we allow Him to use us as He wants.

I am still in Eastern Europe. The living miracles God has done during these days have been a proof of His tender love for His M.C. and our Poor. Let our gratitude be our strong resolution to be only all for Jesus through Mary. Let us be pure and humble like Mary and we are sure to be holy like Jesus.

Humility always is the root of zeal for souls and charity. We see that in Jesus—on the Cross and in the Eucharist. We see it in Mary [who] went in haste to serve as handmaid[18]—not as Mother of God.

So it is very important for us MC to be pure and humble. No MC can live a true MC life and the 4th vow without a pure and humble heart. Because a pure heart can see God in the Poor—a humble heart can love and serve Jesus in the Poor.

Remember the five fingers—

you—did—it—to—Me[19]

Remember—love begins at home—our community—our family.

Remember—works of love are works of peace.

Let us thank Jesus for the 40 years of tender love we have received from Him through each other—and pray that we grow in this love for each other and our Poor—by deepening our personal and intimate love for Jesus and greater attachment to Jesus through prayer and sacrifice.

Try to be Jesus' love, Jesus' compassion, Jesus' presence to each other and the Poor you serve.

All this will be possible if you keep close to Mary the Mother of Jesus and our Mother. She will guide & protect you and keep you only all for Jesus.

Let nothing and nobody ever separate you from the love of Jesus[20] and Mary.—It was at her pleading that the Society was born.—Let it be again at her pleading that the Society gives saints to Mother Church.

Remember wherever you may be—Mother's prayer, love, and blessing will always be with you.

God bless you,
M. Teresa, M.C.[21]

In this letter Mother Teresa touches on many of the central features of the life of the Missionaries of Charity. Among these is the "Gospel on five fingers"—as she liked to say, "You-did-it-to-Me"—one word for each finger. With this, she wanted the Missionaries of Charity to remember the poor—not only to respect the dignity of the child of God in each one, but also to realize the supernatural reality of God's presence in each of them.

She likewise wanted them to remember that "love begins at home." In many of her letters and instructions she had insisted that only by first loving those closest would her religious family become the builders of peace that she wanted them to be. She used to distribute a little card, what she referred to as her "business card," with one of her well-known sayings printed on it, showing the path to peace:

The fruit of silence is prayer,
The fruit of prayer is faith,
The fruit of faith is love,
The fruit of love is service,
The fruit of service is peace. [22]

In the Name of God and in the Name of the Poor

Mother Teresa had been a fearless missionary all her life. She had heard the Voice of God calling her to serve the poor. She had, in turn, become a voice pleading on behalf of the poor. Armed with the weapon of faith, she was not afraid to face and challenge world leaders to protect the interests of the most vulnerable members of human society. An open letter she wrote to the heads of state of the United States and Iraq, in the hope that the looming war could be averted, was one eloquent example of her courage and single-mindedness.

2ND JANUARY, 1991.

Dear President George Bush and President Saddam Hussein
I come to you with tears in my eyes and God's love in my heart to

plead to you for the poor and those who will become poor if the war that we all dread and fear happens. I beg you with my whole heart to work for, to labour for God's peace and to be reconciled with one another.

You both have your cases to make and your people to care for but first please listen to the One who came into the world to teach us peace. You have the power and the strength to destroy God's presence and image, His men, His women, and His children. Please listen to the will of God. God has created us to be loved by His love and not to be destroyed by our hatred.

In the short term there may be winners and losers in this war that we all dread, but that never can, nor never will justify the suffering, pain and loss of life which your weapons will cause.

I come to you in the name of God, the God that we all love and share, to beg for the innocent ones, our poor of the world and those who will become poor because of war. They are the ones who will suffer most because they have no means of escape. I plead on bended knee for them. They will suffer and when they do, we will be the ones who are guilty for not having done all in our power to protect and love them. I plead to you for those who will be left orphaned, widowed, and left alone because their parents, husbands, brothers and children have been killed. <u>I beg you please save them.</u> I plead for those who will be left with disability and disfigurement. They are God's children. I plead for those who will be left with no home, no food and no love. Please think of them as being your children. Finally, I plead for those who will have the most precious thing that God can give us, life, taken away from them. I beg you to save our brothers and sisters, yours and ours, because they are given to us by God to love and to cherish. It is not for us to destroy what God has given to us. Please, please let your mind and your will become the mind and will of God. You have the power to bring war into the world or to build peace. PLEASE CHOOSE THE WAY OF PEACE.

I, my sisters and our poor are praying for you so much. The whole world is praying that you will open your hearts in love to God. You may win the war but what will the cost be on people who are broken, disabled and lost.

I appeal to you—to your love, your love of God and your fellow men. In the name of God and in the name of those you will make poor, do not destroy life and peace. Let love and peace triumph and let your names be remembered for the good you have done, the joy you have spread and the love you have shared.

Please pray for me and my sisters as we try to love and serve the poor because they belong to God and are loved in His eyes, as we and our poor are praying for you. We pray that you will love and nourish what God has so lovingly entrusted into your care.

May God bless you now and always.

> God bless you,
> M. Teresa, M.C.[23]

Mother Teresa was preaching not only by her words but even more by her actions. Wherever a disaster struck or a tragedy occurred, she would be there with her sisters. She did not judge, nor did she criticize; she loved and helped in a simple but effective way. In June of 1991, she wrote to her religious family from Baghdad, where she had opened a home for handicapped children and begun a mobile clinic:

BAGDAD 23/6/91

My dearest children all over the world, every one of you Fathers, Brothers, Sisters, Co-Workers and Lay Missionaries of Charity, This brings you Mother's love, blessing and prayer that you

may all grow in holiness through love for each other and the poor
you serve.

It is one real living miracle of God's tender love that we were
allowed by the Government of Iraq to come in and establish the
M.C. convent in the heart of the city of Baghdad in the house
given by the Gov. [Government] . . .

The fruit of the war is so terrible. One cannot understand
how any human being can do that to another—and for what? Let
us pray that our works of love bring peace, unity and joy.

For the present there is a great shortage of food & medicine
and as hundreds & hundreds of houses have been destroyed, I do
not know how long it will take to rebuild—so let us include Iraq
in our daily prayer. . . .

Looking at the people—the Old Testament becomes so
alive. Tomorrow we will go to see "Babylon." Who ever thought
M.C. will come to these places—to proclaim the Word of God
through works of love? I never thought that our presence would
give so much joy to thousands of people.—So much suffering
everywhere— . . .

Looking at the terrible suffering & fruit of war—same thing, I
was thinking, can happen through uncharitable words & actions.—
We do not destroy buildings—but we destroy the very heart of
love, peace and unity and so break the beautiful building, our
Society—which was built with so much love by Our Lady.—

I know you all love Mother and that you would do anything
to show your love & gratitude. I ask of you but one thing:
Be a true Missionary of Charity and so satiate the thirst of Jesus
for love, for souls by working at the salvation and sanctification
of your community and your family, the poor you serve. Let
us pray.

God bless you,
Mother[24]

"I Satiate Your Thirst with My Love and the Suffering of My Heart"

In his message for Lent 1993, Pope John Paul II insisted on listening to the voice of Jesus "who, tired and thirsty, says to the Samaritan woman at Jacob's well: 'Give me a drink' (Jn 4:7). Look upon Jesus nailed to the Cross, dying, and listen to his faint voice: 'I thirst' (Jn 19:28). Today, Christ repeats his request and relives the torments of his Passion in the poorest of our brothers and sisters." These words greatly struck Mother Teresa:

> After reading Holy Father's letter on "I Thirst," I was struck so much—I cannot tell you what I felt. His letter made me realize more than ever how beautiful is our vocation. How great God's love for us in choosing our Society to satiate that thirst of Jesus, for love, for souls—giving us our special place in the Church. At the same time we are reminding [the] world of His thirst, something that was being forgotten. I wrote Holy Father to thank him. Holy Father's letter is a sign for our whole Society—to go more into what is this great thirst of Jesus for each one. It is also a sign for Mother, that time has come for me to speak openly of [the] gift God gave Sept. 10th—to explain [as] fully as I can what means for me the thirst of Jesus.[25]

In the early years, Mother Teresa had often spoken to the sisters about quenching Jesus' thirst being the one aim of all their labors. In later years she insisted on the means of satiating Jesus' thirst. After the pope's Lenten message, Jesus' thirst again became a recurrent theme in Mother Teresa's letters and instructions to her followers. She was sharing what she had been living. All her labors, her sufferings and her joys were only the means to that end. She had willingly embraced and offered even her agonizing interior darkness to satiate His thirst and was ready to do so with "every single drop of [her] blood."[26]

The most difficult aspect of her continuing interior darkness was her unquenchable thirst for God. She had discovered the meaning of it and learned to live in peace with it, but still she could not satisfy her thirst for the One "whom my heart & soul longs to possess."[27] The growth of her congregation, the success of her mission, the praise of the world, could not appease this thirst for God.

She understood so well Jesus' words "I thirst." She had embodied something of His thirst for souls for over forty years. She knew what Jesus had felt, and in spite of her old age—she was eighty-three years old—she wanted to satiate His thirst for love and for souls. She could stop speaking about her darkness but she could not stop speaking about His thirst.

A year after the Holy Father's Lenten message, she was in Vietnam to open a new house for her community. It was Holy Week, and during this special time she exhorted her community to heed Jesus' thirst:

L.D.M.

VIETNAM,

29-3-94

My dearest Sr. M. Frederick and all in the Mother House and the world,

This brings you all Mother's prayer, love, and blessing.

I hope and pray you are all one heart full of love in the heart of Jesus through Mary.

As this week is a special time for Jesus and for us of greater love and greater union, let us try in a special way to come as close as [the] human heart can come to the Heart of Jesus and try to understand as much as possible Jesus' terrible pain caused to Him by our sins and His Thirst for our love.—He has never felt this pain so much as during this week so precious for Him and for us.—No wonder it came out so clearly in the last moments of His human life when He said "I Thirst." Thank God Our Lady was there to understand fully the thirst of Jesus for love.—She must have straight away said, "I satiate Your thirst with my love and the suffering of my heart."

"Jesus, my Jesus, I love you"—how clear. Her total surrender, her loving trust must have satiated His Thirst for love for souls.— That is why it is very important to keep very close to Our Lady as St. John and St. Mary Magdalen kept.[28] Often I wonder what they felt when they heard Jesus say "I Thirst." That is why, my children, this week is so important to the life of our Society and [this] reason for our existence as M.C., to satiate the thirst of Jesus on the cross for love, for souls, by working at the salvation and sanctification of the poorest of the poor.—Who are the poorest of the poor?—My Sisters, my Brothers, my Fathers, every member of our M.C. family.—That's where this beautiful gift of love—of satiating the thirst of Jesus for love, for souls—begins.

That is why, my children, let us deepen our knowledge of the thirst of Jesus on the Cross, in the Eucharist and in every soul we meet, for this knowledge will help us to be holy like Jesus & Mary. . . .

I hope you are all well wherever you are doing God's work with great love.—I ask you again—please, for the love of God and the love [of] the Society take the trouble to be holy. All for Jesus through Mary.

Holy & Happy Easter to you all.

God bless you,
Mother[29]

Mother Teresa had asked Father Neuner many years earlier to teach her how to grow in a "deep personal union of the human heart with the heart of Christ."[30] She had been drawn to His Sacred Heart and had experienced His thirst. With her love, her service, and especially her darkness she had been satiating Christ's thirsting Heart. Now she was spending the last drops of her energy to instill in the members of her religious family the same longing.

She insisted that her sisters "keep very close to our Lady." Often she had affirmed, "It was at her [the Blessed Mother's] pleading that the Society was born and by her continual intercession it has grown up."[31] For years Mother Teresa had left her sisters wondering about the origins of this statement. Only after her death would they learn about the three visions Mother Teresa had in which Our Lady had pleaded with her to answer the call of Jesus and the call of the poor.

Father Van Exem had been generously helping Mother Teresa and her Missionaries of Charity since the very beginning, and remained a faithful guide and support to the end. In his last letter to Mother Teresa, who was in critical condition in the hospital, he reminded her of Our Lady's essential role on the last part of her journey.

Dear Mother,

Tomorrow morning I shall say Holy Mass

    1. that you may have no operation

    2. that you may be in China by the 7th October 93

    3. that the Lord may take me and not you if that is His Will. His will, not mine.

I am with you and the Sisters, all of them.

There is a Calvary for every Christian. For you the way to Calvary is long, but Mary has met you on the road. You did not go up the hill, this is for later.

I adore the Blessed Sacrament which, I am sure, you have in your room.

Pray for me and all my companions, especially the companions of Jesus with whom I am.

Yours sincerely in O.L. [Our Lord]
C. Van Exem, S.J.[32]

Father Van Exem died four days later.

Without Counting the Cost

Mother Teresa had given her all to answer God's call, without counting the cost. The fruitfulness of her apostolate came at the steep price of many years of sacrifice. The sisters living closest to her could not help but notice:

She must have undergone martyrdom. Her extensive travels in crowded trains, only third class compartments, her daily walks to the slums in the dust and dirt, being tired, hungry, thirsty, not having any privacy—the door of her room being always open—no fan even in the hottest summer, small rooms, small chapels, a narrow, hard iron bed: all these and more, without ever a complaint! . . . She would just say almost daily, "All for Jesus"—just like that, no comment, nothing. . . . And when she had special trials or something, she used to teach us: "You know, this is the chance for greater love."

These were only the sufferings others observed. The excruciating interior ones she had kept well hidden, and those closest to her would be able to comment on them only in retrospect:

Jesus used all the sufferings Mother went through in the dark night of the spirit, to bless the work. His work prospered but

Mother suffered immensely. But Mother was totally surrendered to whatever the Lord wanted.

In the midst of all her activities and in constant interior pain, Mother Teresa was fully involved in community life with her sisters. During her extensive travels, she would at times reach her destination after midnight but she would still be up at 4:40 in the morning, first in the chapel for morning prayers and ready to carry out the day's demanding work schedule. This routine continued until shortly before her death:

During 1994 and 1995 Mother led a normal life, following the whole timetable, meeting visitors, answering the phone, etc. From time to time, she suffered from bouts of cough and colds, malaria, etc. She had broken her shoulder bone and fractured three ribs due to a fall in Rome, but this was not enough to keep Mother in bed. She was always in haste to give Jesus and gave no thought for herself. At the age of over 80 it surely was not easy to have a hectic day followed by handling the mail each night. However, Mother gave herself completely.

When visiting the houses of her congregation, she would share in doing the simplest tasks with her sisters. Her example spoke to them more eloquently than her words, as a sister testifies:

I remember once when Mother came to Baton Rouge, I was watching Mother's every step. After we had lunch, Mother helped us to wash the dishes and she was the first one to take the duster [dishcloth] to clean off the table. People were crowded outside because of Mother, and here Mother is doing the humblest act like a simple sister.

Mother Teresa accepted all the interior and exterior sufferings God gave her as a privilege, using them to fulfill the aim of her congregation. Yet it was not with a sense of helplessness or passive resignation that she lived; rather she radiated the joy of belonging to God, of living with Him. She knew that after the pain of the Passion, the joy of the resurrection would dawn.

"Something Truly Beautiful for God"

Much of Mother Teresa's correspondence in the last years of her life was reduced to short notes, but they convey succinctly her thoughts, her desires, and her prayer. They were often just encouraging exhortations, her simple expression veiling a profound wisdom:

> God is in love with us and keeps giving Himself to the world—through you—through me. . . .
>
> May you continue to be the sunshine of His love to your people and thus make your life something truly beautiful for God.[33]

Doing "something truly beautiful for God" was not just an attractive motto; it was how she had been attempting to show her love for Jesus all these years, doing everything as beautifully as she possibly could for Him. She considered embracing the mystery of the cross in her life an opportunity to do something beautiful for God and carry His love to those living in darkness. She extended this teaching to one of her co-workers:

> In this time of Lent, the time of greater love, when we look at all that Jesus chose to suffer out of love for us, to redeem us, let us pray for all the grace we need to unite our sufferings to His, that many souls, who live in darkness and misery, may know His love and life.

... May Our Lady be a mother to you and help you to stand beneath the Cross with great love.

I pray that nothing may ever so fill you with pain and sorrow as to make you forget the joy of the Risen Jesus.[34]

"I Am So Happy to Give Him This Gift"

At the age of eighty-five, Mother Teresa was still eager to receive advice and spiritual guidance with humility and simplicity. Bishop Curlin was a witness to this characteristic of hers:

I remember especially our last meeting together in Charlotte when she came here in 1995. That evening we spent an hour in private conversation discussing her spiritual life. When I suggested that she offer her spiritual dryness to God as a special gift, she reacted with enthusiasm. She repeated several times, "What a wonderful gift from God to be able to offer Him the emptiness I feel. I am so happy to give Him this gift." ...

In the telephone conversations that followed our last meeting, she invariably mentioned her continuing to make that inner and hidden gift.[35]

Thus, only two years before her death, Mother Teresa was readily welcoming the suggestion to offer to God this inseparable "traveling companion." Since the early 1960s she had been doing so as part of her call to be identified with Jesus and the poorest of the poor. Once more she ratified that offering. And by all existing evidence, she remained in that state of "dark" faith and total surrender until her death, offering to the end this hidden and wonderful gift.

She offered to God not only her darkness, but even the memory

of the light that He had bestowed upon her at the beginning of her
call to serve the poor. One of the sisters remembered:

One afternoon when I was alone with Mother, I told her the
golden Jubilee of our Inspiration Day was coming soon. Mother
said, "Yes, but how strange nobody asked me about the
Inspiration. But it is very difficult to explain. I told Him [Jesus]
to take away everything so that I don't have to explain. I know, I
understand, but I can't explain. When you make it public it loses
its sanctity." This gave me an inkling of the depth of Mother's
humility and detachment. It also made me understand why
Mother always changed the subject whenever we asked her about
the Inspiration.

"She Is Just Looking and Looking and Looking at That Box"

In 1996 Mother Teresa's health took a notable turn for the worse. At
times she required hospitalization. One of her priests recalled her
suffering and the strength she drew from the Eucharist in those hard
moments:

In her last illness [1996] she was often in the hospital. She was
literally pinned to the bed, nailed to the cross. When she became
conscious, she immediately tried to make the sign of the cross,—
even when she had so many needles from machines in her
arms etc. She told me how I could become a holy priest. "First
thing in the morning," she said, "kiss the crucifix. Offer Him
everything you will say, or do or think during the day. Love Him
with a deep, personal, intimate love—and you will become
a holy priest."

Mother had the grace in the latter years, to have the Blessed Sacrament in her hospital room, and she always wanted it with her. . . . [In August] She had another heart failure right before our eyes. A tube was put down into her lungs to assist her breathing and relieve the pressure upon her heart.

Before the tubes were finally removed, [the doctor] . . . said, "Father, go home and bring that box to Mother." For a second I wondered, "what box—shoe box"? He said, "That box, that temple they bring and put in her room and Mother looks at it all the time. If you bring it and put it in the room Mother will become so quiet." I realized he meant the tabernacle with the Blessed Sacrament. He said to me, "When that box is there, in the room, she is just looking and looking and looking at that box." The Hindu doctor was an unknowing witness to the power of the Eucharist over our Mother.[36]

"I Want Jesus"

At the end of the year Mother Teresa was close to death again. Another member of her religious family witnessed her struggles:

In December 1996 the breakdown of her health came to a climax and the whole world was very anxious and preoccupied over her critical condition. Mother Teresa, too, suffered much, not only in body, but also in spirit. She looked sad and downcast. It was clear for those who had known her for years that her spirit was passing through thick clouds and the devil was trying to take advantage of this opportune moment. So much so that one December morning, after Holy Mass in her room, as I was taking leave of her she told me in a very low voice, "Jesus is asking a bit too much." It seemed to me as if her beloved Jesus was reliving His agony in her in order to redeem the world anew from the darkness of sin. After all the hardships and sacrifices Mother Teresa had endured for years for her beloved Spouse, one might have expected a more serene and tranquil end. But instead there she was, a woman of sorrows, familiar with suffering, bearing the sufferings and burdens of the Society and of the poorest of the poor. Her hands became blue as if she was bearing the wounds that the nails had left in Jesus' flesh. Just as "in His wounds we were healed," so now in her wounds, in her pain, we were healed and comforted.[37]

In all simplicity she had admitted, "Jesus is asking a bit too much"; but she still accepted all He requested from her. She belonged to Him and He was her only desire. The sisters who were nursing her at that time were impressed by the amount of suffering she could bear. But they were even more edified that, in what looked like her last agony, she wanted only Jesus. A sister, also a doctor, later recalled:

That year [1996], what suffering she had! I never saw in my life the physical suffering that Mother put up with. She could not talk, she could not move with the respirator and bronchial tube fixed with cello tape. She made a sign for a pen but she could not write my name correctly. For two or three days she tried this. Ultimately, one morning Mother wrote, "I want Jesus." We asked Father Gary to come that morning, early, at 5.00 a.m. After the Mass he was just able to give her a drop of the Precious Blood. She began to improve. And that gave a clue . . . all believers and non-believers realized that her strength came from Jesus, and only with Him, in love and union, could she go through that terrible pain and agony.[38]

Another sister who witnessed this event also reflected on its meaning:

> But the most touching of all was when she wrote on a piece of paper early one morning, the phone number of Mother House and the words "I want Jesus." These words spoke volumes of Mother's suffering and love for God.

"To Be His Victim—to Be at His Disposal"

From this near-fatal illness Mother Teresa recovered. She remained at the head of her congregation until March 1997 (six months before her death), when, to Mother Teresa's great joy, Sister M. Nirmala Joshi M.C. was elected as her successor. In May, against all medical advice, Mother Teresa set out on what was to be her last journey to Rome, New York, and Washington, D.C. Sister Nirmala was aware of the gravity of the situation but also of the motives behind Mother Teresa's determination:

> [The doctor] was absolutely against Mother's traveling to the U.S.A., for it was too dangerous for Mother's life. I understood how important the religious Professions of the Sisters were for Mother. For in each Profession she offered so many consecrated souls to Jesus to quench His thirst for them and for souls. . . . This perhaps was the last time Mother would have the chance of doing it. This was her mission of quenching the thirst of Jesus for love and for souls. And I knew I had to support Mother's decision to go to the U.S.A. for this purpose, even at the risk of her life. If Mother had lost her life during the journey, it would be the consummation of her life in the fulfillment of her mission, for which Jesus had called her. That would be her joy and glory.[39]

When Mother Teresa returned to Calcutta in July, after a hectic and exhausting journey, she quietly told a friend, "My work is done." She was overjoyed to be "back home" at Motherhouse, in her beloved Calcutta, where she had always desired to die. One of the sisters remarked, "After her return from Rome . . . Mother had been extremely happy, joyful, optimistic, and talkative. Her face was always radiant, full of fun. The Lord must have revealed to her the impending end of her life."

A few days before Mother Teresa's death, a sister witnessed a scene that confirmed her heroic fidelity to her private vow not to refuse God anything:

I saw Mother alone, facing . . . a picture of the Holy Face . . . and she was saying, "Jesus, I never refuse you anything." I thought she was talking to someone. I went in again. Again I heard the same: "Jesus, I have never refused you anything."[40]

Mother Teresa had kept her word to God. She had succeeded in not refusing Jesus anything for fifty-five years, welcoming each situation as a new opportunity to be faithful to the love she had pledged.

From the earliest days of her congregation, she had always been keen on instructing her young followers not to refuse God anything and to offer their lives to God without reserve. Her vision of a true Missionary of Charity was demanding indeed, as she wrote in the Explanation of the Original Constitutions of the order:

True love is surrender. The more we love the more we surrender. If we really love souls we must be ready to take their place, to take their sins upon us and face the anger of God. It is only thus that we make ourselves their means and them our end. We must be living holocausts, for the world needs us as such. For by giving the little we possess, we give all—and that there is no limit to the love that prompts us to give. To give oneself completely to God is to be His Victim—the victim of His unwanted love—the love that made the heart of God love men so much. This [is] the Spirit of our Society—one of complete giving to God. We cannot be pleased with the common. What is good for other religious may not be sufficient for us. We have to satiate the thirst of an infinite God, dying of love. Only total surrender can satisfy the burning desire of a true Missionary of Charity. To be His Victim—to be at His disposal.

This is what she herself had been for decades now—a true Missionary of Charity, a victim for others. And through all the suffering that this entailed she lived with a deep joy originating from her wholehearted response to Jesus' call. While her last days continued to be marked with physical and spiritual pain, those around her could see that she was consciously preparing for the moment of meeting God, and the thought of "going home to God" filled her with joy. One of the sisters remembered:

Towards the last, Mother spoke . . . so much of heaven and she showed so much concern for every Sister. . . . Mother was very loving and affectionate; she was very joyful and radiant.

And one of the Missionaries of Charity fathers recalled:

As she approached the end of her life when she spoke, you could hear in her message her own longing (thirst) to be with Jesus, her longing to "go home to God." If someone begged, "Mother, don't leave us. We can't live without you." She would simply say: "Don't worry. Mother can do much more for you when I am in heaven."[41]

On September 5, 1997, after 8 P.M. Mother Teresa complained of severe back pain; soon her condition was aggravated by the inability to breathe. The sisters at the motherhouse were alarmed. All was done to help her; a doctor and a priest were called in. Unexpectedly the electricity failed and the whole house was in darkness. Foreseeing an emergency, the sisters had secured two independent electric supplies. But both lines went out at the same time; such a thing had never happened before. Prompt and expert medical aid could not help, as the breathing machine (Bi-PAP) could not be started. It was 9.30 P.M. While Calcutta was in darkness, the earthly life of the one who had brought so much light to this city and to the whole world was extinguished. Even so, her mission continues: from heaven she still responds to Jesus' call, "Come be My light."

Conclusion

In a dark time she is a burning and a shining light;
in a cruel time, a living embodiment of Christ's gospel
of love; in a godless time, the Word dwelling among us,
full of grace and truth. For this, all who have the
inestimable privilege of knowing her, or knowing
of her, must be eternally grateful.
—Malcolm Muggeridge[1]

Be My Light — Carry Me into the Holes of the Poor

"Mother, you were a source of light in this world of darkness," proclaimed one of the countless banners put up by the citizens of Calcutta at the time of Mother Teresa's funeral. The secret of the abundant light and love that Mother Teresa radiated has been the topic of this book.

That secret lies in the depth and intimacy of

her relationship with God. She was a "woman madly in love with God," and even more she was a woman who understood that "God was madly in love with her." Having experienced God's love for her, she desired ardently to love Him in return—even as He had never been loved before.

At the beginning of her "call within a call," Mother Teresa had been inundated with light. The Voice that she had heard spoke to her tender words of love, flooding her soul with consolations, and the closer she drew to Him, the more she longed for Him. The light of His presence, however, was soon veiled by the darkness of His apparent absence. As intense as the consolations had been were the desolations that followed.

She was called to share in a distinct way in the mystery of the Cross, to become one with Christ in His Passion and one with the poor she served. Through this sharing she was led to a deep awareness of the "painful thirst" in the Heart of Jesus for the poorest of the poor.

The darkness she experienced and described in her letters, in which the strength and beauty of her soul shines forth, was a terrible and unrelenting torment. In the lives of the saints, it is almost without parallel; only the experience of St. Paul of the Cross is comparable in length.

Throughout this ordeal, Mother Teresa remained steadfast and faithful to her call, spending herself unremittingly and cheerfully in the mission entrusted to her. Rising above the pain of feeling "unloved and unwanted" by Jesus, she did her utmost to show her love for Him, the Beloved of her soul, and to give joy to Him through all that she did. She sought Him in each person she met, especially in the poorest of the poor, holding fast to His words, "As you did it to one of the least of these my brethren, you did it to me."

Her painful darkness mysteriously united her so intimately with her crucified Spouse, that He became the sole "object of her thoughts and affections, the subject of her conversations, the end of her actions and the model of her life."[2] Her total surrender to His will and her determination not to refuse Him anything allowed Him to manifest through her His love for each individual. It was the light and love of Jesus Himself that radiated from her—in the midst of her own darkness—and that had such an impact on others.

Through embracing her interior darkness, Mother Teresa became a "saint of darkness." Jesus' call *"Come—carry Me into the holes of the poor.—Come be My light,"*[3] urged her "to give [herself]—without any reserve to God in the poor of the slums and the streets."[4] Disregarding her own suffering, she reached out to others whose suffering seemed greater than her own, bringing the light of God's love to the hopeless and the helpless, to the poorest of the poor. Though she had carried Jesus into many "dark holes," there were many more; and even when her strength was notably failing, her spirit remained resolute. She carried on.

She Always Led Us to Jesus

Mother Teresa was able to lift up those who had fallen, to encourage the faint, to rekindle hope in the disheartened.

> She seemed to delight in you. It was not something of charity that was burdensome, which destroys the dignity of the poor, but it was something that she delighted in. . . . You had the sense that she considered it a privilege to do this. She comforted you when you were sad. She encouraged you when you were doubting whether you could do something.[5]

Another of her followers noted, "She always led us to Jesus, especially in very difficult moments."[6] All were astonished, however, to discover that she had been living in agonizing pain for almost fifty years, clinging to Jesus in pure faith. Her closest collaborators were totally unaware of it, as her successor, Sister Nirmala shared:

> From May 1958 onward, I have been with Mother and I can testify none of us could imagine what Mother was going through interiorly. Exteriorly, Mother was full of life as a Missionary of Charity. God was blessing the work: Vocations were coming, houses were being opened in India and outside India, and the work was being recognised and appreciated very much. And Mother had to pay the price.

It was not the suffering she endured that made her a saint, but the love with which she lived her life through all the suffering. She knew that everyone can, with God's grace and one's own resoluteness, reach holiness, not in spite of the mystery of suffering that accompanies every human life, but through it. She was able to convey this conviction to her followers, as one of them testified:

> She would say to me in difficult times, "Don't give in to your feelings. God is permitting this." This really taught me that the best and the worst in life would pass and if I will learn myself to accept the cross, to be quiet, humble and hopeful, that all will pass. By renewing hope in me, I was able to come through that period without making a bad judgement, by acting on my feelings.

Mother's Pledge

Mother Teresa believed her mission would continue beyond her death. Her mission statement says this plainly: "If I ever become a saint—I will surely be one of "darkness." I will continually be absent from heaven—to light the light of those in darkness on earth."[7] Her encouraging words in an instruction to her sisters also affirmed her conviction:

> Mother is here to help you, guide you, lead you to Jesus. Time is coming closer when Mother also has to go to God. Then Mother will be able to help each one of you more, guide you more and obtain more graces for you.[8]

Mother Teresa's help, guidance and intercession are for everyone, especially those who find themselves in darkness for whatever reason. As she had pledged, she would be "absent from heaven" to bring them light.

Having taken to heart Christ's words "Love one another as I have loved you,"[9] and made them a reality in her life, she invites us to travel along the same path:

> And today God keeps on loving the world. He keeps on sending you and me to prove that He loves the world, that He still has that compassion for the world. It is we who have to be His love, His compassion in the world of today. But to be able to love we must have faith, for faith in action is love, and love in action is service."[10]

Mother Teresa's life shows us that holiness can be reached by simple means. Starting by loving the unloved, the unwanted, the lonely closest to us, in our own homes, in our communities and neighborhoods, we can follow her example of loving until it hurts, of doing always a little more than we feel ready to do.

The Light She Lit in my Life
Is Still Burning

In a book resonating with Mother Teresa's voice it seems appropriate to grant her the last word. The following is a story she told that wonderfully expresses the heart of her life and mission. It also invites each one to "be His light" by partaking in these humble deeds of love and compassion that may seem insignificant but are, in fact, nothing less than the means of radiating God's love to each person we meet, thus transforming, little by little, the darkness of the world into His light:

> I will never forget the first time I came to Bourke and visited the sisters. We went to the outskirts of Bourke. There was a big reserve where all the Aborigines were living in those little small shacks made of tin and old card-board and so on. Then I entered one of those little rooms. I call it a house but it's only one room, and inside the room everything. So I told the man living there, "Please allow me to make your bed, to wash your clothes, to clean your room." And he kept on saying, "I'm alright, I'm alright." And I said to him, "But you will be more alright if you allow me to do it." Then at the end he allowed me. He allowed me in such a way that, at the end, he pulled out from his pocket an old envelope, and one more envelope, and one more envelope. He started opening one after the other, and right inside there was a little photograph of his father and he gave me that to look at. I looked at the photo and I looked at him and I said, "You, you are so like your father." He was so overjoyed that I could see the resemblance of his father on his face. I blessed the picture and I gave it back to him, and again one envelope, second envelope,

third envelope, and the photo went back again in the pocket near his heart. After I cleaned the room I found in the corner of the room a big lamp full of dirt and I said, "Don't you light this lamp, such a beautiful lamp. Don't you light it?" He replied "For whom? Months and months and months nobody has ever come to me. For whom will I light it?" So I said "Won't you light it if the Sisters come to you?" And he said "Yes." So the sisters started going to him for only about 5 to 10 minutes a day, but they started lighting that lamp. After some time he got into the habit of lighting. Slowly, slowly, slowly, the Sisters stopped going to him. But they used to go in the morning and see him. Then I forgot completely about that, and then after two years he sent word—"Tell Mother, my friend, the light she lit in my life is still burning."[11]

APPENDIX A

Rules handwritten by Mother M. Teresa M.C., attached to the letter from Mother M. Teresa, M.C., to Archbishop F. Perier, S.J., dated Corpus Christi 1947

The Rules

1. *The End*

The General End of the Missionaries of Charity is to satiate the thirst of Jesus Christ on the Cross for love and souls by the Sisters, [through] absolute poverty, angelic chastity, cheerful obedience.

The Particular End is to carry Christ into the homes and streets of the slums, [among] the sick, dying, the beggars and the little street children. The sick will be nursed as far as possible in their poor homes. The little children will have a school in the slums. The beggars will be sought and visited in their holes outside the town or on the streets.

2. To be able to do all these—the Sisters must learn first to live real interior lives of close union with God—and seek and see Him in all they do for the poor.

3. There will be no difference amongst the Sisters—they must all

learn farming, cooking, nursing and a little teaching—and be ready always to do any of these works if obedience requires.

The Dress

4. The Sisters will dress in simple Indian dress in India. A white habit with long sleeves and a light blue saree—a white veil, sandals, a girdle and a crucifix.

The Aspirants

5. Catholic girls from the age of 16 upwards, full of love and zeal. Women who can so love God and the poor as to forget themselves entirely. Who will possess strong wills, to be able to live without all, so as to live to God alone. They must be souls of prayer and penance and filled with the simplicity of [the] Christ Child.

6. They need be healthy in body and mind so as to be able to bear the hardships of continual abnegation for souls.

7. If the rich and highly educated girls desire to enter—they may be accepted, but their riches or education will make no difference—they will be one of the Sisters.

8. Souls desiring to consecrate their lives as victims—but on account of bad health are unable to join the fighting forces—they too will be accepted, for from their continual suffering, the work of the Sisters will bear fruit.

9. Girls of any nationality will be accepted—only they must learn the language of the country where they will work thoroughly.

10. Before entering, the aspirants must spend 3 months in the mission field with the Sisters, so as both sides could choose.

11. They must be well examined by a priest who knows the spirit of the Missionaries of Charity.

The Novices and the Novitiate

12. For the present the novitiate will begin at Cossipore, where the Sisters will be able to have that complete separation from the world and spend a year in contemplation and manual labour. For this reason to this house no secular, not even relations, may be admitted.

13. For the second year the novices will move to a house in Calcutta Sealdah if possible, where the Sisters will be able to undergo a short training in maternity and other nursing and some teaching.

14. A month before the end of this second year, the Sisters will make a month's retreat, thereby [preparing] her heart for the taking of the three vows—absolute poverty, angelic chastity and cheerful obedience. Only then the Sister will receive the habit of the Institute.

15. The novices must be well taught of the interior life—and their religion. They must be given every possible care and help to understand and live lives of close union with God. They must learn to be contemplatives in the streets and slums just as much as in their convents.

16. Before taking their vows they must be well examined—so that the Sister well understands what a life of total forgetfulness and abnegation for souls is—and if she is willing to lead such a life cheerfully.

The Vows

17. *Absolute Poverty*—By this vow the Sister binds herself to absolute poverty. She renounces the right of possessing anything whatsoever as her own. To the temporal things of this world, she shall be like one dead.

18. The clothes will be kept, washed and mended in common. They shall also eat, sleep and work in common.

19. The food will be cooked and served according to the rules of the country in which they live.

20. The Missionaries of Charity will not possess buildings of their own but depend for shelter on the charity of the Bishop under whom they work.—The best room and the best of what they have must [be] used for the chapel.

21. The house may possess a bus, a bicycle, a boat which the Sisters will learn to use when on the mission field.

22. The Superior with another Sister will sometimes go begging for food, clothes, medicine for the poor. None of these are to be used by the Sisters.

23. For their own maintenance, the Sisters will work at the farm, make different things which can be sold, and cash used to provide food and clothing for the Sisters.—We need nothing else.

24. Things which will help the world to creep in must never be accepted by any one—not even Superiors. We must be free from all. The things that are most necessary will be carefully and kindly provided by the Superior.

25. But if a Sister falls ill she must be given everything that the doctor thinks necessary.—She must be put in a room where she could easily hear Holy Mass and have daily Holy Communion if she so wishes.

26. The Sisters will have no servants.—All the work of the house must they do.—And if the numbers permit—their clothes and food must be the fruit of their hands.

27. *Angelic Chastity*—By this vow the Sister binds herself to remain a virgin and to abstain from any act which is opposed to chastity.

28. Angelic purity must be the aim of each Sister, and to preserve it they must have a personal love for the Most Pure Heart of Mary and guard their hearts free from any affection however small. For a pure heart will easily see God in his poor and forget herself.

29. Any difficulties or temptations arising from their continual intercourse with the poor, must be revealed to the confessor sincerely and simply.

30. *Cheerful Obedience*—By this vow the Sister binds herself to obey the lawful Superior—in things which are connected with the life of the Missionaries of Charity.

31. The Sisters will obey cheerfully, promptly, blindly and simply. They should remember, that it is not her or she whom they obey, but He, Jesus Christ, for whose sake and whom they obey in all.

32. Perfect obedience—the powerful guardian of peace, brings joy to the heart and unites the soul closely to God—to His Holy Will.

Spiritual Exercises

33. As each Sister is to do the work of a priest—go where he cannot go, and do what he cannot do, she must imbibe the spirit of Holy Mass, which is one of total surrender and offering. For this reason Holy Mass must become the daily meeting place, where God and His creature offer each other for each other and the world.

34. The Sisters should use every means to learn and increase in that tender love for Jesus in the Blessed Sacrament.

35. Confession being one of the best means of making the soul strong—should be used according to the need and choice of the Sister. She must be a child in confession—simple and open.

36. Daily the Sisters shall make half an hour's Meditation. Twice a day the examination of conscience.—The full rosary—the litanies of Our Lady and Saints and half an hour of spiritual reading. On Thursdays and Sundays the hour of reparation.

37. The Sisters shall spend one day in every week, one week in every month, one month in every year, one year in every six years in the motherhouse, where in contemplation and penance together with solitude she can gather in the spiritual strength, which she might have used up in the service of the poor. When these Sisters are at home, the others will take their place in the Mission field.

Penance and Self-Denial

38. As each sister is to be a victim of Christ and do His work, she will understand what God and the Institute expects from her. No half measure.—We must give to God all or nothing and keep up that total surrender—cost what it may.

In the practice of corporal penances the Sisters shall be guided by the judgment of the confessor alone. For any public penance the permission of the Superior is required.

The Work Amongst the Poor of a City

39. The Sisters shall after Holy Mass and Communion go in pairs to the different slums of Calcutta.

School

With the help of the parish priest—they shall get a little house in the slums or close by where they can gather the little ones of that locality.— First get them clean—tend to their little wants—teach them little prayers and especially how to love God—play with them—teach them plenty of hymns—some reading, writing and a little of arithmetic. Prepare them for the Sacraments, and on Sundays take them to church.—On some big feast ask the priest to offer Mass amongst them.

Home Nursing

The other pair will visit the sick from house to house.—They will wash and tend the sick—and if the person has nobody to look after, they will prepare the food for the day, clean & sweep her room. If necessary the other two sisters will assist the mother at child's birth and see that both mother and child get the required care and attention.—They will encourage the sick, even if not dying, to ask for Holy Communion—for which they will also carry the required things and have the place and the sick ready for Our Lord's coming. They will notify the priest in time as to how many people wish to receive Our Lord.

The Dying

The sisters will use every tenderness and love for those who are leaving this world—so that the love of Jesus will attract them and make them make their peace with Him.—They will pray near the dying and make sure that the priest is called in time.—If the person has not got anybody—the sisters will prepare his or her body for the burial.—They should gather the money from the poor neighbours for a Mass the next morning at which the family and the neighbours with the sisters should go.

The Beggars

Two other Sisters will visit the beggars—nurse them and see to their wants if sick.—In their visit of their holes, they will gradually try to teach them self-respect and a desire for self-help.—And those who take in the lesson should be given work in the field—where they could bring their family also.

The Home for the Outcasts of Human Society

There are those that are not wanted amongst the poor—the lame—the blind—the sick.—For them when the Bishop thinks fit—will the home be opened—and there the sisters will take care of their body and soul.—This of course is only for the little children.

40. *The Work in the Villages*

In the villages the sisters will do the same work. They will go from place to place—with the missionary—who will do his priestly work while the sisters will tend the sick, teach the little children and prepare the adults for the receiving of the Sacraments. While there the Sisters will use the hut which will be used as a church also. They must not make a permanent stay in any village. If the priest thinks that the harvest is great—he may ask for the Daughters of St. Anne to whom the work would be joyfully handed to continue. They should be back home for the fourth week.

41. No boarding school or high or middle school work will ever be accepted by the Sisters—they must be free to go in search of souls and not be bound to the few.

42. If there are poor orphans left—then the parish priest should be told, and he is sure to do his duty to them.—The Sisters will not bind themselves to any such obligations.

All things to the Greater Glory of God.

Glory be to the Father and to the Son

And to the Holy Ghost.

Amen

FIRST DAY[1]

<u>Under the guidance of Jesus, Our Risen Lord.</u>

AIM: To realize more deeply that the purpose of my life is to do the Holy Will of God.

EXAMINATION: Let me try to answer the following questions sincerely:

1. Do I really try to praise, reverence and serve God? *I want but I don't.* Do I put this into daily practice? *No.* In ALL my actions? *Except for the first offering to the S.H. [Sacred Heart] in the morning—the rest of the day is like a stone. Yet my heart is all and only His—my mind & will are fixed on Him—the whole time.*[2]

2. Do I value the salvation of my soul? *I don't believe I have a soul. There is nothing in me.* Am I working in earnest for the salvation of the souls of others? *There was a burning zeal in my soul for souls from childhood until I said "yes" to God & then all is gone. Now I don't believe.*[3]

3. What use am I making of creatures? *I have no attachment.*[4]

4. Am I truly indifferent to my work, the companions with whom I work, my health, my success, my failure? *Yes.* Am I indifferent to the love and affection of my companions and of the people for whom I work? *Yes.*

READINGS: Book of Psalms, Chapter 32.

THE IMITATION OF CHRIST: Book I, Chapter 20; Book 3, Chapters 9 & 10.

REFLECTION FOR THE DAY: St. Augustine wrote these beautiful words: "Thou hast made us for Thyself, and our hearts are restless unless they rest in Thee."

N.B. The Readings are optional. The Examination should be made carefully every day.

* * *

SECOND DAY

<u>Under the patronage of my Guardian Angel.</u>

AIM: To acquire the sentiments which are necessary for a perfect Act of Contrition.

EXAMINATION:

1. Do I realize that sin is a possibility for me and that I must always be on my guard? *Yes.*

2. Which are the dangerous occasions of mortal sin to which I am exposed? *my eyes*

3. I must find out the habits and inclinations, which, if left unchecked, will lead me to grievous sin. *I am inclined to be harsh & quick. Inclined to look. Fear of deceiving of being deceived.* Do I try to overcome semi-deliberate venial sins? *Yes.*

4. My rules are given to me by God to keep me from all dangers. Do I neglect any of them habitually? *No, but sometimes also I have fallen.* What remedies should I take to improve matters? *Guard my eyes—sweetness.*[5]

READINGS: Book of Psalms, Chapter 11.

IMITATION OF CHRIST: Book I, Chapters 21 and 25; Book 3, Chapter 52.

REFLECTION FOR THE DAY:

—What HAVE I DONE for Christ? *I have loved Him blindly, totally, only.*

—What AM I DOING for Christ? *I use every power in me—in spite of my feelings—to make Him loved personally by the Sisters & people.*

—What SHOULD I DO for Christ? *I will let Him have a free hand with and in me.*[6]

Lead, kindly light, amid the encircling gloom,
    LEAD THOU ME ON!
The night is dark, and I am far from home,
    LEAD THOU ME ON!
Keep thou my feet I do not ask to see
The distant scene—one step enough for me.
[Cardinal John Henry Newman]

* * *

THIRD DAY

<u>Under the patronage of St. Mary Magdalen.</u>

AIM: To purify my heart.

EXAMINATION:

1. Do I make use of the means of Purification which God has given me? *I struggle against it, but I accept.*[7]

2. How do I make my Examination of Conscience? *Many times negligently & few times made it very badly. I pick up the things I have done wrong and spend my time in saying sorry to God.*

Do I insist on Perfect Contrition *not so fervently* and a Firm Purpose of Amendment? *Not always.*

3. How do I make my Particular Examination? *I don't mark*[8]—
but I keep a point "Sweetness of Jesus" for many years.

Am I sincere in my Confession? Y*es.* Am I humble? *I want
too [be].*

4. Manifestation of Conscience. Am I perfectly sincere to my
Superior? *I find it more and more difficult to speak—it is just closed. To
give you these papers it is one of the greatest sacrifices of the retreat, my
gift for the Sisters.*[9]

READINGS: St. Luke's Gospel, Chapter 7, verses 36 to 50;
Chapter 15, verses 11 to 32.

IMITATION OF CHRIST: Book I, Chapters 22, 23 and 24.

REFLECTION FOR THE DAY: "Many sins are forgiven her
because she has loved much." (St. Luke, Chap. 7, vs. 47).

* * *

Please destroy every paper I give you.

FOURTH DAY

Under the patronage of St. Ignatius.

AIM: To acquire an intense desire and a firm determination to
follow Christ my King wherever He may lead me.
"Master I shall follow Thee wheresoever Thou goest"
(St. Matthew, Ch. 8, v. 19).

EXAMINATION:

1. How do I perform my daily exercises of piety? *Very badly.*
Do I keep to the prescribed time? *Yes.* Do I have internal and
external reverence? *Yes.*[10]

2. Do I really consider Holy Mass to be the greatest action of
my day? *I want but it is not like that.* Do I receive Holy Communion
with faith and love? *No.*

3. When visiting the Blessed Sacrament, do I really visit Jesus

as my Friend, telling Him everything? *He has always been the One to share, know everything in details—but now, it is not like that.*[11]

4. Do I say my Rosary with fervour? *I want to love her [Our Lady], but no love enters my heart.*[12]

READINGS: St. Luke's Gospel, Chapters 1 & 2.

IMITATION OF CHRIST: Book 2, Chapters 7 & 8; Book 3, Chapter 13.

REFLECTION FOR THE DAY: Jesus says to me: "I AM THE WAY, THE TRUTH AND THE LIFE." [Jn 14:6]

*   *   *

But the city of God, enriched with flowing waters, is the chosen sanctuary of the Most High, God dwells within her, and she stands unmoved; with break of dawn He will grant her deliverance.[13]

FIFTH DAY

Under the patronage of St. Joseph.

AIM: To obtain a clear knowledge of the treachery of Satan and his followers and to live the "true" life which has been revealed to us by Our Lord.

EXAMINATION: My love of Poverty:

—Do I desire to be poor with Christ's poor? *With my whole heart.*

—Do I keep anything precious or superfluous, even though I may have permission for it? *No.*

Rule frees us   —Do I always ask permission for what I receive?

"no personal gifts"   —What is my attitude towards receiving gifts? Do I do my very best to avoid

receiving presents from others? When out of politeness I receive something do I receive it only with permission?

Whatever is given to the Sister goes naturally to the Superior.

—Am I inclined to share gifts only with some members of the community or do I, like a good religious, put these gifts at the disposal of my Superior?

—Am I happy to share in hardships which my state of life imposes on me? *Yes, very.*

—Do I really love Poverty as "My Lady Poverty" (St. Francis of Assisi) *Yes, with my whole heart.*[14]

READING: BOOK OF PSALMS: Psalms 45, 61.
ST. PAUL'S 1st Epistle to the Corinthians, Chapter 1, 18–31.
IMITATION OF CHRIST: Book III, Chapters 32 & 33.
From your CONSTITUTION: Chapter VI, Nos. 42–56;
Chapter IX, Nos. 74 & 75.
REFLECTION: "The Son of Man hath not where to lay His head." [Mt 8:20]

* * *

*I am not humble but I am too small to be proud.
For 20 years in Loreto I prayed fervently to be forgotten,
nothing to the world, to be ignored and held for nothing—and this
is how the Lord has answered my prayer,*[15] *but I still keep on
saying the same prayer.
My greatest humiliation & the daily sacrifice I have to make
continually is meeting people, priests, etc. How horrible
I feel inside when I have to speak to people. With the Sisters
& the poor I don't feel like that.*[16]

SIXTH DAY

<u>Under the patronage of St. Francis Xavier.</u>

AIM: To follow the beautiful example of Christ's Humility and Obedience.

EXAMINATION: My love of Humility

—Have I habitually got a lowly opinion of myself? *Yes.* Or do I judge others harshly in thoughts and express these in words? *No.*

—Without any morbidity, can I truly say that I enjoy humiliations, since these make me similar to Christ? *Yes—*

—Do I show my humility by my perfect sincerity to my Superior and to my Confessor? *Yes.* Do I hide things from them? *No—*

—Do I avoid trying to "shine" in front of outsiders? *No chance to hide.*

—Do I try to appear better than I truly am? *No.*

—Do I have obedience of the will and judgment? *Yes.*

—Do I desire for humble offices, for being ignored and humiliated? *All our works are of this type.*

—What are my reactions when I am just forgotten by my Sisters or by outsiders? *I am very happy.*

READINGS: Your Constitution: Chapter XIII, Nos. 97–132.

BOOK OF PSALMS: Psalms 107, 128.

IMITATION OF CHRIST: Book 3, Chapter 54.

REFLECTION: "Learn of Me, for I am meek and humble of heart." (Matthew XI, 29)

Fr. Joseph Rickaby writes: "How does the work of God suffer at my hands? This is the question of questions to put oneself during a Retreat. In my Retreat I want to get at <u>facts</u>, to think straight, to find out betimes now the truth that will come in upon me at death, to ascertain as nearly as may be how I stand with my God, to have my relations with my Creator dissected out."

At this stage of the Retreat I should be getting my Resolutions ready:

These resolutions must be 1) according to the present needs of my soul. 2) Something which may seem trivial to others, but which is of vital importance to me just now. 3) Something practical which I can put into practice immediately.

* * *

EIGHTH DAY[17]

<u>Under the patronage of the Holy Apostles.</u>

AIM: To make my plan of Life for the years following my Final Profession. My plan must be made with great clarity, courage and supernatural outlook.

EXAMINATION: Fraternal Charity. *Rule 1*[18] *& 86*[19] *were the Rules I loved best. My heart & soul were in it. But now nothing.*

Before there was so much love & real tenderness for the Sisters & the people—now I feel my heart is made of stone.

Sometimes I am even harsh.[20]

1. Do I observe my Rules No. 86 and 87? Do I love each of my Sisters with an intense love, without being concerned at all about nationality or social standing?

2. Rule 104: Do I try to make the children I teach happy? Do I respect the good name of my pupils and not talk carelessly of their faults?

3. Rule 106: In what spirit do I visit and look after the sick? Am I an angel of comfort and consolation?

4. Rule 112: My care for the Dying.

5. Rule 120: My love for the poor. Does Christ radiate and live his life in me in the slums. (Rule 86)

6. Rule 125: Supernatural outlook in my work—seeing Jesus in all strangers.

—Do I seek to encourage my Sisters, making them happy? *Yes.*

—Do I consider myself as their servant in Christ? *No—a mother.*

—Do I accept the unavoidable little difficulties of community life, patiently? forgivingly? with a sense of proportion and a sense of humour?

—Am I charitable to my Superiors? seeking by my behaviour to lighten their burden; defending rather than criticizing their decisions.

READINGS: Imitation of Christ, Book I, Chapters 14 and 16.
ST. LUKE: Chapter X, verses 25–37.
REFLECTION: "Whatsoever you have done to the least of my Brethren, you have done it to ME." [Mt 25:40]

* * *

In 1942 I think it was on this day I bound myself to God under pain of mortal sin not to refuse Him anything. This is what hides everything in me. [21]

NINTH DAY

Under the patronage of the Holy Martyrs and Virgins.
AIM: To finalize all my resolutions and to be quite definite about what Christ expects from me.
EXAMINATION: My duties of State:

—Do I observe all my Rules? *One rule I don't observe the going with a companion. I do it with a purpose—a Sister would be very tired etc. if she had to go to so many places.* [22]

—Do I give my best effort to the different duties? and works assigned to me? *Letter writing I do with a great effort.* [23]

—Do I show preference for one work rather than another.

No. Do I let everybody know when the work I have is not liked by me? *No.*

—Do I avoid interfering in another's work? *Yes—*

—Do I pray for the success of the work of the other Sisters? *Very much.*

READINGS: Imitation of Christ, Book III, Chapter 54.
REFLECTION: "Be ye perfect as your Heavenly Father is perfect." [Mt 5:48]

* * *

For the love of Jesus please destroy every paper. I don't know why He wants me to open my soul to you—I do it because I can't "refuse."

TENTH DAY

<u>With Jesus in His Agony.</u>

AIM: To spend a day in reparation for the sufferings I have made Jesus bear for me.
EXAMINATION: My spirit of Mortification.

EXTERIOR PENANCE

—Do I perform all these penances in the spirit of faith? *Yes.*

—How do I take the discomforts due to the climate, ill-health, common life, poverty, etc. . . . ? *As part of the call.* [24]

INTERIOR PENANCE

—Am I resigned interiorly to the trials which God sends me? *As gifts.* [25]

—Do I try to hide the little sufferings of my daily life? *Yes.* [26]

—Do I accept Desolation as readily as Consolation? Do I accept

Dryness in Prayer as a grace of God? *Being always in darkness—no chance of choosing.*

—Do I put up with the defects of others? *Yes.*

Please Father, don't let me deceive you—the torture within me is great.—Thank God.

READINGS: Imitation of Christ, Book 2, Chapters 11 and 12.
ST. JOHN'S GOSPEL: Chapters 14 and 17.
REFLECTION FOR THE DAY: "Father, he said, if it pleases thee, take away this chalice before me; only as Thy will is, not as mine is." [Lk 22:42]

* * *

*"I can [relieve] the sufferings of Jesus.
I can take a part from His suffering."*
Thank you for telling me.—This was a tremendous grace to me.

ELEVENTH DAY

With Mary, the Mother of Sorrows.

AIM: To spend the day in union with the sorrow of Jesus and Mary in order to strengthen my resolutions.
EXAMINATION: My desire to die to the world and to self love. *I have a great & deep desire to be nothing to the world and the world to be nothing to me.*

—Do I keep my Rule No. 88?[27] This Rule tells me to love humility so earnestly that I may accept humiliation readily, even with joy? *Yes.*

—Do I receive correction and admonition in the spirit of faith without excuse or complaint? *When Sisters say harsh & hurtful things I feel sorry for them—but personally I feel very happy.*[28]

—Am I ready to accept suffering out of love for Jesus and Mary? *Yes*—

Humility holds a great grip on my soul. I don't think I am humble for I am convinced of my smallness & nothingness, but I long to be meek & humble of heart like Jesus' Heart is. I don't know for how many years I have tried to make my own this meekness & humility of the Heart of Jesus—up to now nothing.

READINGS: Book of Isaias, Chapter 53.

IMITATION OF CHRIST: Book 3, Chapter 19. Any passage from the Passion of Christ (New Testament).

REFLECTION FOR THE DAY: "O my people, what have . . ."[29]

* * *

Thank you Father—you have helped me. I am <u>determined</u> to <u>become</u> a saint of the Sacred Heart—meek & humble. Ask Jesus for one grace only—to give me "the smiling face of a child." The darkness maybe is deeper, the loneliness harder, but I want it to be so—because it is His Holy Will.

TWELFTH DAY

<u>Under the patronage of Mary, Queen of Heaven.</u>

AIM: Union with the Risen Jesus in His great glory. To acquire a great confidence in goodness and greatness of my Redeemer.

EXAMINATION: My love for the Church. *I am determined to show my love for the Church by <u>becoming</u> very holy.*

—Do I really look upon the Church as the "Mystical Body of Christ"? *Nothing inside of me.*

—Do I burn with zeal to make the Church known and loved by all men?

—Do I try to conform my judgements with the directions given by the Church through the Encyclicals, Pastoral Letters, Directions, etc. . . . ? *Yes.*

READINGS: PSALM 65. "*All things being equal choose the hard thing. No one is going to force me to be holy. It lies in my own hands and I will be inferior, moderate or very fervent just as I choose.*
But one cares—Jesus Christ."
ST. MATTHEW'S GOSPEL, Chapter 28.
ST. MARK'S GOSPEL, Chapter 16.
ST. LUKE'S GOSPEL, Chapter 24.
ST. JOHN'S GOSPEL Chapters 20 & 21.
THE IMITATION OF CHRIST: Book III, Chapter 49.
REFLECTIONS:
"Joy to thee, O Queen of Heaven
He whom thou was meet to bear
As He promised, hath arisen
Pour for us to Him thy prayer.[30]

When we stand, sooner or later, at His judgement seat, the questions put to us will ~~not be~~:[31]

"What have you done?" *Nothing God. I have only tried to be a willing instrument.*

~~or~~ "How have you done it?" *My best.*

~~but~~ "WHY did you do it? *For You alone.*

* * *

THIRTEENTH DAY

<u>Under the protection of the Immaculate Heart of Mary,
Cause of our Joy.</u>
AIM: To put myself in the right dispositions for my final offering.
EXAMINATION: Am I ready to make this final offering with real love and complete surrender? <u>Yes</u>.
Take and receive, O Lord, my liberty,
Take all my will, my mind, my memory.
All things I have, and all I own are Thine;
Thine was the gift, to Thee I all resign.

Do Thou direct and govern all and sway,
Do what Thou will, command and I obey,
Only Thy grace, Thy love on me bestow,
Possessing these, all riches I forgo."[32] *Amen*
READINGS: Imitation of Christ, Book 3, Chapter 10.
REFLECTION: Let me have full confidence in the Sacred Heart
of Jesus and the Immaculate Heart of Mary, the Cause of our Joy.

Say with fervour the following prayer:[33]

ENDNOTES

Preface

1. "Very often I feel like a little pencil in God's Hands. He does the writing, He does the thinking, He does the movement, I have only to be the pencil." Mother Teresa's speech in Rome, March 7, 1979.

Introduction

1. Mother M. Teresa, M.C., to Father Joseph Neuner, S.J., March 6, 1962.
2. Mother Teresa to Father Neuner, undated, but most probably written during the retreat of April 1961.
3. Malcolm Muggeridge, *Something Beautiful for God* (New York, Evanston, San Francisco, London: Harper & Row, 1971), p. 18.
4. Mother Teresa to Archbishop Ferdinand Périer, S.J., February 8, 1956.
5. Mother Teresa to Archbishop Périer, March 30, 1957.
6. Mother Teresa to Archbishop Périer, December 18, 1960.
7. Father Céleste Van Exem, S.J., to Archbishop H. D'Souza, March 12, 1993.
8. Father Albert Huart, S.J., "Mother Teresa: Joy in the Night," *Review for Religious*, 60, no. 5 (Sept.–Oct. 2001), p. 501.

ONE: "Put Your Hand in His Hand, and Walk Alone with Him"

1. Mother Teresa's Instructions to the Missionaries of Charity Sisters, May 24, 1984.
2. Mother Teresa's Instructions to the M.C. Sisters, 1992.

3. Mother Teresa to Malcolm Muggeridge quoted in Malcolm Muggeridge, *Something Beautiful for God* (New York, Evanston, San Francisco, London: Harper & Row, 1971), p. 84.

4. Mother Teresa to Father Neuner, July 24, 1967.

5. Gonxha Bojaxhiu to the superior general of Loreto, June 28, 1928. Mother Teresa's baptismal name is Gonxha Agnes Bojaxhiu. However, as her letter to the superior general was written in Serbo-Croatian, she signed her name in that language (a common practice in Skopje at the time): Gonđa Bojađijević.

6. Mother Teresa to Archbishop Périer, January 25, 1947.

7. Mother Teresa, from the Mediterranean Sea to *Blagovijest* (the local Catholic magazine in Skopje), March 25, 1929, pp. 3–4.

8. The poem was written in Serbo-Croatian, a language Gonxha had become proficient in as a citizen of Yugoslavia. In every stanza the first line rhymes with the third and the second with the fourth. The language was so rich that the editors of the magazine deemed it necessary to add a footnote to one of the words she used, as it would be a word they would not expect an average reader to know. Translated from Serbo-Croatian by Dr. Tom Butler.

9. The "Te Deum" is a traditional hymn of joy and praise sung in thanksgiving to God and used in the Church's liturgy. The title derives from the original Latin text "Te Deum Laudamus" that translates "We praise Thee, O God."

10. Mother Teresa to *Katoličke Misije* [Mission magazine published by the Jesuits in Yugoslavia], January 6, 1929, p. 58.

11. Subsequently she renewed her vows every year for three years and then once for three years before being admitted to final profession.

12. Mother Teresa to Anka Čavčić, 1931.

13. "Medium" referred to the language in which the classes were taught, either English or Bengali.

14. Mother Teresa to *Blagovijest*, November 1932. Cf. Matthew 28:19. Bible citations are taken from the Revised Standard Bible, Catholic Edition, unless otherwise indicated.

15. Father Franjo Jambreković, S.J., (1890–1969), Croatian Jesuit, pastor of the Sacred Heart Parish in Skopje, from 1924 to 1930.

16. Cf. Matthew 16:24.

17. The tertianship was a period of intense preparation for final profession that took place in the Loreto convent in Darjeeling.

18. Cf. Luke 2:51 and Matthew 27:33.

19. She did not mean for him to stop his formal prayers and only work. She would later explain to her sisters, "Work is not prayer; prayer is not work, but we must pray the work for Him, with Him and to Him."

20. Sister Teresa to Father Jambreković, February 8, 1937. Sister Teresa used to sign her name in the language in which she was writing. To avoid confusion, her name has been replaced by its original "Teresa."

21. "In the same proportion as charity grows, the fear of suffering diminishes and that of sin increases without the weakening of trust." Father Reginald Garrigou-Lagrange, O.P., *The Three Ages of Interior Life: Prelude of Eternal Life*, vol. 2, trans. Sister M. Timothea Doyle, O.P. (St. Louis, MO: B. Herder Book Co., 1948, Rockford, IL: Tan Books and Publishers, Inc., 1989), pp. 463–64.

22. Sister Teresa to Father Jambreković, February 8, 1937.

23. St. John of the Cross (1542–1591), Spanish Founder (with St. Teresa of Avila) of the Discalced Carmelites, mystic, poet, Doctor of the Church.

24. Archbishop Périer was born on September 22, 1875, in Anvers, Belgium. He was ordained a priest of the Society of Jesus (Jesuits) in 1909, consecrated a bishop on December 21, 1921, and appointed coadjutor archbishop of Calcutta. He succeeded the archbishop of Calcutta on June 23, 1924, and remained in office until his retirement in 1960.

25. With self-deprecatory humor, Mother Teresa observed that her pride got in the way of her totally belonging to Jesus, ironically referring to her "reverend" or exalted self.

26. Cf. Matthew 20:22 and 26:39, 42.

27. Mother Teresa to Father Jambreković, November 25, 1937.

28. Sister Mary Gabrielle, I.B.V.M., to Father Jambreković, November 25, 1937.

29. Testimony of Sister Francis Michael Lyne, I.B.V.M.

30. Sister Marie-Thérèse, I.B.V.M., quoted in Navin Chawla, *Mother Teresa* (Rockport: Element Books, 1996), p. 12.

31. A Loreto nun with final vows was not addressed with the Bengali "Ma" but with the English "Mother." Thus it was Sister Teresa's love for her people that earned her the well-deserved title "Ma"—an expression of their closeness and affection for her.

32. Sister Teresa to *Katoličke Misije*, October 1937, p. 25.

33. Ibid.

TWO: Something Very Beautiful for Jesus

1. Mother Teresa to Archbishop Périer, September 1, 1959. In the other two references she makes to the vow, Mother Teresa uses the common expression "under pain of mortal sin."

2. Mother Teresa to Father Neuner, May 12, 1962.

3. Mother Teresa to Father Lawrence Trevor Picachy, S.J., April 4, 1960.

4. Mother Teresa's Retreat Notes, March–April 1959. p. 357.

5. Explanation of the Original Constitutions of the Missionaries of Charity, handwritten by Mother Teresa, undated. Mother Teresa is quoting P. Johanns, S.J., The Little Way, Light of the East Series, No. 15 (Calcutta: F. G. Gomes at the Bengal Litho Press), pp. 90, 91, 92.

6. Fr. William Doyle, S.J., was born on March 3, 1873, in Dalkey, Ireland, and died on August 16, 1917, in Flanders while serving as an army chaplain.

7. Alfred O'Rahilly, Father William Doyle, S.J., *A Spiritual Study* (London, New York, Toronto: Longmans, Green and Co., 1925) p. 288. This vow is also recorded in the book *Merry in God* (Father William Doyle, S.J.). (London, New York, Toronto: Longmans, Green and Co., 1939) p. 137, which Mother Teresa read.

8. Sister Benigna Consolata Ferrero, a religious of the Visitation Order of Como, Italy, was born on August 6, 1885, and died on September 1, 1916— the First Friday of the month.

9. The Community Circular of Como, translated by M.S. Pine, Sister Benigna Consolata Ferrero (Chicago: John P. Daleiden Company, 1921) pp. 41, 128.

10. Pope Pius XI, Vehementer exultamus hodie, Bull of Canonization of St. Thérèse of the Child Jesus in *Saint Thérèse of Lisieux: The Little Flower of Jesus,* trans. Rev. Thomas N. Taylor (P.J. Kennedy & Sons, New York, 1927), p. 279.

11. Mother Teresa's Instructions to the M.C. Sisters, January 19, 1983.

12. The Constitutions of the Loreto Sisters encouraged "perfect" obedience, that is, conforming one's own will and judgment to that of one's superior.

13. Mother Teresa to Father Neuner, May 12, 1962.

14. Ibid. A mortal sin is "a grave violation of God's law; it turns man away from God, who is his ultimate end and his beatitude, by preferring an inferior good to him" (Catechism of the Catholic Church, 1855; hereafter abbreviated as CCC). If mortal sin "is not redeemed by repentance and God's forgiveness, it causes exclusion from Christ's kingdom and the eternal death of hell" (CCC, 1861). Conditions for a mortal sin are grave matter, full knowledge, and complete consent (CCC, 1858–59).

15. Mother Teresa to Father Picachy, April 4, 1960.

16. Sister Marie-Thérèse, I.B.V.M., quoted in Navin Chawla, *Mother Teresa* (Rockport: Element Books, 1996), p. 11.

17. Speaking from her own life, in her instructions to her sisters she would insist that "submission for someone who is in love is more than a duty, it is a blessedness." She was in fact paraphrasing the thought that with time had become her own, taken from Louis Colin, C.S.S.R.: "Submission, for someone who is in love, is more than a duty: it is more than a necessity; it is a taste of blessedness" (*The Practice of the Rule* [Cork, Ireland: The Mercier Press Limited, 1964], p. 11).

18. Mother Teresa's Instructions to the M.C. Sisters, March 31, 1987.

19. Cf. 2 Corinthians 9:7.

20. Explanation of the Original Constitutions.

21. St. Thérèse of Lisieux, *Story of a Soul*, trans. John Clarke, O.C.D. (Washington, D.C.: Institute of Carmelite Studies, 1976), p. 196.

22. Mother Teresa to the M.C. Sisters, First Friday, November 1960.

23. Mother Teresa's Instructions to the M.C. Sisters, October 30, 1981.

24. Mother Teresa to Archbishop Périer, September 1, 1959.

25. See *Katoličke Misije*, February 1942.

26. Statement of Sister Letitia, D.S.A.

27. Father Ante Gabrić, S.J., quoted in Juraj Gusić, S.J., *Majke Odbačenih* (Zagreb, Croatia: privately printed, 1976), p. 54.

28. "Godown" was the common word in India for a storage room.

29. Sister M. Francesca, I.B.V.M., quoted in Navin Chawla, *Mother Teresa* (Rockport: Element Books, 1996), p. 14.

30. Mother Teresa quoted in Eileen Egan, *Such a Vision of the Street: Mother Teresa—The Spirit and the Work* (New York: Image Doubleday, 1985), p. 24.

31. Explanation of the Original Constitutions.

THREE: "Come, Be My Light"

1. Mother Teresa to Malcolm Muggeridge, quoted in Muggeridge's *Something Beautiful for God* (New York, Evanston, San Francisco, London: Harper & Row, 1971), pp. 85–86.

2. When a new sister enters the congregation, her personal data is recorded in the "entrance register." One important piece of information is the date that sister entered the Missionaries of Charity.

3. Mother Teresa to the M.C. Sisters, April 24, 1996.

4. Mother Teresa to the Co-Workers, Christmas 1996.

5. John 19:28.

6. Explanation of the Original Constitutions. From the beginning, Mother Teresa and the sisters connected the profession of the vows with quenching Jesus' thirst; for example, they drew a cross with the words "I thirst" as the heading of the paper on which they wrote their vows for their profession ceremony.

7. Cf. John 19:25–27.

8. Explanation of Original Constitutions.

9. On the wall of every chapel of the Missionaries of Charity, the words of Jesus "I thirst" are placed next to the crucifix as a reminder of the aim of the Institute's spirituality and mission.

10. Mother Teresa to the M.C. Sisters, Brothers and Fathers, March 25, 1993.

11. Constitutions of the Missionaries of Charity Sisters, 5.

12. Cf. Luke 10:33–35.

13. Matthew 25:40.

14. Mother M. Teresa to Archbishop Périer, Feast of Corpus Christi, June 5, 1947.

15. Locutions (or supernatural words) are "manifestations of God's thought" which may come through words heard externally (exterior or auricular locutions) or in the imagination (interior imaginative locutions) or immediately without any words (interior intellectual locutions). See Reginald Garrigou-Lagrange, O.P., *The Three Ages of the Spiritual Life: Prelude of Eternal Life,* vol. 2 (St. Louis, MO: B. Herder Book Co., 1948; Rockford, Ill.: Tan Books and Publishers, Inc., 1989), pp. 589–90; and Augustin Poulain, S.J., *Revelations and Visions: Discerning the True and Certain from the False or the Doubtful,* trans. L. L. Yorke Smith (1910; repr., New York: Alba House, 1998), pp. 1–18. Mother Teresa received interior imaginative locutions.

16. The words of Jesus that Mother Teresa heard by interior locution are italicized throughout the book.

17. Mother Teresa to *Katoličke Misije,* February 1935, p 25.

18. Mother Teresa to *Katoličke Misije,* October 1937.

19. Mother Teresa to Archbishop Périer, January 13, 1947.

20. Mother Teresa to Mother M. Gertrude Kennedy, I.B.V.M., January 10, 1948. This was the classic Catholic response to such extraordinary manifestations of the divine presence. The unanimous opinion of the masters of spirituality is that the first step in testing such communications is to turn aside from them, to refuse to become obsessed by them. If they are genuine, they will maintain themselves of their own strength. If they are not, they will fade away.

21. Saint Frances Xavier Cabrini (1850–1917), Italian nun and foundress of the Missionary Sisters of the Sacred Heart of Jesus, an order that worked with Italian immigrants in the United States. She founded hospitals, orphanages, nurseries, and schools. In 1946 she was the first American citizen to be canonized.

22. Cf. Luke 10:38–42.

23. Cf. Matthew 27:35.

24. Cf. Philippians 2:8.

25. Cf. Luke 23:34, 43.

26. St. Francis of Assisi (1181 or 1182–1226), Italian founder of the Franciscans and known for his practice of radical poverty.

27. St. Benedict of Nursia (c. 480–543), Italian founder of Western monasticism, whose motto was *"Ora et labora"* (Pray and Work).

28. A piece of rope that serves as a belt.

29. Grade two of primary school.

30. Mother Teresa to Archbishop Périer, January 13, 1947.

FOUR: "To Bring Joy to the Suffering Heart of Jesus"

1. A religious superior responsible for a number of convents grouped in a region or "province."

2. Mother Gertrude to Archbishop Périer, January 25, 1948.

3. Archbishop Périer to Mother Gertrude, January 13, 1948.

4. Ibid.

5. In the letter of January 13, 1947, Mother Teresa had quoted Jesus as saying, *"Ask His Grace to give Me this in thanksgiving of the 25 years of Grace I have given him."*

6. Mother Teresa and Father Van Exem.

7. Mother Teresa to Archbishop Périer, January 25, 1947.

8. Archbishop Périer to Mother Teresa, February 19, 1947.

9. Cf. 1 Corinthians 9:22.

10. St. Francis Xavier (1506–1552), one of the first members of the Society of Jesus (Jesuits), a great missionary in India, and Japan.

11. Mother Teresa to Archbishop Périer, sometime before March 7, 1947.

12. Father Joseph Creusen, S.J., to Archbishop Périer, June 28, 1947.

13. Archbishop Périer to Mother Teresa, March 7, 1947.

14. Cf. Matthew 10:42.

15. Mother Mary of the Passion (1839–1904), French foundress of the Franciscan Missionaries of Mary.

16. Mother Teresa is referring to Pope Pius XII's encyclical *Quemadmodum* (Pleading for the Care of the World's Destitute Children), promulgated on January 6, 1946.

17. Mother Teresa is referring to the civil unrest and riots that took place in India immediately before India's independence on August 15, 1947.

18. Boys Own Home, a school located in Cossipore, an area in northern Calcutta, was founded by Swami B. Animananda Rewachand (1868–1945). It had been vacated at the beginning of 1946.

19. Mother Teresa to Archbishop Périer, March 30, 1947.

20. The archbishop's question is whether a group of laywomen could accomplish Mother Teresa's objective without taking on the commitments of religious living in a community.

21. Archbishop Périer to Mother Teresa, April 7, 1947. The numbering and underlining in this letter are Mother Teresa's.

22. Ibid.

23. Father Van Exem to Archbishop Périer, June 14, 1947.

24. Ibid.

25. The liturgical feast of the Holy Eucharist, celebrated on the Thursday after Trinity Sunday.

26. "Mem" is short for "Memsabib," literally "big lady." Formerly in

India a term of respect used for a married European woman. In this context, Mother Teresa was implying that life in a European order is unlike the simple and poor lifestyle she envisioned for her sisters.

27. Mother Teresa to Archbishop Périer, Feast of Corpus Christi, June 5, 1947.

28. She drafted the Rules during the novena preceding Pentecost. In 1947 Pentecost Sunday was May 25, so the novena was from May 15 to May 24. See Appendix A.

29. Father Van Exem to Archbishop Périer, June 14, 1947.

FIVE: "Delay No Longer. Keep Me Not Back."

1. Mother Gertrude to Archbishop Périer, January 25, 1948.

2. Father Van Exem to Archbishop Périer, August 8, 1947.

3. Ibid. (Father Van Exem is quoting Mother Teresa in his letter to the archbishop).

4. Ibid.

5. Ibid.

6. Ibid.

7. Father Van Exem to Archbishop Périer, October 26, 1947.

8. Father Van Exem to Archbishop Périer, August 8, 1947.

9. Ibid.

10. Ibid.

11. Thomas Dubay, *Fire Within: St. Teresa of Avila, St. John of the Cross, and the Gospel—on Prayer* (San Francisco: Ignatius Press, 1989), p. 265.

12. Mother Teresa to the Lord, undated.

13. Mother Teresa to Father Neuner, undated, but most probably written during the retreat of April 1961. Sweetness, consolation, and union are some of the effects of genuine locutions and visions. Father Augustin Poulain, S.J., quotes St. John of the Cross: "The effects which these (imaginative) visions in the soul produce are quiet, illumination, joy like that of glory, sweetness, purity, love, humility, and the inclination or elevation of the mind to God." Some of these spiritual favors were evident in Mother Teresa's soul, and this was further incentive to Father Van Exem to believe that the call was authentic. See Augustin Poulain, *Revelations and Visions* (New York: Alba House, 1998), p. 16.

14. Father Van Exem to Archbishop Périer, August 8, 1947.

15. Archbishop Périer to Mother Teresa, October 24, 1947.

16. Saint Thérèse of the Child Jesus and the Holy Face, commonly known as St. Thérèse of Lisieux.

17. Mother M. Teresa to Archbishop Périer, October 1, 1947.

18. Mother Teresa writing to Jesus in 1959 (see chapter 9, endnote 25).

19. Mother Teresa changed her opinion about not destroying the letters once the congregation was established; at that point she thought that the letters were of no further use.

20. Father Joseph Creusen, S.J. (1880–1960), was a professor at the Gregorian University in Rome. Mother Teresa had inquired as to whether he had seen the rule and, if so, what had been his opinion. According to the archbishop, this was not her concern.

21. Mother Teresa to Father Van Exem, October 19, 1947.

22. Ibid.

23. Father Van Exem to Archbishop Périer, August 8, 1947.

24. Father Van Exem to Archbishop Périer, October 20, 1947.

25. Father Van Exem to Archbishop Périer, October 26, 1947.

26. Archbishop Périer to Father Van Exem, October 28, 1947.

27. Cf. Acts 5:38–39.

28. Cf. John 14:13.

29. Mother Teresa to Archbishop Périer, October 24, 1947.

30. Mother Teresa to Father Van Exem, October 28, 1947.

31. Mother Teresa to Archbishop Périer, November 7, 1947.

32. Cf. Luke 18:2–8.

33. Cf. Philippians 4:13.

34. Mother Teresa to Archbishop Périer, November 7, 1947.

35. Mother Teresa to Archbishop Périer, December 3, 1947.

36. Father Creusen to Archbishop Périer, June 28, 1947.

37. Father Jerome Sanders, S.J., to Archbishop Périer, December 8, 1947.

38. Father Creusen to Archbishop Périer, June 28, 1947.

39. Archbishop Périer to Mother Gertrude, January 13, 1948.

SIX: To the "Dark Holes"

1. Through an indult of secularization, a religious receives a dispensation from his or her religious vows, thereby becoming a layperson. By an indult of exclaustration, the religious formally remains a member of his or her religious institute bound by religious vows but lives outside the religious house. Many rights and obligations cease.

2. Mother Teresa to Mother Gertrude, January 10, 1948.

3. "Someday it [permission] is sure to come—and then you will, I am sure be the first to give the young institute all the help it will need." Mother Teresa to Archbishop Périer, most probably before March 7, 1947.

4. Mother Teresa to Father Van Exem, October 19, 1947.

5. Mother Teresa to Archbishop Périer, January 28, 1948.

6. Ibid.

7. Archbishop Périer to Father Van Exem, January 12, 1948.

8. Ibid.

9. Since she was from Yugoslavia, English was not her first language; as a result, she was not assigned to teach in English.

10. Archbishop Périer to Mother Gertrude, January 13, 1948.

11. It was actually less than three weeks, because her letter to Mother Gertrude was written on January 10 and this letter to the archbishop was written on January 28.

12. Neither of these young women joined, but this shows Mother Teresa's confidence that vocations would come.

13. Mother Teresa to Archbishop Périer, January 28, 1948.

14. Mother Teresa to Archbishop Périer, January 13, 1947.

15. "Instant" means the present or current month.

16. Archbishop Périer to Mother Teresa, January 29, 1948.

17. Ibid.

18. Mother Gertrude to Archbishop Périer, January 25, 1948.

19. Mother Gertrude to Mother Teresa, January 25, 1948.

20. Mother Teresa to the Cardinal Prefect, Sacred Congregation of Religious, February 7, 1948.

21. Archbishop Périer to the Cardinal Prefect, Sacred Congregation of Religious, February 20, 1948, translation from the original French.

22. Mother Teresa to Archbishop Périer, April 14, 1948.

23. The month of May is traditionally dedicated to Our Lady.

24. Mother Teresa to Archbishop Périer, May 13, 1948.

25. Archbishop Périer to Mother Teresa, May 18, 1948.

26. Ibid.

27. Archbishop Périer to Mother M. Columba, I.B.V.M., dated August 7, 1948.

28. In remembrance of this important day, Mother Teresa chose this date as the day of final profession for the first group of Missionaries of Charity, as well as for a good number of subsequent groups.

29. Mother Teresa to Archbishop Périer, March 30, 1947.

30. Mother Teresa to the Cardinal Prefect, Sacred Congregation of Religious, February 7, 1948.

31. "Punjab mail" train.

32. Mother Teresa to Archbishop Périer, August 15, 1948.

33. Testimony of Navin Chawla.

SEVEN: "The Dark Night of the Birth of the Society"

1. Eileen Egan, *Such a Vision of the Street* (New York: Image Doubleday, 1985), p. 32.

2. Mother Teresa to Archbishop Périer, August 24, 1948.

3. Ibid.

4. This prayer, dictated by Jesus to Visitation Sister Benigna Consolata Ferrero (1885–1916), was copied by Mother Teresa on the first page of her Medical Notebook in Patna, dated 1948. In it, besides medical terms, diseases, and corresponding treatments, she wrote recipes for various cookies and names and addresses of potential benefactors.

5. The motto of St. Ignatius of Loyola.

6. Mother Emmanuel, I.B.V.M., to Mother Teresa, August 15, 1948.

7. An affectionate term involving a pun that the two of them understood.

8. Mother M. Joseph, I.B.V.M., to Mother Teresa, August 15, 1948,

9. Mother M. Gabrielle, I.B.V.M., to Mother Teresa, September 3, 1948. Mother Teresa's feast—St. Thérèse's feast—was actually on October 3, so possibly Mother Gabrielle made a mistake in dating the letter.

10. Mother Teresa to Father Van Exem, September 17, 1948.

11. Father Julien Henry, S.J., was born on August 18, 1901, in Dampremy, Belgium. He joined the Society of Jesus in 1918 and was ordained in 1931. In 1938, he came to India and in 1940 began his apostolate in St. Teresa's Parish. He also served as spiritual father to the girls' Sodality in Entally, Calcutta. He supported Mother Teresa from the beginning of her work among the poorest of the poor and was advisor and confessor of the MCs from 1949 to the end of his life in 1979.

12. A town in India. Mother Teresa was referring to a convent there.

13. Mother Teresa to Father Van Exem, September 17, 1948.

14. Ibid.

15. Then a poor area of Calcutta. Mother Teresa was referring to a convent there.

16. Mother Teresa to Father Van Exem, September 17, 1948.

17. Ibid.

18. Mother M. Pauline Dunne, I.B.V.M., to Sister M. Teresa, October 29, 1948.

19. Cf. Luke 2:7.

20. Mother Teresa to Mother Pauline, November 9, 1948.

21. Testimony of Sister M. Gertrude, M.C.

22. Veronica Gomes, a Sodality member at St. Teresa's, was working in the parish; she was Mother Teresa's guide to the poor areas of the city.

23. Record of the First Days, written from December 21–23, 1948.

24. Cf. Luke 4:43.

25. Journal of Mother Teresa, January 24, 1949 (hereafter Journal). This record of events was mandated by Archbishop Périer and written from Christmas 1948 to June 11, 1949.

26. Mother Teresa to Archbishop Périer, February 10, 1949.

27. Mother Teresa to Archbishop Périer, January 13, 1947.

28. Mother Teresa to Archbishop Périer, February 21, 1949.

29. Journal, February 28, 1949.

30. Journal, February 16, 1949.

31. Cf. John 2:3.

32. Journal, February 2, 1949.

33. Journal, March 19, 1949.

34. Mother Teresa to Archbishop Périer, June 29, 1949.

35. Archbishop Périer to Cardinal Prefect of the Sacred Congregation of Religious, Rome, August 4, 1949, translated from the French.

36. Mother Teresa to Pope Pius XII, March 1, 1950.

37. Mother Teresa to Archbishop Périer, July 23, 1950.

38. Mother Teresa to Archbishop Périer, June 21, 1950.

39. Decree of Erection of the new congregation: the Missionary Sisters of Charity.

40. Mother Teresa to Archbishop Périer, September 23, 1950.

41. Ibid.

42. Testimony of Sister M. Dorothy, M.C.

43. John 12:24–25, Douay-Rheims Bible.

44. Explanation of the Original Constitutions.

45. Mother Teresa to Archbishop Périer, January 20, 1951.

46. Mother Teresa to Archbishop Périer, March 20, 1951.

47. Mother Teresa to Archbishop Périer, October 26, 1950.

48. Mother Teresa to Father Jambreković, November 25, 1937.

49. Mother Teresa is referring to the devotion to Mary presented by Saint Louis de Montfort in *The Secret of Mary* which "consists in surrendering oneself in the manner of a slave to Mary, and to Jesus through her, and then performing all our actions with Mary, in Mary, through Mary, and for Mary." Saint Louis de Montfort, *The Secret of Mary* (New York: The Montfort Publications, 1984), p. 24.

50. Mother Teresa to Archbishop Périer, April 15, 1951.

51. Explanation of the Original Constitutions.

52. Mother Teresa to Archbishop Périer, July 30, 1951.

53. Archbishop Périer to Mother Teresa, July 31, 1951.

54. The Daughters of St. Anne was the religious branch affiliated with Loreto, of which Mother Teresa had been in charge while in St. Mary's Entally.

55. Mother Teresa to Archbishop Périer, July 30, 1951.

56. Mother Teresa to Archbishop Périer, August 11, 1951.

57. Mother Francis Xavier Stapleton, I.B.V.M., to Mother Teresa, August 9, 1951.

58. Mother Teresa to Archbishop Périer, February 8, 1952.

59. Mother Teresa to Archbishop Périer, April 4, 1952.

60. Mother Teresa to Archbishop Périer, July 6, 1952.

61. In gratitude to Our Lady, Mother Teresa wanted to have all her homes named after the Immaculate Heart.

62. Archbishop Périer to Mother Teresa, October 1, 1952.

63. Mother Teresa to Archbishop Périer, October 6, 1952.

64. Mother Teresa's speech, Synod of Bishops, Rome, October 1980.

65. Mother Teresa obtained the concept of a "second self" from Jesuit Father Alphonsus Rodriguez: "This [loving one's friend as oneself] makes me look on my friend as my *second self*, and on me as a *second self* to him; and in fine, of us both it makes only one." V. F. Alphonsus Rodriguez, S.J., *The Practice of Christian and Religious Perfection*, Vol. 1, The Fourth Treatise, Chapter 1 (Dublin: James Duffy and Sons, 1882), p. 155.

66. Mother Teresa to the Co-workers, March 1, 1995.

67. Cf. Philippians 4:13.

68. Mother Teresa to Jacqueline de Decker, January 13, 1953.

69. Mother Teresa to Jacqueline de Decker, March 15, 1953.

70. Mother Teresa to Archbishop Périer, July 15, 1958.

EIGHT: The Thirst of Jesus Crucified

1. Mother Teresa to Archbishop Périer, March 18, 1953.

2. Archbishop Périer to Mother Teresa, March 20, 1953.

3. Mother Teresa to Archbishop Périer, April 1, 1953.

4. Archbishop Périer to Mother Teresa, April 12, 1953.

5. Archbishop Périer to Mother Teresa, December 22, 1954.

6. Mother Teresa to Archbishop Périer, April 17, 1953.

7. Mother Teresa to Archbishop Périer, August 6, 1953.

8. Mother Teresa wished to grant the request of this aspirant who wanted to make her religious profession before dying. Since she was not yet a novice, this was not possible. Mother Teresa nonetheless considered her to be a Missionary of Charity, even if this was not formally the case.

9. Mother Teresa to Archbishop Périer, September 8, 1953.

10. Mother Teresa to Archbishop Périer, Feast of Corpus Christi (June 5), 1947.

11. Mother Teresa to Archbishop Périer, October 23, 1953.

12. Mother Teresa to Archbishop Périer, December 19, 1953.

13. Mother Teresa to Archbishop Périer, February 26, 1954.

14. Mother Teresa to Jacqueline de Decker, March 25, 1954.

15. Mother Teresa had added her own name after Jacqueline's.

16. Cf. John 10:38.

17. Cf. Matthew 1:1–3.

18. Mother Teresa to Jacqueline de Decker, October 17, 1954.

19. From the prayer "Radiating Christ," prayed daily after Mass by the M.C.s.

20. A popular prayer to Mary: "Remember, O most gracious Virgin Mary, that never was it known that anyone who fled to your protection, implored your help, or sought your intercession, was left unaided. Inspired with this confidence, I fly to you, O Virgin of virgins, my Mother, to you I come, before you I stand, sinful and sorrowful. O Mother of the Word Incarnate! Despise not my petitions, but, in your mercy hear and answer them. Amen." The title is derived from the first word of the prayer in Latin, "Memorare."

21. Mother Teresa to Sister Margaret Mary, M.C., January 15, 1955.

22. Mother Teresa to Archbishop Périer, January 21, 1955.

23. Archbishop Périer to Mother Teresa, January 23, 1955.

24. Mother Teresa to Archbishop Périer, January 31, 1955.

25. This is the way Mother Teresa addresses the sick and suffering co-workers in this letter.

26. Cf. Col 1:24.

27. Mother Teresa to sick and suffering co-workers, March 9, 1955.

28. Mother Teresa to Archbishop Périer, March 30, 1957.

29. The sixth day of her retreat.

30. Mother Teresa to Archbishop Périer, April 4, 1955.

31. Cf. Luke 14:12–14.

32. Mother Teresa is referring to the religious celebrations of the Hindus and Muslims.

33. During Advent an empty crib and a basket filled with straw was placed in the chapel next to the altar. The sisters placed a wisp of straw in the crib for every sacrifice made in preparation for the coming of Jesus at Christmas.

34. Mother Teresa to Archbishop Périer, December 15, 1955.

35. Mother Teresa to Archbishop Périer, February 8, 1956.

36. Archbishop Périer to Mother Teresa, February 9, 1956.

37. Ibid.

38. Ibid.

39. Mother Teresa to Archbishop Périer, March 27, 1956.

40. Father Lawrence Trevor Picachy, S.J., was born in Lebong, Darjeeling District, on July 8, 1916. He entered the Society of Jesus in 1934 and was ordained in 1947. He was Rector of St. Xavier's Calcutta from 1954 to 1960; parish priest at Basanti (Dt. 24-Parganas) from 1960 to 1962; received Episcopal Ordination at Golmuri, Jamshedpur, on September 9, 1962; became archbishop of Calcutta on July 10, 1969; and in 1976 he was named cardinal. Starting in 1979 he served as one of the presidents of the Synod of Bishops on the Family in Rome. He resigned his office in 1986 and died in Calcutta on November 29, 1992.

41. Mother Teresa to Father Picachy, April 4, 1960.

42. Mother Teresa's Retreat Notes, March–April 1959, p. 358.

43. Mother Teresa to Archbishop Périer, April 10, 1956.

44. Ibid.

45. Mother Teresa to Jacqueline de Decker, July 18, 1956.

46. St. Bernadette Soubirous (1844–1879), to whom Our Lady appeared in Lourdes, France, in 1858.

47. St. Ignatius of Loyola (1491–1556), founder of the Society of Jesus.

48. Archbishop Périer to Mother Teresa, July 29, 1956.

49. Mother Teresa to Archbishop Périer, September 25, 1956.

50. Mother Teresa to Archbishop Périer, June 21, 1950.

51. Mother Teresa to Archbishop Périer, November 17, 1956.

52. Mother Teresa to Father Picachy, January 26, 1957.

53. Mother Teresa to Archbishop Périer, February 28, 1957.

54. Mother Teresa to Archbishop Périer, March 30, 1947.

55. That Mother Teresa was sensitive to small expressions of thoughtfulness can be seen from her reaction to Archbishop Périer's not sending her a greeting for her feast day: "I missed your letter for my feast. In 20 years this is the first time" (Mother Teresa to Archbishop Périer, October 4, 1956).

56. Cf. Matthew 11:29.

57. Mother Teresa to Archbishop Périer April 8, 1957.

58. The Sacred Heart of Jesus is traditionally honored on the first Friday of each month.

59. Mother Teresa to Archbishop Périer, September 12, 1957.

60. Mother Teresa to Mother Gertrude, January 10, 1948.

61. Mother Teresa to Archbishop Périer, March 30, 1947.

62. Mother Teresa to Archbishop Périer, Feast of Corpus Christi (June 5), 1947.

63. Mother Teresa to Archbishop Périer, September 12, 1957.

64. Yeti, "Battle in Busteeland," *The Statesman,* January 22, 1958.

65. Mother Teresa to Archbishop Périer, January 29, 1958.

66. Mother Teresa to Father Picachy, April 25, 1958.

67. Mother Teresa to Father Picachy, June 28, 1958.

68. Ibid.

69. Sacred Returns were the statistics of the religious activities submitted each year by parish priests or religious superiors to the bishop or his vicar general.

70. Mother Teresa to Archbishop Périer, July 15, 1958.

71. Mother Teresa to Eileen Egan, May 15, 1958.

72. Mother Teresa to Eileen Egan, July 20, 1958.

73. Pope Pius XII died on October 9, 1958.

74. Mother Teresa to Archbishop Périer, November 7, 1958.

75. Mother Teresa to Archbishop Périer, November 16, 1958.

NINE: *"My God, How Painful Is This Unknown Pain"*

1. Mother Teresa did not include Archbishop Périer here, as he was the bishop and her religious superior.

2. Mother Teresa to Father Picachy, August 15, 1957.

3. Mother Teresa to Father Picachy, November 22, 1957.

4. These letters have not been preserved.

5. Mother Teresa to Father Picachy, November 6, 1958.

6. From Punjab, a state in northwestern India.

7. Mother Teresa to Father Picachy, November 23, 1958.

8. Mother Teresa to Father Picachy, December 2, 1958. Mother Teresa was referring to the book *Garlic for Pegasus* by Father Wilfred P. Schoenberg, S.J.

9. Schoenberg, *Garlic for Pegasus: The Life of Brother Benito de Goes of the Society of Jesus* (Westminster, MD: Newman Press, 1955), p. 194.

10. "Third year" or "tertianship." The sisters in this period of formation were known as tertians. These tertians were the ten sisters of the first group. This retreat would be the one immediately before final vows.

11. Mother Teresa to Father Picachy, January 24, 1959.

12. Mother Teresa to Father Picachy, March 7, 1959.

13. Ibid.

14. "Holy time" in this letter refers to Holy Week, not to the time of retreat. Mother Teresa wrote this letter on Saturday, March 21, 1959, the day before Palm Sunday and the beginning of Holy Week.

15. Mother Teresa to Archbishop Périer, March 21, 1959.

16. See Appendix B, Retreat Notes of Mother Teresa. Mother Teresa's answers appear in italics.

17. Mother Teresa to Archbishop Périer, April 5, 1959.

18. Mother Teresa to Archbishop Périer, April 12, 1959.

19. Acceptance of nomination, attached to Mother Teresa's letter to Archbishop Périer, April 15, 1959.

20. Mother Teresa to Archbishop Périer, May 28, 1959.

21. Sister Agnes became the assistant general and local superior of the motherhouse.

22. Mother Teresa to Father Picachy, April 26, 1959.

23. Mother Teresa to Father Picachy, July 3, 1959.

24. There are only three letters written by Mother Teresa to Father Picachy that refer to a written description of her interior state: the letter of November 6, 1958, referring to "three letters"; the letter of September 3, 1959, to which a letter to Jesus is attached; and this one of July 3, 1959. It is very unlikely that the undated "paper" she sent with the July 3rd letter, beginning "In the darkness," is one of the three letters mentioned in the letter

of November 6. Therefore it is most probably linked to the letter of July 3. In any case, this "paper" clearly belongs to this time period.

25. Mother Teresa to the Lord, undated.

26. Testimony of Sister Margaret Mary.

27. This may be referring to Jesus' words in the letters of January 12, and December 3, 1947: "You will suffer and you suffer now—but if you are my own little Spouse—the Spouse of the Crucified Jesus—you will have to bear these torments on your heart." Or they may be words of Jesus she had written in her notes but did not place in the letters.

28. Mother Teresa to Sister Margaret Mary, 1959.

29. Mother Teresa to Father Picachy, August 2, 1959.

30. Mother Teresa to Father Picachy, August 25, 1959.

31. Mother Teresa to Archbishop Périer, September 1, 1959.

32. Mother Teresa's letter to Jesus, enclosed with her letter to Father Picachy, September 3, 1959.

33. Ibid.

34. Ibid.

35. Like her patroness St. Thérèse of Lisieux during her trial of faith in the last eighteen months of her life, Mother Teresa feared that her thoughts were blasphemous. St. Thérèse rarely spoke about her trial of faith, except with her sister, Pauline (Mother Agnes of Jesus), because she feared that her words might be a cause of scandal or temptation to others.

36. See Appendix B, p. 351.

37. Mother Teresa to Father Picachy, September 6, 1959.

38. Cf. Luke 1:28–37.

39. Cf. Matthew 1:20–23.

40. Cf. Luke 2:19, 51.

41. Mother Teresa to the M.C. Sisters, September 20, 1959.

42. Cf. Luke 2:51.

43. A ticket costing 3 rupees. Either she received a discount or someone made a donation.

44. Mother Teresa to Father Picachy, October 27, 1959.

45. Ibid.

46. Mother Teresa to Father Picachy, November 21, 1959.

47. Mother Teresa to Father Picachy, December 13, 1959.

48. Mother Teresa to Father Picachy, December 26, 1959.

49. A town about 55 miles south of Calcutta.

50. Mother Teresa to Father Picachy, April 4, 1960.

51. The feast of St. Lawrence, Father Picachy's name day, is celebrated on August 10.

52. Mother Teresa to Father Picachy, August 7, 1960.

53. Mother Teresa to Father Edward Le Joly, S. J., quoted in Edward Le

Joly, S. J., *Mother Teresa of Calcutta: A Biography* (San Francisco, Cambridge, Hagerstown, New York, Philadelphia, London, Mexico City, Sao Paulo, Singapore, Sydney: Harper & Row, Publishers, 1983), p. 179.

54. Mother Teresa to Monsignor McCarthy, July 29, 1960.

55. Mother Teresa to a friend, August 10, 1960.

56. Mother Teresa to Eileen Egan, August 9, 1960.

57. Mother Teresa chose Mary, the Mother of Jesus, as companion and support in her darkest hours. In her meditation, which without her realizing it was a prayer of union with Jesus in agony, she turned to Mary with a line of the "Stabat Mater" (a hymn that dates back to the Middle Ages and celebrates the sentiments of Our Lady at the foot of the Cross): "Let me share with thee His pain."

58. Mother Teresa to Father Picachy, October 20, 1960.

59. In his study of the reparatory night of the spirit, Father Reginald Garrigou-Lagrange, O.P., using the example of the founder of the Passionist order, St. Paul of the Cross, asserts: "The reading of the works of St. John of the Cross leads one to consider the night of the spirit chiefly as a personal passive purification, which prepares the soul for the perfect union with God, called the transforming union. This purification, which in its passive aspect is a mystical state and implies infused contemplation, appears thus as necessary to remove the defects of proficients of whom the author speaks in *The Dark Night* (Bk. II, chap. 10). . . . The lives of some great servants of God especially dedicated to reparation, to immolation for the salvation of souls or to the apostolate by interior suffering, make one think, however, of a prolongation of the night of the spirit even after their entrance into the transforming union. In such cases, this trial would no longer be chiefly purificatory; it would be above all reparative. . . . The common opinion is that the servants of God are more particularly tried, whether it be that they need a more profound purification, or whether, following the example of our Lord, they must work by the same means as He used for a great spiritual cause, such as the foundation of a religious order or the salvation of many other souls." The long duration of this trial is one of the striking common traits between the night of St. Paul of the Cross and that of Mother Teresa. See Reginald Garrigou-Lagrange, O.P., *The Three Ages of Interior Life: Prelude of Eternal Life*, vol. 2, trans. Sister M. Timothea Doyle, O.P. (St. Louis, MO: B. Herder Book Co., 1948; Rockford, IL: Tan Books and Publishers, Inc., 1989), pp. 502–3, 504.

60. Mother Teresa to Father Picachy, October 20, 1960.

61. Mother Teresa to Kay Brachen, August 10, 1960.

62. Mother Teresa to Eileen Egan, October 2, 1960.

63. Mother Teresa to Eileen Egan, July 24, 1960.

64. Mother Teresa's speech, Thirtieth National Convention of the National Council of Catholic Women, Las Vegas, 1960.

65. Mother Teresa to Mrs. Ann Blaikie, November 29, 1960.

66. Mother Teresa to Archbishop Périer, December 18, 1960.

67. Reference to the motherhouse of the M.C. Sisters located at 54A Lower Circular Road, Calcutta.

68. This request was a further expression of her reverence for "God's wonderful work." She was only an instrument and wanted no attention drawn to her person; it would only harm the work. "God's tender love for His children" was the only story she wanted told.

69. Mother Teresa to Eileen Egan, 1960.

70. For these visits she would usually take the night train (without reservation of a berth), so as not to lose time, and then spend the next day with the sisters, without extra rest, as if she had not traveled. After a few days she would return to Calcutta, usually again on the night train, and carry on with her ordinary schedule.

71. Mother Teresa to Father Picachy, December 20, 1960.

72. Mother Teresa to Father Picachy, undated.

73. Mother Teresa to Father Picachy, January 23, 1961.

TEN: "I Have Come to Love the Darkness"

1. Father Joseph Neuner was born on August 19, 1908, in Feldkirch, Austria. He joined the Society of Jesus in 1926, was ordained in 1936 in Munich, Germany and went to India in 1938 to teach theology at the newly established De Nobili College in Pune. During the war he was interned in India. From 1948 to 1950 he earned his doctorate in theology at the Gregorian University in Rome and returned to India in 1950 to resume teaching theology at Jnana Deepa Vidyapeeth in Pune. He participated at the Second Vatican Council as a theologian serving in the Commissions on priestly formation, missionary activity, and the relation of the Church to non-Christian religions. From 1960 onward he often lectured at Morning Star College in Calcutta and kept in contact with Mother Teresa. Their correspondence continued until 1980.

2. Morning Star College was a seminary of the Archdiocese of Calcutta.

3. Testimony of Father Neuner, about Mother Teresa.

4. Father Neuner removed the little he considered irrelevant.

5. In her previous correspondence, Mother Teresa clearly affirms that she made her private vow in 1942. Hence her statement here "about 17 years now" is indeed approximate.

6. Father Neuner comments that "it seems she wrote 'loving' first and then corrected it with 'living.'"

7. Mother Teresa is referring to the instructions she was giving to the sisters, usually daily.

8. Mother Teresa to Father Neuner, undated, but most probably written during the retreat of April 1961.

9. Testimony of Father Neuner.

10. Mother Teresa to Father Neuner, most probably April 11, 1961.

11. Mother Teresa to Archbishop Périer, January 25, 1947.

12. Father Neuner, S.J., "Mother Teresa's Charism," *Review for Religious,* 60, no. 5 (2001): pp. 484–5.

13. This retreat resolution was the same one she had taken during the retreat of the previous year.

14. Mother Teresa to Father Neuner, dated 1961.

15. Mother Teresa to Co-workers, April 22, 1961.

16. "When the night of the spirit is chiefly purificatory, under the influence of the grace that is exercised mainly by the gift of understanding, the theological virtues and humility are purified of all human alloy. . . . The soul thus purified can pass beyond the formulas of mysteries and enter into 'the deep things of God,' as St. Paul says (Cf. 1 Corinthians 2:10). Then, in spite of all temptations against faith and hope, the soul firmly believes by a direct act in a most pure and sublime manner which surmounts temptation; it believes for the sole and most pure motive supernaturally attained: the authority of God revealing. It also hopes for the sole reason that He is ever helpful, infinite Mercy. It loves Him in the most complete aridity, because He is infinitely better in Himself than all the gifts which He could grant us. . . . When this trial is chiefly reparatory, when it has principally for its end to make the already purified soul work for the salvation of its neighbor, then it preserves the same lofty characteristics just described, but takes on an additional character more reminiscent of the intimate sufferings of Jesus and Mary, who did not need to be purified." Reginald Garrigou-Lagrange, O.P., *The Three Ages of Interior Life: Prelude of Eternal Life,* vol. 2, trans. Sister M. Timothea Doyle, O.P. (St. Louis, MO: B. Herder Book Co., 1948; Rockford, IL: Tan Books and Publishers, Inc., 1989), pp. 508–9. By all indications this was the case with Mother Teresa. With Father Neuner's help, she began to understand that her trial was a part of her mission, indeed an opportunity for greater charity, and thus she began to love her darkness.

17. Mother Teresa to Father Picachy, June 1961.

18. Colossians 1:24.

19. Mother Teresa to the M.C. Sisters, First Friday, July 1961.

20. Mother Teresa to Father Picachy, September 1, 1961.

21. Cf. Matthew 16:24.

22. Mother Teresa's Instructions to the M.C. Sisters, May 17, 1981.

23. Vatican diplomatic representative, appointed by the pope to represent him to the government of the country to which he is assigned.

24. Here "theologians" refers to the seminarians studying theology in preparation for priestly ordination.

25. Mother Teresa to Father Neuner, October 16 1961.

26. A friend of Eileen Egan's.

27. Mother Teresa to Eileen Egan, February 27, 1961.

28. Mother Teresa to Father Neuner, October 16, 1961.

29. "But how shall I show my love, since love proves itself by deeds? I, the little one, will strew flowers, perfuming the Divine Throne with their fragrance. I will sing Love's canticle in silvery tones. Thus will my short life be spent in Thy sight, O my Beloved! To strew flowers is the only means of proving my love, and these flowers will be each word and look, each little daily sacrifice. I wish to make profit out of the smallest actions and do them all for Love. For Love's sake I wish to suffer and to rejoice: So shall I strew my flowers. Not one that I see but, singing all the while, I will scatter its petals before Thee. Should my roses be gathered from amid thorns, I will sing notwithstanding, and "the longer and sharper the thorns, the sweeter will grow my song." [emphasis added]. From *Saint Thérèse of Lisieux: The Little Flower of Jesus,* trans. Rev. Thomas N. Taylor (New York: P. J. Kennedy & Sons, 1927), p. 205.

30. Mother Teresa to Father Neuner, October 23, 1961.

31. Mother Teresa to Father Neuner, November 3, 1961.

32. Mother's instructions to the M.C. Sisters, October 5, 1984.

33. Mother's Instructions to the M.C. Sisters, May 13, 1982.

34. Mother Teresa to Father Neuner, dateable as November 8, 1961. Mother Teresa made every effort to put her time to the best use. She did much of her letter writing while traveling.

35. Mother Teresa to Father Neuner, December 18, 1961.

36. Mother Teresa to Father Neuner, February 17, 1962.

37. The Padma Shri is an award given to Indian citizens for distinguished service in various fields of activity. Mother Teresa is referring to the announcement of the award; it was actually presented on April 28, 1962, in New Delhi.

38. Mother Teresa to Eileen Egan, February 21, 1962.

39. Statement of Father Neuner.

40. Cf. Luke 1:39.

41. Reference to the motherhouse of the Missionaries of Charity at 54A Lower Circular Road, Calcutta.

42. In the pre-Vatican II liturgical calendar of the Catholic Church, the second Sunday before Lent (or the eighth Sunday before Easter) was called Sexagesina Sunday.

43. Mother Teresa to Father Neuner, March 6, 1962.

44. 2 Corinthians 12:9.

45. Mother Teresa to Eileen Egan, March 20, 1962.

46. Mother Teresa was referring to a meeting with her co-workers that took place after her stay in Las Vegas.

47. Cf. John 15:19.

48. Mother Teresa to Eileen Egan, March 20, 1962.

49. St. Margaret Mary (1647–1690) was a religious of the Order of the Visitation in Paray-le-Monial (France). She was an apostle of devotion to the Sacred Heart of Jesus. Mother Teresa was referring to Margaret Trouncer, *The Nun* (New York: All Saints Press Book Guild Press, 1965).

50. Cf. Acts 10:38.

51. Mother Teresa to Father Neuner, May 12, 1962.

52. Quoted in Malcolm Muggeridge, *Something Beautiful for God* (New York, Evanston, San Francisco, London: Harper & Row Publishers, 1971), pp. 73–74.

53. Desmond Doig, *Mother Teresa: Her People and Her Work* (New York: Harper & Row, 1976), p. 159.

54. Cf. Luke 4:18.

55. Mother Teresa, Charity: Soul of Mission, January 23, 1991.

ELEVEN: "At His Disposal"

1. She was referring to receiving the Padma Shri award on April 28, 1962.

2. Mother Teresa to Father Picachy, May 18, 1962.

3. Mother Teresa to Father Picachy, June 27, 1962.

4. When Father Picachy became bishop, Mother Teresa usually addressed him as "My Lord" or "Your Lordship," yet she would remind him, "Please do not address me 'Reverend' as I look up to you as my spiritual guide" (Mother Teresa to Bishop Picachy, August 20, 1963).

5. Mother Teresa to Father Picachy, July 20, 1962.

6. Mother Teresa received the Ramon Magsaysay Award for International Understanding on August 31, 1962, in Manila, Philippines.

7. Mother Teresa to Eileen Egan, August 29, 1962.

8. Mother Teresa to Father Neuner, September 10, 1962.

9. Mother Teresa to Bishop Picachy, September 21, 1962.

10. Archbishop Albert Vincent D'Souza (1904–1977) served as archbishop of Calcutta from August 8, 1962, to May 29, 1969.

11. Mother Teresa to Father Neuner, January 15, 1963.

12. Mother Teresa to Bishop Picachy, February 3, 1963.

13. Mother Teresa to Bishop Picachy, February 13, 1963.

14. Cf. Matthew 3:1–6.

15. Cf. John 3:29.

16. Mother Teresa to Father Neuner, February 25, 1963.

17. Mother Teresa to Bishop Picachy, March 23, 1963.

18. Mother Teresa to Bishop Picachy, undated; this letter is addressed to

Bishop Picachy, so it had to be written after September 9, 1962, when Father Picachy was consecrated bishop. In the file folder containing Mother Teresa's letters to Picachy, it was placed after the letter of March 23, 1963.

19. Mother Teresa's Retreat Notes, March–April 1959, p. 351.

20. Mother Teresa to Bishop Picachy, April 7, 1963.

21. Quote from the prayer *Stabat Mater*, actually addressed to the Blessed Virgin Mary. Here it seems that Mother Teresa is directing the prayer to Jesus.

22. Mother Teresa to Father Neuner, April, 11, 1963.

23. Mother Teresa to Eileen Egan, September 1, 1963.

24. Father Neuner was going to Rome to participate at the Vatican Council as theologian, in the commissions for priestly formation, missionary activity and relations of the Church to non-Christian religions.

25. Mother Teresa to Father Neuner, September 3, 1963.

26. On the way home from Jamshedpur on the train.

27. Cf. Matthew 26:47.

28. Mother Teresa to Bishop Picachy, January 8, 1964.

29. Mother Teresa to Eileen Egan, January 8, 1964.

30. Ibid.

31. Mother Teresa to Eileen Egan, January 24, 1964.

32. Mother Teresa to Bishop Picachy, March 20, 1964.

33. Mother Teresa to Eileen Egan, April 15, 1964.

34. Mother Teresa to Father Neuner, May 17, 1964.

35. Mother Teresa to Eileen Egan, October 4, 1964. Cf. Mark 12:30.

36. Mother Teresa to the Superiors of the M.C. Sisters, November 17, 1964.

37. Mother Teresa to the Apostolic Nuncio, Archbishop James R. Knox, December 27, 1964.

38. Mother Teresa to Bishop Picachy, December 29, 1964.

39. Mother Teresa to Father Neuner, before January 8, 1965.

40. Cf. 2 Corinthians 5:21; 1 Peter 2:24.

41. Cf. Matthew 26:36–45.

42. Cf. Matthew 27:46.

43. Cf. Matthew 3:17.

44. Cf. Matthew 17:5.

45. Mother Teresa's Instructions to the M.C. Sisters, April l, 1981.

46. "In this case [reparatory night] the suffering makes one think of that of a lifesaver who, in a storm, struggles heroically to save from death those who are on the point of drowning. Spiritual life-savers, like St. Paul of the Cross, struggle not only for hours and months, but sometimes for years in order to snatch souls from eternal death; and, in a way, these reparative souls must resist the temptations of the souls they seek to save that they may come efficaciously to their assistance." Reginald Garrigou-Lagrange, O.P., *The*

Three Ages of Interior Life: Prelude of Eternal Life, vol. 2, trans. Sister M. Timothea Doyle, O.P. (St. Louis, MO: B. Herder Book Co., 1948; Rockford, IL: Tan Books and Publishers, Inc., 1989), p. 509.

47. Mother Teresa to Archbishop Périer, December 3, 1947.

48. Mother Teresa to Bishop Picachy, April 4, 1965.

49. John 3:30.

50. Mother Teresa to Father Neuner, May 15, 1965.

51. Mother Teresa to Archbishop Knox, June 19, 1965.

52. Ibid.

53. Mother Teresa to Archbishop Knox, July 1, 1965.

54. Mother Teresa to Bishop Picachy, July 11, 1965.

55. Mother Teresa to Archbishop Knox, July 20, 1965.

56. Mother Teresa was referring to the courage of the sisters in the new foundation in Cocorote, Venezuela.

57. Mother Teresa to Archbishop Knox, July 28, 1965.

58. Mother Teresa often referred to herself in the third person, not only in her general letters to the sisters or in her instructions, but also when writing to others.

59. Mother Teresa to Archbishop Knox, October 13, 1965.

60. Mother Teresa to Bishop Picachy, May 16, (most probably 1965 or 1966).

61. Mother Teresa to Father Neuner, March 30, 1966.

62. "[T]he more souls advance in the spiritual life, the more their interior sufferings resemble those of Jesus and Mary. The common opinion is that the servants of God are more particularly tried, whether it be that they need a more profound purification, or whether, following the example of our Lord, they must work by the same means as He used for a great spiritual cause, such as the foundation of a religious order or the salvation of many other souls. St. John of the Cross and St. Teresa almost continually experienced this, as the facts clearly show." From Reginald Garrigou-Lagrange, O.P., *The Three Ages of Interior Life: Prelude of Eternal Life,* vol. 2, trans. Sister M. Timothea Doyle, O.P. (St. Louis, MO: B. Herder Book Co., 1948; Rockford, IL: Tan Books and Publishers, Inc., 1989), p. 504.

63. Mother Teresa to Archbishop Knox, May 9, 1966.

64. Mother Teresa to Archbishop Knox, June 6, 1966.

65. Mother Teresa to Bishop Picachy, September 2, 1966.

66. Mother Teresa to Bishop Picachy, October 8, 1966.

67. Mother Teresa to Archbishop Knox, September 8, 1966.

68. Mother Teresa to Bishop Picachy, February 4, 1967.

69. Luke 1:49.

70. Whatever is said in praise of her and the work.

71. Mother Teresa to Father Neuner, July 24, 1967.

72. Mary's song of praise when she visited her relative Elizabeth (Luke 1:46–55).

73. Mother Teresa to Father Neuner, July 24, 1967.

74. Ibid.

75. Mother Teresa died on a first Friday of the month of September, a day traditionally dedicated to the Sacred Heart.

76. Mother Teresa to the author, quoted in Desmond Doig, *Mother Teresa: Her People and Her Work* (New York: Harper & Row, 1976), pp. 23–24.

77. Ibid.

78. Translation used in the Mass, taken from the Douay-Rheims Bible used at that time in the liturgy. In the RSV and other translations the verse is Psalms 69:20.

79. Image of Jesus after the scourging and the crowning with thorns. Cf. John 19:5.

80. Mother Teresa's Instructions to the M.C. Sisters, February 24, 1989.

81. *Shanti* means "peace" and *nagar* means "city," thus City of Peace.

82. Mother Teresa (on the train to Bhagalpur, Patna, Ranchi) to Eileen Egan, September 2, 1967.

83. Mother Teresa to Patty and Warren Kump, December 1, 1967.

84. Mother Teresa to Father Neuner, January 28, 1968.

85. Mother Teresa to Bishop Picachy, January 8, 1969. Cf. Nehemiah 8:10.

86. Cf. John 14:6.

87. Cf. John 8:12.

88. Most probably a reference to her chronic headaches.

89. Hebrews 13:8.

90. Mother Teresa to Patty and Warren Kump, August 22, 1969.

91. Cf. Matthew 25:40.

92. Cf. Nehemiah 8:10.

93. Cf. John 14:6.

94. Cf. John 8:12; 9:5.

95. Cf. John 14:6; 11:25.

96. Cf. 1 John 4:8; 16.

97. Mother Teresa to Eileen Egan, October 13, 1969.

98. Mother Teresa to Father Neuner, November 27, 1969.

99. Testimony of Father Neuner.

100. In May 1969, Bishop Picachy was appointed archbishop of Calcutta.

101. Mother Teresa to Archbishop Picachy, December 21, 1969.

TWELVE: "God Uses Nothingness to Show His Greatness"

1. Father Michael van der Peet, S.C.J., was born in Alkmaar, Netherlands, in 1924. In 1953 he was ordained to the priesthood in the Congregation of the Priests of the Sacred Heart (SCJ). From 1955 until 1970 he taught in the seminaries of his community in the United States. From 1970 until 1986 he was involved full-time in retreat ministry.

2. Margaret Plevak, "Chance encounter led to a 22-year friendship: Local priest in Rome working on Mother Teresa's sainthood cause," Milwaukee *Catholic Herald*, 133, no. 8, (February 21, 2002), p. 9.

3. Mother Teresa to Father van der Peet November 16, 1975.

4. Mother Teresa to Father van der Peet, March 6, 1976.

5. Mother Teresa's letter to Jesus, enclosed with her letter to Father Picachy, September 3, 1959.

6. Mother Teresa to Father Picachy, November 21, 1959.

7. Mother Teresa to Bishop Ransch, February 25, 1976.

8. Margaret Plevak, "Chance encounter led to a 22-year friendship; Local priest in Rome working on Mother Teresa's sainthood cause," Milwaukee *Catholic Herald*, 133, no. 8, (February 21, 2002), p. 9.

9. This "cardboard box" was the box where she kept her awards, honorary degrees, and other tributes. The awards were instrumental in proclaiming the presence of the poor, and she was convinced that they belonged to the poor.

10. Three days of prayer.

11. The contemplative branch of the Missionaries of Charity Sisters. The following year the name was changed to Missionaries of Charity Contemplative Sisters.

12. Mother Teresa to Father van der Peet, May 29, 1976.

13. See p. 214 "I have come to love the darkness," Mother Teresa to Father Neuner, most probably April 11, 1961.

14. Mother Teresa to Father Don Kribs, December 13, 1976. Cf. John 6:35, 48; Matthew 25:35.

15. Mother's Instructions to the M.C. Sisters, May 17, 1978. Cf. Matthew 12:34.

16. Mother Teresa to Father van der Peet, June 19, 1976. Letter written "on my way to New York," i.e., on the plane.

17. Cf. John 1:14.

18. Cf. Luke 4:34–41.

19. Mother Teresa to Father Don Kribs, February 7, 1974.

20. Mother Teresa to Cardinal Picachy, June 27, 1976.

21. Mother Teresa to Father Don Kribs, July 23, 1976.

22. Margaret Plevak, "Chance encounter led to a 22-year friendship;

Local priest in Rome working on Mother Teresa's sainthood cause," Milwaukee *Catholic Herald*, 133, no. 8, (February 21, 2002), p. 9.

23. 1070 Union Ave., Bronx, New York, address of the M.C. Contemplative Sisters.

24. Mother Teresa attended the Forty-first Eucharistic Congress in Philadelphia on August 6, 1976.

25. Cf. Matthew 26:26–28; Luke 22:19–20.

26. Mother Teresa to Father van der Peet, November 26, 1976.

27. Mother Teresa's Retreat Notes, March–April 1959, p. 360.

28. Cf. John 3:1ff.

29. Cf. Matthew 18:3.

30. Mother Teresa is referring to Jesus as the Bread of Life in the Eucharist.

31. Mother Teresa to Malcolm Muggeridge, November 12, 1970.

32. Mother Teresa's speech, Cambridge, June 10, 1977.

33. Mother Teresa to Sister Marie of the Trinity, O.P., undated.

34. "I read that sorrow & suffering is the kiss of Jesus. His gift to you— for being His" (Mother Teresa to Sister. M. John Francis, S.S.N.D., August 3, 1976). Most probably she had read this in Paul de Jaegher, S.J., *The Virtue of Love* (New York: P. J. Kenedy & Sons, 1955), p. 123: "Our sufferings then, borne as they should be, are, as we have said, as kisses bestowed upon our crucified Jesus. But suffering is also the kiss of Jesus crucified upon our soul. Ordinary souls generally see in suffering nothing but a punishment from God, a proof of his justice or his displeasure. The generous soul, on the contrary, finds in it a proof of his love for it. It does not see the bare cross, but rather sees Jesus crucified on it, Jesus who embraces it with love and who expects from it in return a generous and loving assent. . . . For me, the Cross of Jesus is all that causes me to suffer. The kisses of Jesus upon my soul, however strange this may seem, are the numerous petty sufferings of my daily life."

35. Mother Teresa to Eileen Egan, December 14, 1976.

36. Mother Teresa to an M.C. sister, April 8, 1977.

37. Mother Teresa's Instructions to the M.C. Sisters, May 9, 1979.

38. Mother Teresa to a friend, March 29, 1977.

39. Mother Teresa to Father van der Peet, June 20, 1977.

40. Cf. Matthew 25:35–40.

41. Cf. John 15:13.

42. Mother Teresa to Father van der Peet, February 17, 1978.

43. Constitutions of the M.C. Sisters, 29.

44. Mother's Instructions to the M. C. Sisters, October 5, 1984.

45. Cf. 2 Corinthians 8:9.

46. Cf. Galatians 2:20.

47. Mother Teresa to Father Neuner, June 23, 1978; Cf. Galatians 2:20.

48. Galatians 2:20.

49. Mother Teresa, Charity: Soul of Mission, January 23, 1991.

50. Mother Teresa to Eileen Egan, July 1, 1978.

51. Mother Teresa's speech, Regina Mundi Institute, Rome, December 20, 1979.

52. Mother Teresa is referring to the tiny bird that sits by Mary's feet at the base of the Statue of Our Lady of Fatima.

53. Mother Teresa to Cardinal Picachy, November 30, 1978.

54. Since the sisters in 1975, the Home for the Dying (Kalighat) in 1977 and the first group of sisters in 1978 celebrated silver jubilees, Mother Teresa decided to give Jesus a silver jubilee as well by opening twenty-five new foundations in 1978.

55. Mother Teresa to Father van der Peet, April 30, 1979.

56. Father Leo Dehon (1843–1925), French founder of the Congregation of the Priests of the Sacred Heart (Dehonian Fathers).

57. Mother Teresa to Father van der Peet, September 22, 1979.

58. Cf. 2 Corinthians 9:7.

59. Cf. 2 Corinthians 8:9.

60. Cf. Hebrew 4:15.

61. Cf. John 12:24.

62. Cf. Matthew 26:40.

63. Mother Teresa to Father Sebastian, M.C., October 12, 1979.

64. Cf. Luke 22:39–46.

65. Mother's Instructions to the M.C. Sisters, February 15, 1983.

66. Matthew 25:40.

67. Cf. Isaiah 49:15–16.

68. Mother Teresa's Nobel Peace Prize acceptance speech, Oslo, Norway, December 11, 1979.

69. Mother Teresa to a doctor, October 12, 1988.

70. Mother Teresa's speech, National Prayer Breakfast in Washington, D.C., February 3, 1994.

71. Mother Teresa to Father Neuner, January 9, 1980.

72. Ibid.

73. Mother Teresa's Instruction to the M.C. Sisters, October 17, 1977.

74. Mother Teresa to Father van der Peet, October 18, 1980.

75. Mother Teresa's letter to Jesus, enclosed with her letter to Father Picachy, September 3, 1959.

76. According to tradition, Veronica wiped the face of Jesus with her veil as He made His way to Calvary.

77. Simon of Cyrene helped Jesus carry His Cross on the way to Calvary (Cf. Luke 23:26).

78. Mother Teresa's speech, Synod of Bishops, October 1980, from *The Catholic Leader,* October 26, 1980.

79. Explanation of the Original Constitutions.

80. Mother Teresa to Father Neuner, December 15, 1980.

81. Ibid.

82. Mother Teresa to the M.C. Sisters, March 15, 1980.

83. Mother Teresa to the M.C. Sisters, November 23, 1980.

84. A reference to the constant stream of requests for her presence at public events.

85. Mother Teresa's Instructions to the M.C. (Contemplative) Sisters, June 18, 1981.

86. Mother Teresa to Cardinal Picachy, September 28, 1981.

87. Dear Jesus, help me to spread Your fragrance everywhere I go. Flood my soul with Your spirit and life. Penetrate and possess my whole being so utterly that my life may only be a radiance of Yours. Shine through me and be so in me that every soul I come in contact with may feel Your presence in my soul. Let them look up, and see no longer me, but only Jesus! Stay with me and then I will begin to shine as You shine, so to shine as to be a light to others. The light, O Jesus, will be all from You; none of it will be mine. It will be You, shining on others through me. Let me thus praise You in the way You love best, by shining on those around me. Let me preach You without preaching, not by words but by my example, by the catching force, the sympathetic influence of what I do, the evident fullness of the love my heart bears for You. Amen.

THIRTEEN: Radiating Christ

1. Mother Teresa to the M. C. Sisters, August 19, 1982.

2. Mother Teresa's meditation in the hospital in Rome, 1983.

3. Mother Teresa rose every morning at 4:40 a.m. and, after community prayers and meditation on the Word of God from 5:00 a.m. to 6:00 a.m., attended Holy Mass. After breakfast, Mother Teresa and the sisters would start their apostolate in the slums, visiting families or serving in the homes for the dying and for children, or in various dispensaries. (In later years Mother Teresa was no longer able to go regularly to the slums or the homes for the poor because of her many travels, the needs of the sisters, the administration of the congregation, and the numerous visitors.) At 12:30 p.m., community prayers were followed by lunch, half an hour rest, and half an hour of spiritual reading. Then she and the sisters would go back to their work with the poor. At 6:00 p.m. there was an hour of adoration before the Blessed Sacrament (since 1973), followed by the liturgy of the hours and supper. After the evening meal and half an hour of recreation, at 9:00 p.m. the sisters would end the day with their night prayer. Mother Teresa would often stay up to answer the mail until late in the night.

4. Mother Teresa to Cardinal Picachy, September 16, 1985.

5. Mother Teresa to Cardinal Picachy, February 17, 1986.

6. Father Alber Huart, S.J., was born on March 28, 1926, in Namur, Belgium. He joined the Society of Jesus on August 10, 1943, came to India on November 3, 1953, and was ordained a priest on April 27, 1957. He preached the retreat for the members of the General Chapter in 1985. He was confessor to the Missionaries of Charity community at motherhouse from 1984 to 1998. To date he serves as confessor to various communities in Calcutta.

7. Testimony of Father Huart.

8. Father Albert Huart, S.J., "Mother Teresa: Joy in the Night," *Review for Religious,* vol. 60, no. 5 (Sept.–Oct. 2001), p. 495.

9. Bishop William G. Curlin was born on August 30, 1927, in Portsmouth, Virginia. He was ordained to the priesthood on May 25, 1957, for the Archdiocese of Washington and became an auxilliary bishop there on December 20, 1988. On April 13, 1994, he was installed as bishop of the Diocese of Charlotte, North Carolina. He retired in 2001.

10. Testimony of Bishop Curlin.

11. "8,000 feeding," that is, with 8,000 people to feed.

12. Mother Teresa to Father van der Peet, January 7, 1985.

13. Excerpts from Pope John Paul II's speech on the occasion of his visit to Nirmal Hriday, *L'Osservatore Romano,* weekly edition, February 10, 1986.

14. Mother Teresa to Father van der Peet, January 1, 1988.

15. Mother Teresa to the M.C. Sisters, October 10, 1988.

16. Mother Teresa to Brother Roger of Taizé, December 16, 1989.

17. Mother Teresa to the M.C. Sisters, April 23, 1991.

18. Cf. Luke 1:39–56.

19. Cf. Matthew 25:40.

20. Cf. Romans 8:35–39.

21. Mother Teresa to M.C. Sisters, Brothers, Fathers, Lay Missionaries and Co-workers, June 1990.

22. Mother Teresa to the M.C. Sisters, January 31, 1980.

23. Open letter of Mother Teresa to President George Bush and Saddam Hussein, January 2, 1991.

24. Mother Teresa to her religious family, June 23, 1991.

25. Mother Teresa to M.C. Sisters, Brothers, and Fathers, March 25, 1993.

26. Mother Teresa's letter to Jesus, enclosed with her letter to Father Picachy, September 3, 1959.

27. Mother Teresa to Father Neuner, January 1965.

28. Cf. John 19:25–26.

29. Mother Teresa to Sister M. Frederick, M.C., and the M.C. Sisters, March 29, 1994.

30. Mother Teresa to Father Neuner, July 24, 1967.

31. Mother Teresa to the M.C. Sisters, May 15, 1995.

32. Father Van Exem to Mother Teresa, September 16, 1993.

33. Mother Teresa to Father van der Peet, February 2, 1993.

34. Mother Teresa to a friend, February 25, 1994.

35. Testimony of Bishop Curlin.

36. Testimony of Father Gary, M.C.

37. Testimony of Father Sebastian, M.C.

38. Testimony of Sister Gertrude.

39. Testimony of Sister M. Nirmala, M.C.

40. Testimony of Sister Margaret Mary

41. Testimony of Father Gary.

Conclusion

1. Malcolm Muggeridge, *Something Beautiful for God* (New York, Evanston, San Francisco, London: Harper & Row Publishers, 1971), p. 146.

2. M.C. Sisters' Prayer Book.

3. Mother Teresa to Archbishop Périer, December 3, 1947.

4. Mother Teresa to Mother Gertrude, January 10, 1948.

5. Testimony of Father Joseph, M.C.

6. Testimony of Brother Yesudas, M.C.

7. Mother Teresa to Father Neuner, March 6, 1962.

8. Mother Teresa's Instructions to the M.C. Sisters, October 1, 1977.

9. John 15:12.

10. Mother Teresa's speech, Cambridge, June 10, 1977.

11. Mother Teresa's speech, Corpus Christi College, Melbourne, October 8, 1981.

Appendix B: Retreat Notes

1. The retreat started on Easter Sunday evening, March 29, 1959, with meditation points for the following morning. The retreat was preached by Jesuit Father Picachy following the Spiritual Exercises of St. Ignatius Loyola.

2. The first offering to the Sacred Heart that Mother Teresa referred to is a prayer said by the Missionaries of Charity upon rising: "O Jesus, through the most pure Heart of Mary, I offer You the prayers, works, joys and sufferings of this day for all the intentions of Your Divine Heart. In union with all the Masses being offered throughout the Catholic world, I offer You my heart. Make it meek and humble like Yours." This prayer gave her some consolation.

3. From all her other correspondence it is clear that her answer, "Now I don't believe," portrays her feelings, not a lack of faith.

4. Though in utter darkness, she did not turn to others to compensate for the lack of consolation she experienced. She had reached a considerable degree of emotional maturity and interior freedom to be so detached.

5. Her profound self-knowledge was accompanied with a true repentance for her faults and imperfections, and she immediately identified the practical solution to her weakness.

6. In spite of her feelings, which she made no attempt to hide, all her responses were based on an outstanding faith and love that guided and preserved her throughout this trial.

7. Though she felt she had no faith, it was faith that prompted her to see her interior sufferings as a "means of purification" and to surrender to it. She did not, however, deny the struggle that it required of her.

8. Following the Spiritual Exercises of St. Ignatius of Loyola, Mother Teresa is referring to the practice of keeping a journal and marking successes versus failures of a particular defect one has chosen to overcome or of a virtue one has chosen to improve.

9. The sacrifice that she made then for her sisters bears fruit even now for all who are privileged to benefit from it.

10. Though she could sincerely state, "My heart is all and only His—my mind & will are fixed on Him—the whole time," and though she strictly kept to the prescribed times and external manifestations of reverence, still judging from her own feelings, she had a poor opinion of her devotional practices.

11. One can detect the loneliness and nostalgia for His felt presence between the lines of this statement, for the One who "knew everything in detail" seems to have disappeared.

12. Even her relationship with Mary was affected by the darkness. Nonetheless, the rosary was at this time and to the end of her life one of her favorite devotions.

13. Psalms 46:4–5 touched her and reminded her of God's dwelling within her; this gave her both stability and hope. Though only a day earlier she had remembered with regret that at present Jesus was no longer there "to share, know everything in detail," she may have hoped that the time of suffering would come to an end and that she would again experience the same union they had previously shared.

14. In spite of all the interior suffering, she remained steadfast in her conviction and did not draw back from the radical commitment she had made earlier in life. Her concept of poverty comes very close to the "absolute poverty" on which she had insisted with Archbishop Périer when discerning her new call.

15. This was her desire and prayer, but it was not answered in the way she expected or would have liked. Instead of being set aside, she was becoming the center of attention. While she prayed to be forgotten, her popularity

was rapidly growing. Only within was she "left totally alone." It was in the company of Jesus that she desired to be, yet she was able to forgo her own desires and concern herself with others.

16. Mother Teresa was a sociable person; her company was pleasant and enjoyable. Yet she found it hard to be a public figure. It was only out of love for Jesus and others that she ignored her preferences and adapted to the demands of the mission entrusted to her.

17. The notes for the seventh day of the retreat are missing.

18. Rule 1: "The General aim of the Society is to quench the thirst of Jesus Christ on the Cross for love of souls, by the Sisters' observance of the four Vows of absolute Poverty, Chastity, Obedience and of devoting themselves to work among the poor according to the Constitutions."

19. Rule 86: "As each Sister of this Society is to become a co-worker of Christ in the slums, she ought to understand what God and the Society expect from her. Let Christ radiate and live His Life in her and through her in the slums. Let the poor seeing her be drawn to Christ and invite Him to enter their homes and their lives. Let the sick and the suffering find in her a real angel of comfort and consolation; let the little ones of the streets cling to her because she reminds them of Him, the Friend of the little ones."

20. This statement painfully evokes the memory of the intense consolations and the effect they had on her feelings of charity for others.

21. This comment was written on the top of the ninth page. The retreat started on March 29, 1959, with the meditation point for the next day. The first day of the retreat was March 30. The ninth day is therefore April 7, 1959. In 1942 Easter was on April 5; therefore Mother Teresa made her private vow on Easter Tuesday, April 7, 1942. It was in these days that the Bengali section of St. Mary's school was evacuated to Morapai because of the war; the exact date is unknown (see Mother M. Colmcille, I.B.V.M., *First the Blade* [Calcutta: Firma K. L. Mukhopadhyay, 1968]), p. 291–292. While such extreme circumstances were the context and perhaps even the occasion of the vow, they were by no means the cause of Mother Teresa's binding herself in such a radical way, as is verified by the crucial role the vow played throughout her life.

22. The rule demanded that a sister go out of the convent always with another sister as a companion. Mother Teresa was able to place charity above the letter of the rule. Besides her great concern and thoughtfulness toward her sisters, her wholehearted labor and zeal are striking: Her companions were in their twenties and she was approaching her fiftieth birthday—and they still could not keep up with her!

23. During her life Mother Teresa wrote thousands of letters. The "great effort" she expended on them was another consequence of her private vow and an expression of her love.

24. In 1947, while asking Archbishop Périer to let her begin her new life, Mother Teresa had written: "You might think that I am looking only at the joy of giving up all, and bringing Joy into the Heart of Jesus[.] Yes, I look at these most, but I see also what suffering the fulfillment of these two will bring. By nature I am sensitive, love beautiful and nice things, comfort and all the comfort can give—to be loved and love—I know that the life of a Missionary of Charity—will be minus all these. The complete poverty, the Indian life, the life of the poorest will mean a hard toil against my great self-love. Yet, Your Grace, I am longing with a true sincere heart, to begin to lead this kind of life—so as to bring joy to the Suffering heart of Jesus—Let me go, Your Grace. Let us trust Him blindly—He will see to it, that our faith in Him, will not be lost." This was now the reality, and her answer on this tenth day of retreat confirmed her awareness of it.

25. Accepting suffering as a gift was Mother Teresa's own attitude and one she encouraged in others. This did not mean that she thought one should make no effort to remove suffering. In fact, Mother Teresa spent the greater part of her life in alleviating it. But at least the first step is to accept one's present suffering. In sum, "accept, offer and (depending on the circumstances) act" is a concise expression of Mother Teresa's response when faced with suffering.

26. Her religious training encouraged silent suffering in union with Jesus Crucified; one was not expected to "parade" one's sufferings but rather hide them. Mother Teresa strived for perfection in this practice: Her smile was one of the most effective ways that she hid suffering.

27. Rule 88: "Let them love humility so earnestly that they may accept humiliation readily, and even with joy. Therefore they shall receive correction and admonition in the spirit of Faith without excuse or complaint."

28. Her attitude was the fruit of her humility. She was happy to resemble Jesus in the humiliations of His Passion and in His benevolence toward the offender.

29. A hymn called "Reproaches" (based on Micah 6) and sung for veneration of the Cross during the Good Friday liturgy:

P: O my people, what have I done to you? How have I offended you? Answer me! I led you out of Egypt, from slavery to freedom, but you have led your Savior to the cross.

C: Holy is God! Holy and strong! Holy immortal One, have mercy on us.

P: For forty years, I led you safely through the desert. I fed you with manna from heaven and brought you to a land of plenty, but you have led your Savior to the cross.

C: Holy is God! Holy and strong! Holy immortal One, have mercy on us.

P: What more could I have done for you? I planted you as my fairest vine, but you yielded only bitterness; when I was thirsty, you gave me vinegar to drink, and you pierced your Savior's side with a spear.

C: Holy is God! Holy and strong! Holy immortal One, have mercy on us!

30. "The Queen of Heaven" *(Regina Coeli)* is an ancient Latin Marian hymn of the Catholic Church, recited from Easter Sunday to Pentecost.

31. Mother Teresa crossed out the words "not be" and wrote above them, "if they were"; she also crossed out the words "or" and "but." She seems to mean: "If the questions put to us were . . ."

32. Prayer of St. Ignatius Loyola.

33. The next—and last—page of the retreat notes is missing.

ACKNOWLEDGMENTS

A book such as this could not have come about without the contribution of many. Accordingly, my heartfelt thanks goes to all those who have in various ways contributed to making this book a reality.

First, we owe a huge debt of gratitude to the Jesuits and others who had the foresight to preserve Mother Teresa's letters for future generations of the Missionaries of Charity (MC) and the Church. Thankfully, Mother Teresa did not get her wish to have such an abundance of precious material destroyed. Sincere appreciation goes also to those who have enriched our knowledge and understanding of the foundress of the MC family by sharing their memories of her.

I am indebted to the MC sisters in the postulation office and archives who spent numerous hours transcribing and organizing the documents. I am deeply grateful to the MC sisters working in the Mother Teresa Center in Tijuana, Kolkata, and Rome. Without their generous and diligent assistance, this book would not be what it is.

Special thanks to Claudia Cross of Sterling Lord Literistic for her encouragement, care, and expert assistance. It has been a joy working with Bill Barry, publisher, and Trace Murphy, editorial director, of Doubleday Religion. They were enthusiastic about this project from the beginning and have demonstrated a pursuit of excellence throughout. Our friends Henry Hockeimer, Jamie Bischoff, Corey Field, and Stephen Kim at Ballard Spahr Andrews & Ingersoll have so generously assisted us all along the way—thank you.

A number of people reviewed all or parts of the book and offered constructive suggestions. Among these, I would like to especially thank Fr. Matthew Lamb, Jim Towey, Fr. Paul Murray, O.P., Fr. Thomas Dubay, S.M., Fr. Benedict Groeschel, C.F.R., Fr. Pascual Cervera, and Tim S. Hickey as well as Professor Tom Butler, Ph.D., who spent hours in translating Mother Teresa's poem.

I am particularly grateful to Sr. Nirmala, M.C., successor to Mother Teresa as Superior General of the Missionaries of Charity Sisters, who has supported the activities of the Mother Teresa Center and this project, to the MC sisters, to the active and contemplative MC brothers, and to my own confreres in the MC Fathers, especially Fr. Robert Conroy, M.C., for their brotherly support and encouragement. A special word of thanks goes to the contemplative branch of the MC sisters and to the many who have supported this work through their prayers and sacrifices.

I am very grateful to Archbishop Lucas Sirkar, S.D.B, Archbishop of Calcutta, for permission to quote from the letters of Archbishop Ferdinand Périer, S.J., to Fr. George Pattery, S.J., provincial of the Calcutta Province of the Society of Jesus for permission to quote from the letters of Fr. Céleste Van Exem, S.J., to Fr. Joseph Neuner, S.J., to Fr. Albert Huart, S.J., to the Jesuits of the Province of Croatia, to Fr. Michael van der Peet, S.C.J., and to Bishop William G. Curlin, DD for their valuable contribution and assistance. The Loreto Sisters have always responded readily to our queries and have graciously permitted the use of various letters from their archives for which we are truly thankful. Grateful acknowledgement goes to TAN Books and Publishers, Inc. for quotes from Fr. Reginald Garrigou-Lagrange, O.P., to Ravindra Kumar, editor of *The Statesman Ltd.* and Nachiketa Publications for permission to use material from the interviews of Desmond Doig, to David Higham Associates, on behalf of Malcolm Muggeridge's literary estate, for the permission to use his words and to the editors of the *Review for Religious,* the *Catholic Leader,* and the Milwaukee *Catholic Herald* for permission to use excerpts from several articles in their journals.

Even with all this help errors may still have occurred, for which I take sole responsibility.

INDEX